I0824763

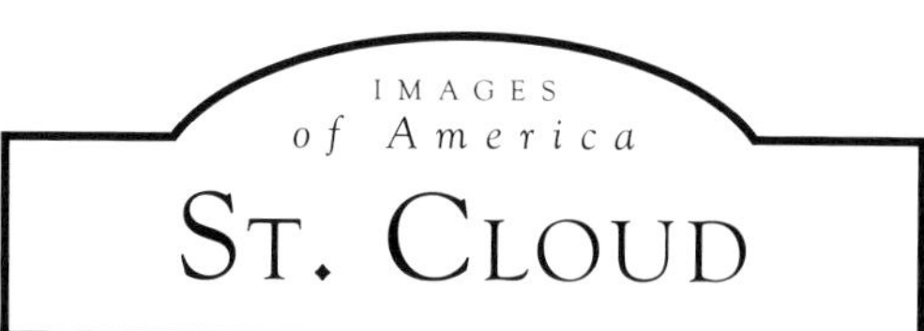
IMAGES
of America
ST. CLOUD

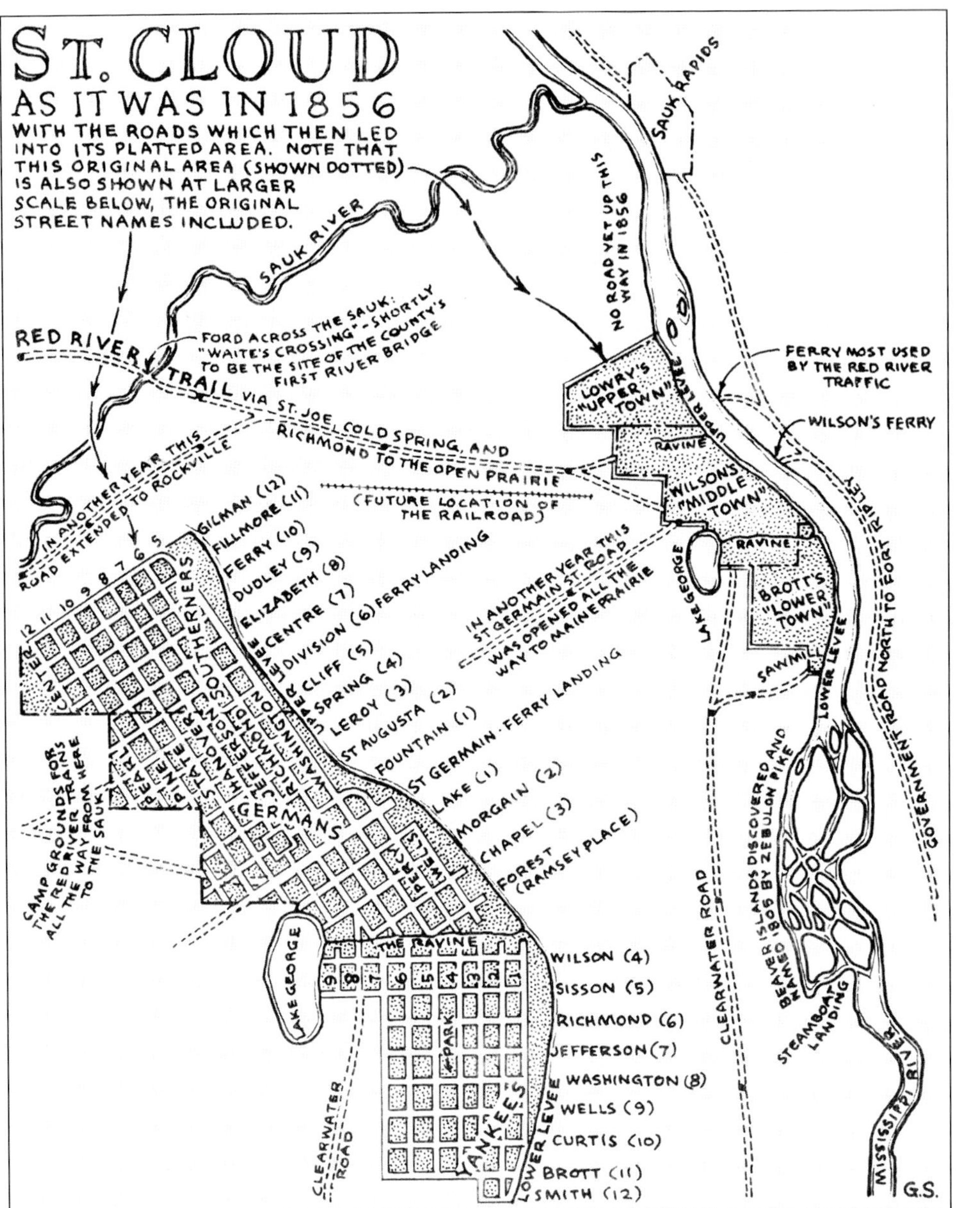

Designer and St. Cloud native Glanville Smith illustrated this map for the cover of John Dominik's *Three Towns Into One City: St. Cloud*, a history of St. Cloud published in 1978. The right side of the map provides a broad view of the St. Cloud area as it appeared in 1856. The left side provides a closer look at St. Cloud with its streets labeled. The three settlements incorporated into St. Cloud proper are clearly delineated. (Courtesy of Stearns History Museum.)

ON THE COVER: *St. Cloud Times* photographer Myron Hall captured this quintessential Christmas scene in downtown St. Cloud near the corner of St. Germain Street and Eighth Avenue South. It is one of a series of photographs taken that day, with a separate photograph published December 10, 1942, and captioned, "Christmas shoppers were given 'A White Christmas' atmosphere Wednesday afternoon in downtown St. Cloud." (Courtesy of Stearns History Museum.)

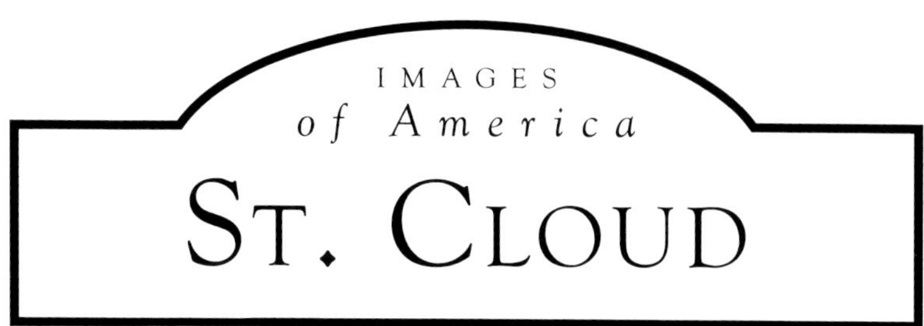

Miranda Stueckrath and Grant Wilson
with the Stearns History Museum
Foreword by John Decker

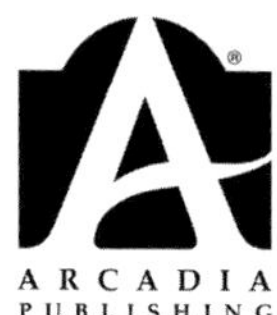

ISBN 978-1-4671-6325-5

Published by Arcadia Publishing
Charleston, South Carolina

Printed in the United States of America

Library of Congress Control Number: 2025948911

For all general information, please contact Arcadia Publishing:
Telephone 843-853-2070
Fax 843-853-0044
E-mail sales@arcadiapublishing.com

Visit us on the Internet at www.arcadiapublishing.com

To all staff, patrons, and volunteers who have given their time, energy, and love to shape, safeguard, and celebrate the history here. This book is yours.

—Miranda

To all those who breathed new life into the Stearns County Historical Society in the 1970s and were instrumental in building the Stearns History Museum, especially Edward Zapp Jr., Ruth Knevel, John Decker, and Dave Ebnet.

—Grant

Contents

FOREWORD

Working in the Research Center and Archives at the Stearns History Museum has been a blessing. When I look back, my university studies were merely a primer for the nearly 50 years of on-the-job training I was about to experience. My hope is that the talented authors of this book, Grant Wilson and Miranda Stueckrath, realize the work they are performing now at the museum will make a difference for generations to come. I am currently a volunteer who has known and worked with Miranda and Grant for a number of years. Both are well-educated professionals, dedicated, and experienced in their fields. Both have transformed my former workplace to a higher level by using advanced methods to collect, preserve, and disseminate information. I am proud of them.

Why was this book published? I believe the authors wanted an old-fashioned way to tell us about local history by text and image. Their writing flows and is to the point. The use of interdisciplinary research is evident as you read through the table of contents. Each chapter gives you a collective idea as to how the St. Cloud area became what it is today. The photographic image selection is thoughtful and connects with the reader. You will see images that reach back to the 1860s as well as photographs that were taken by local photographers such as Myron Hall.

In conclusion, Grant and Miranda have done their homework. Publishing this book is a true testament to their perseverance. It captures how folks who resided in the St. Cloud and surrounding area lived their everyday lives over the last 170 years. If you enjoy a concise local history read or simply enjoy viewing first-rate images from the past, this book is for you. It will be a go-to book on my library shelf.

—John Decker

ACKNOWLEDGMENTS

Much of the research for this book came from the Stearns History Museum Research Center's biographical and subject files, compiled over the last 50 years by museum staff and volunteers, which contain many resources, including *St. Cloud Times* articles documenting the city's history. Special recognition is due to local historian Sr. Owen Lindblad, OSB, for her history columns published in the *St. Cloud Times* between 1998 and 2001 as well as history columnists Mike Moran and Bill Morgan. Other local historians to be thanked are William Bell Mitchell, John Dominik, and Gertrude Gove. Thank you to Dr. Christopher P. Lehman for his assistance and expertise in the early years of St. Cloud and to Tom Steman, archivist of St. Cloud State University. Special recognition is also due to Myron Hall, a former *St. Cloud Times* photographer from 1937 to 1976. Hall donated his entire body of work to the Stearns County Historical Society in 1988, and many of the photographs featured in this book are of his creation.

Thank you to Stearns History Museum staff Caitlin Carlson, Eric Cheever, Amy Degerstrom, Ann Marie Johnson, and Michelle Bue for their suggestions and assistance as well as volunteers Marian Rengel, Mike Knaak, and John Decker. Thank you to the *St. Cloud Times,* St. Cloud State University Archives, and the Minnesota Historical Society for permission to use their photographs.

Unless otherwise noted, all photographs are from the Stearns History Museum archival collections.

Introduction

Long before the arrival of white Europeans, nearly all of present-day Minnesota belonged to the Dakota. Their position in northern Minnesota was contested in the 17th century when the Ojibwe of the Quebec region migrated westward. Ojibwe tradition holds that they conquered the Dakota lands of northern Minnesota, while Dakota tradition says they voluntarily migrated southward to follow buffalo herds. Either way, this marked the beginning of tensions between the two peoples in Minnesota. By the 1800s, Minnesota was generally divided between the Ojibwe in the north and the Dakota in the south. Central Minnesota—including the area that became St. Cloud and greater Stearns County—acted as a borderland between the two tribes. That borderland became a battleground at times but also acted as a space of cooperation during times of scarcity in the winter months.

A few years after the establishment of the Minnesota Territory in 1849, the US government opened lands west of the Mississippi to white settlement. Near the confluence of the Sauk and Mississippi Rivers settled the "Father of St. Cloud," J.L. Wilson. Wilson was a native of Columbia, Maine, and of French Huguenot descent. He was a millwright, constructing mills along the Mississippi River from St. Anthony near the Twin Cities to Little Falls. Wilson arrived in Sauk Rapids, Minnesota, in 1851. In the summer of 1853, he relocated just across the Mississippi River, platting a claim he purchased from Ole Bergeson. He moved into Bergeson's cabin and hired two Frenchmen to build a fence around his recently acquired property. One summer day, as his hired hands were working outside, Wilson read a passage about Napoleon's summer home in St. Cloud, France. Inquiring about his wife, who was staying at the summer home, Napoleon asked a messenger, "How are things in St. Cloud?" Shortly after reading this exchange, Wilson's hired hands came inside the cabin to take a break from their work. Jokingly, Wilson asked them, "Boys, how are things in St. Cloud?" All three being of French descent, they permanently adopted the impromptu name given to the blooming settlement. In addition to naming the city, Wilson fathered St. Cloud by giving land to newly arrived settlers for free on the condition that they build on the land. He also donated land to the city and county governments for civic buildings and parks.

In the 1850s, swaths of German Catholic families came to settle in central Minnesota. Fr. Francis Xavier Pierz, a missionary priest to the Ojibwe and Dakota of central Minnesota, implored German Catholics to immigrate to the region. Father Pierz wrote glowingly of the state, describing its beautiful weather and fertile soil. His words of entreaty were printed in German-language newspapers and periodicals across the eastern United States and Germany: "Hasten, then, my dear German people . . . and settle in Minnesota." By 1855, over 50 German families accepted the invitation and arrived in central Minnesota. J.L. Wilson convinced those Germans who were on their way to Sauk Rapids to settle in St. Cloud and contribute to its development.

Two ravines to the north and south enclosed Wilson's St. Cloud, also known as Middle Town. Across those ravines were two other fledgling communities: Sylvanus B. Lowry's Acadia, or Upper Town, to the north and George Brott's St. Cloud City, or Lower Town, to the south. For this reason, St. Cloud has been called the "Triplet City" by local historians.

Sylvanus B. Lowry was a slaveholding Democrat from Tennessee who came into possession of hundreds of acres across the northern ravine from Wilson's settlement in 1853, later known as Upper Town. He made his money in the Northwest United States through the fur trade and, once he arrived in St. Cloud, by selling land to other southern slaveholders who belonged to his father's church. Profits from these land deals were used to develop Upper Town, fund Lowry's businesses, and fund St. Cloud newspapers, one of which would combine with other local papers to become the *St. Cloud Times*. In its earliest years, Upper Town was the central business district of the three towns, due to its proximity to Sauk Rapids, a popular vacation spot for Southerners, and its accessibility to the Mississippi River. However, after the Panic of 1857, the purchase of land in Upper Town came to a standstill, and at the outbreak of the Civil War, its preeminence declined even further.

If Wilson is the father of St. Cloud proper, and Lowry of Upper Town, then George Brott is the father of Lower Town. Brott headed west from New York in 1850, arriving in St. Anthony Falls, Minnesota, around 1851. He built his wealth through real estate, and in 1854, he purchased land across the southern ravine from Wilson's Middle Town. Brott promoted his new settlement in New England and the mid-Atlantic states, attracting merchant Protestant Yankees. Lower Town developed quickly, and by 1857, it contained a hotel, mills, churches, a factory, and a school.

Although the three settlements were founded independently, they quickly grew together and united. In 1856, the three settlements were incorporated into the city of St. Cloud.

In the years that followed, St. Cloud continued to grow, but Sauk Rapids remained the central hub of commerce in the St. Cloud area. This trajectory was permanently altered when, in April 1886, a massive cyclone devastated both cities. Sauk Rapids sustained the most damage, with every business except one flattened by the cyclone, destroying the bridge that connected the two communities. St. Cloud rebounded from the disaster quickly, taking its place as the focal point of business and commerce in central Minnesota for years to come.

In 1920, the Prohibition era came with the passage of the 18th Amendment. Stearns County's two-to-one referendum against the amendment's ratification foreshadowed the county's derision of the government's attempt to prohibit the production and distribution of alcohol. Stearns County townships from Melrose to Holding, Avon, and Collegeville were hotbeds for moonshining and bootlegging. As the county seat, St. Cloud was the center for federal activity in Stearns County with a high concentration of federal agents, but local law enforcement, court officials, and even Catholic clergy were sympathetic and lenient towards violators. Speakeasies and other establishments covertly offering liquor dotted the St. Cloud area, including Hayward Farm, the Blue Tavern, Oak Grove Pavilion, and the Spaniol Hotel. Federal agents raided area moonshining operations and transported the contraband to the county seat, St. Cloud. Here, alcohol was poured into the Mississippi River, and the Stearns County jailhouse grew to a burgeoning population. In 1933, Prohibition was repealed by the 21st Amendment. At a rate of almost five to one, St. Cloud voted in favor of repealing the 18th Amendment.

When the Great Depression hit, St. Cloud's close connection to its rural surroundings shaped how the community endured the crisis. Many farm families who lost their land to foreclosure stayed on as tenant farmers, while others moved from larger cities back to the countryside, hoping for stability. On July 29, 1932, local farmers gathered in St. Cloud to form the Minnesota Farmers Holiday Association. Their 30-day strike, aimed at halting foreclosures, pressured the state legislature to declare a state of emergency for farmers and pass a mortgage moratorium. That same year, the federal government introduced major relief programs, including the Agricultural Adjustment Act, which paid farmers subsidies to cut production, and the Federal Emergency Relief Act, which provided jobs for both rural and urban residents.

St. Cloud also launched its own efforts to support struggling families. The city set up an unemployment agency at the Salvation Army, and Mayor Murphy proposed a $25,000 bond to fund public works projects under what was called the "Make Work Program." The plan called for 400 men to be employed on city improvements ranging from streets to parks, with money raised through bonds, subscriptions, and the city budget. Voters, however, turned it down by a two-to-one margin. In response, Wheelock Whitney led a private charity drive asking every wage earner to contribute the equivalent of four days' pay. The community effort quickly exceeded its $25,000 goal, and within months, a larger "War on Depression" campaign raised an impressive $800,000 to fund jobs and boost local businesses.

Alongside these local initiatives, St. Cloud reaped the benefits of New Deal programs that reshaped communities across the nation. Programs like the Civilian Conservation Corps (CCC), Public Works Administration (PWA), Emergency Relief Association (ERA), and Relief Works Administration (RWA) brought jobs and infrastructure improvements. But the Works Progress Administration (WPA) left the most visible mark. WPA projects in St. Cloud included construction of the Alice Whitney Park Dam on the Sauk River in 1938, riverbank steps and trails, and Clark Field at Technical High School, developed in partnership with the National Youth Administration (NYA). At St. Cloud State Teachers College, WPA crews built the granite retaining walls along First Avenue in 1936, using stone quarried from the campus itself, improvements that reflected both practical needs and a sense of civic pride.

The WPA's impact went far beyond construction. In 1937, workers helped move St. Cloud's 1902 post office four blocks on rollers, transforming it into a new city hall that later displayed New Deal–era murals and reliefs celebrating local industry and landscape. Selke Field, another WPA project, provided athletic facilities for the college and later became housing for veterans and married students after World War II. The New Deal also invested in public art and memorials. In 1939, thousands attended the dedication of the James J. Hill monument at Lake George, its granite base and parkway crafted by WPA crews. That same year, the WPA and NYA erected a granite marker east of town, honoring St. Cloud's first commercial quarry. Together, these projects not only provided employment during the Depression but also left lasting landmarks that continue to shape St. Cloud's landscape today.

St. Cloud's history is marked by perseverance and transformation, influenced by the convergence of diverse communities, unique challenges, and innovation that defined each era. The city's prolific landmarks and sites and community traditions reflect the perseverance and collaborative efforts of its citizens across every generation. As St. Cloud evolves, its rich past provides lessons in unity and innovation that resonate today.

One

Many Paths, One Home

The history of St. Cloud is a story of movement, settlement, and belonging. Everyone except the Indigenous Dakota and Ojibwe, who had lived, traveled, and traded here for generations, arrived as immigrants or newcomers. Fur traders, farmers, laborers, and refugees all faced the challenge of building a home in unfamiliar surroundings while negotiating coexistence with those who came before them.

The first non-Indigenous arrivals were fur traders at Sauk Rapids, just north of present-day St. Cloud. By the 1850s, the fertile Sauk Valley drew settlers, and three distinct communities emerged: Upper, Middle, and Lower Town. Upper Town attracted Southerners, including slaveholders, reflecting the national conflicts of the era. Middle Town was shaped by German Catholics recruited by Fr. Francis Xavier Pierz, who established the cultural and economic heart of the city. Lower Town was settled by Yankees from New England, whose businesses and civic institutions reflected their entrepreneurial spirit. From the start, the city was divided by culture and vision, yet these settlements eventually merged into one city.

By the late 19th century, immigration diversified further. Polish families settled near the railroads and granite quarries, founding their own parish at St. John Cantius. African Americans, migrating north between the 1890s and 1920s, formed a small but visible community, though they faced rising racism. During World War I, German Catholics, long central to the city's life, faced suspicion and repression, with churches pressured to abandon the German language.

Following the Vietnam War, Rev. Richard Leisen led local efforts to resettle refugees, welcoming the first families into his own home. Between 1975 and 1987, more than 1,400 Southeast Asian refugees, including Vietnamese, Laotian, and Hmong, made central Minnesota their home, bringing new traditions and cultures into the city.

In the 1990s and 2000s, Somali refugees arrived, transforming St. Cloud into a hub for East African immigrants. They established businesses, mosques, and cultural organizations that remain vital today. The Islamic Center, founded in 2006, provides a spiritual and community anchor, while the establishment of a Muslim section at North Star Cemetery in 2014 affirmed its permanence.

From fur traders and frontier farmers to Somali grocery stores and Islamic schools, St. Cloud's history reveals a central truth: it has always been a city of immigrants. Each wave of settlers arrived as strangers, faced challenges of belonging, and left lasting legacies that continue to shape the community.

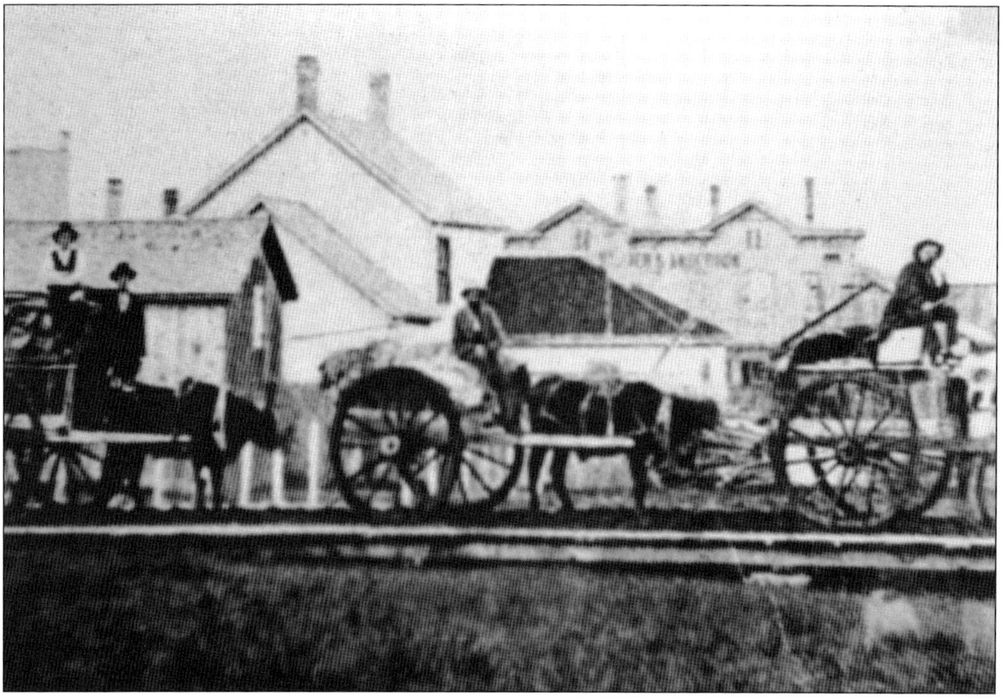

RED RIVER OXCARTS, C. 1860. On March 3, 1849, Pres. James K. Polk created the Minnesota Territory, a vast region that included parts of today's Dakotas. Pioneers and traders traveled the Red River Trails. The "Middle Trail" ran through Stearns County from St. Cloud to Sauk Centre. These rough paths carried furs, goods, soldiers, and settlers seeking new lives on the frontier.

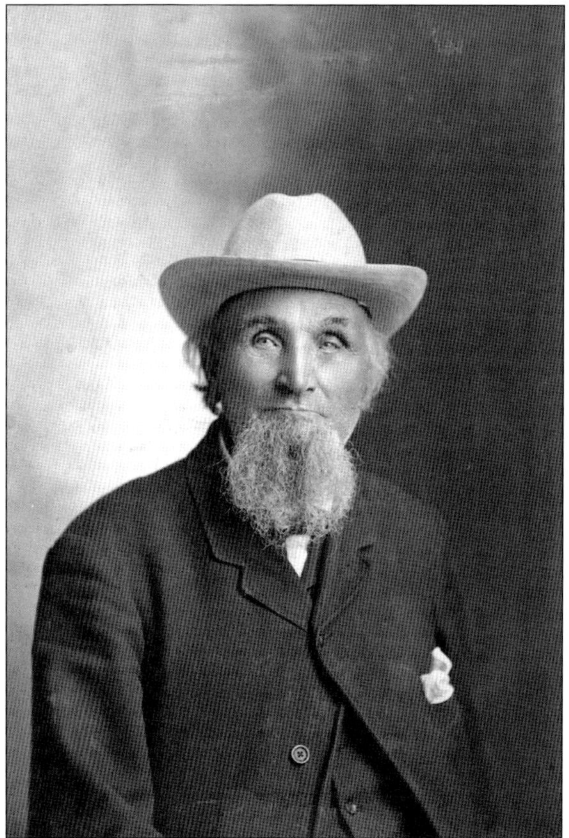

JOHN LYMAN WILSON, 1900. In 1851, John Wilson traveled west to Minnesota to work in the lumber industry. For $100, he purchased a land claim located between two ravines. That property would later become the heart of St. Cloud's business district.

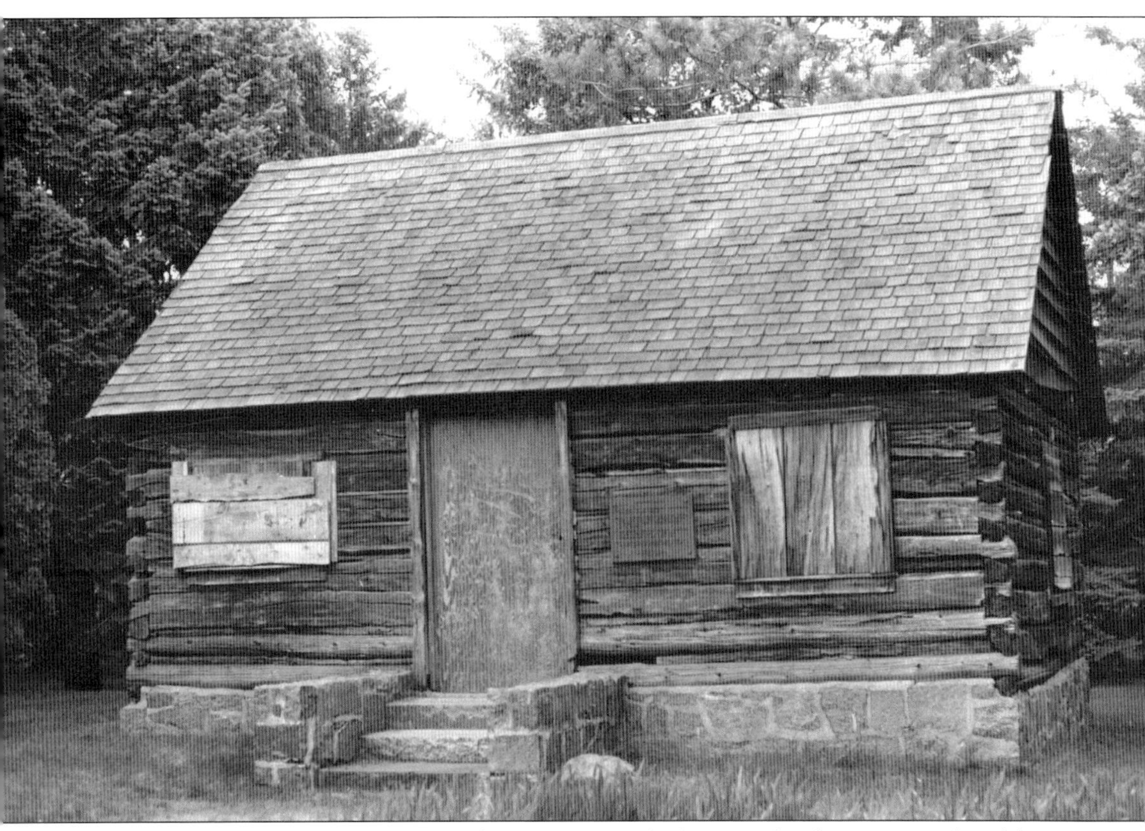

OVERBECK CABIN, C. 1968. Constructed in 1855, a year before St. Cloud incorporated, Balthasar Rosenberger hired Joseph Niehaus to build him a cabin. It was 16 by 20 feet and constructed of nine-inch-high squared hand-hewn logs, dovetailed at the corners. Hand-crafted wooden shingles made up the roof, and it had two windows. It was purchased in 1858 by Barney Overbeck, and he saw it serve many frontier needs: a jail, hotel, courtroom, and a saloon. Overbeck became the city's first police chief, tax collector, and coroner. Overbeck turned the basement into a jail and added rooms for travelers, reflecting the resourcefulness and rough character of pioneer life in early St. Cloud. Although the cabin was moved and rebuilt over the years, pieces of the cabin reside in Riverside Park, and markers that tell the story of the cabin.

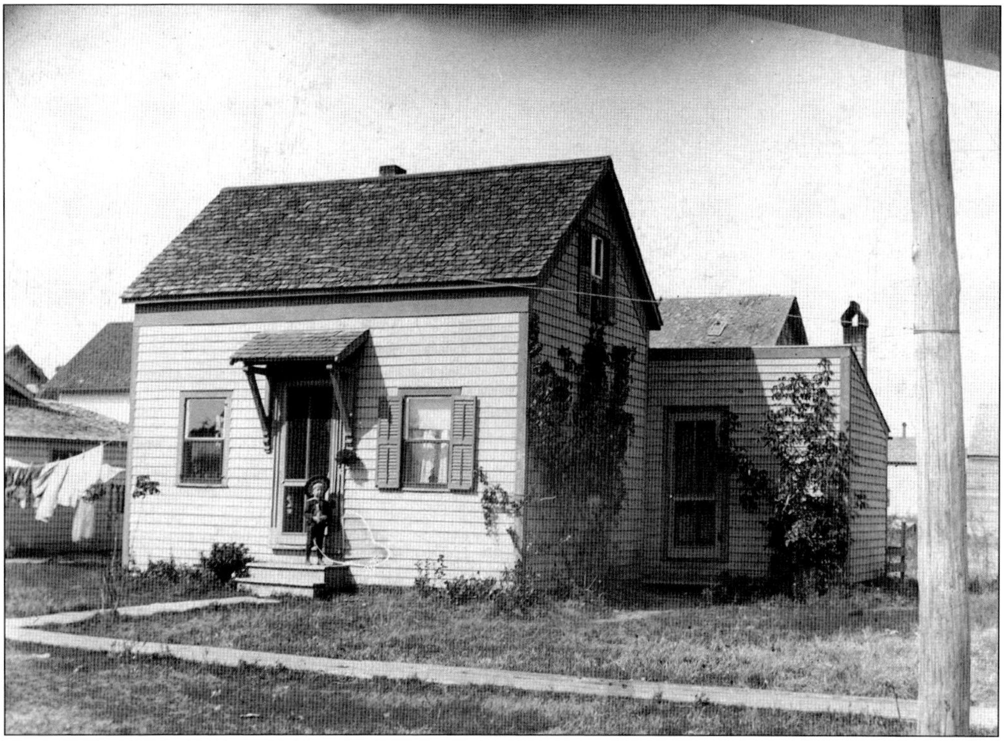

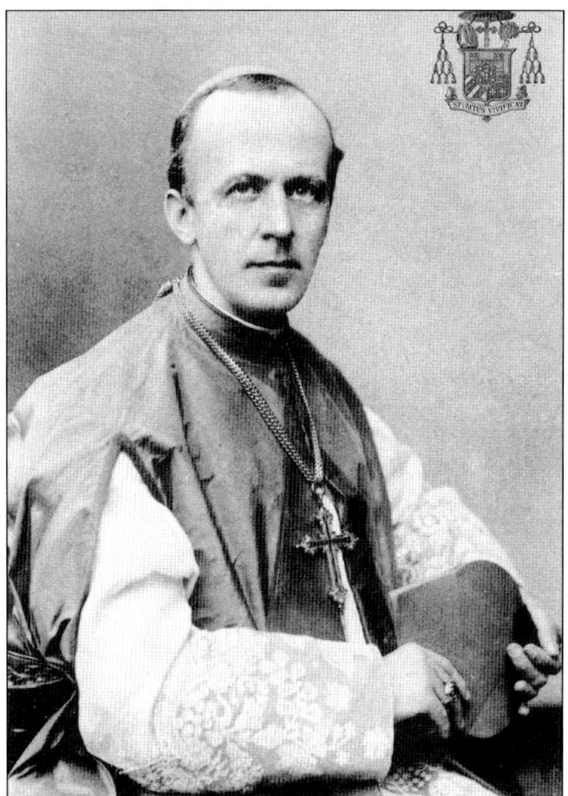

First Frame House, St. Cloud, c. 1895. In addition to platting the original city, serving as a judge of probate court and as a city justice, and being a member of the territorial legislature, the Stearns County Board of Commissioners, and the St. Cloud City Council, Wilson also built the first frame house in St. Cloud.

Bishop Otto Zardetti, c. 1890. Bishop John Joseph Frederick Otto Zardetti became the first bishop of the Diocese of St. Cloud in 1889. At the time, parishes were small and divided by nationality, with most settlers German but also Polish, French Canadian, and Irish. Zardetti worked to unite these isolated communities, establish a diocesan identity, and build a leadership team. Through determination, local communities built the churches and schools that became the foundation of Catholic life in central Minnesota.

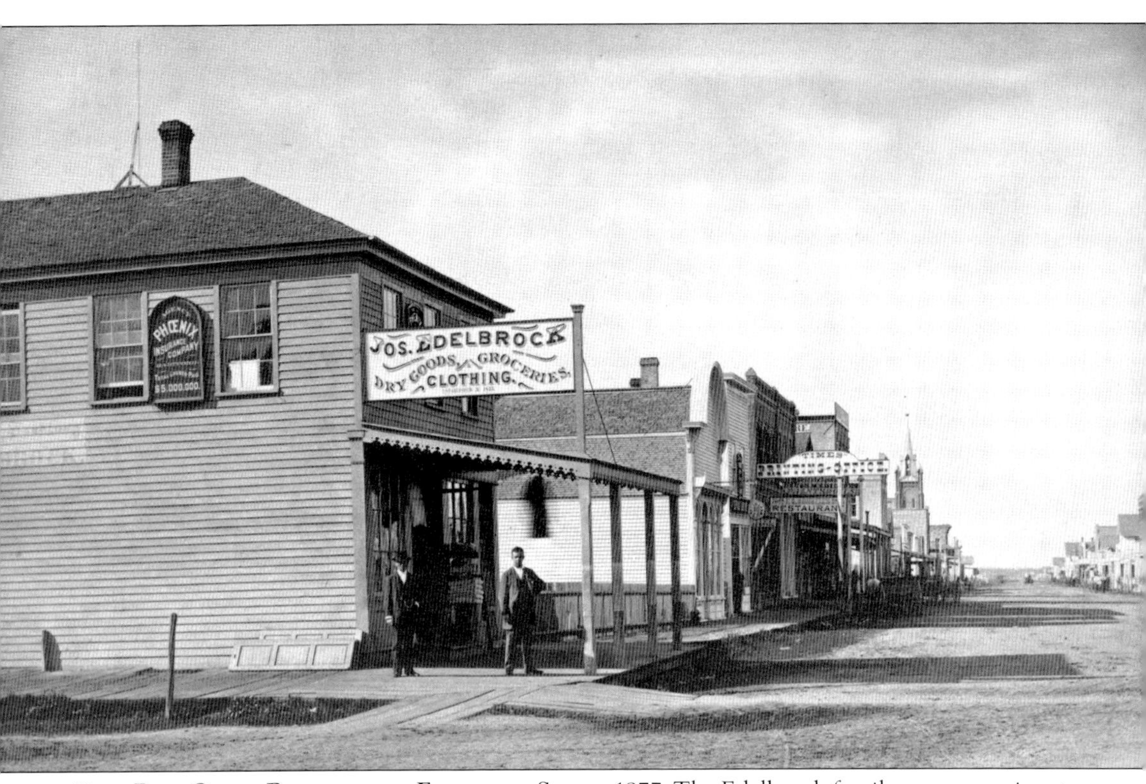

First Post Office Building and Edelbrock Store, 1877. The Edelbrock family was a prominent pioneer family in St. Cloud, playing a vital role in the city's early development. Joseph Edelbrock arrived in 1855 and quickly established himself as a key civic leader and entrepreneur. He opened one of the city's first general stores, which also served as St. Cloud's first post office, and he held several important positions, including mayor, alderman, postmaster, and school board member. The Edelbrock residence was not only a home but also a center of community life; notably, the attic of the house hosted the first Benedictine Mass in St. Cloud, marking its significance in the religious and cultural history of the area. Edelbrock's leadership and business acumen helped shape the city's infrastructure and social fabric during its formative years.

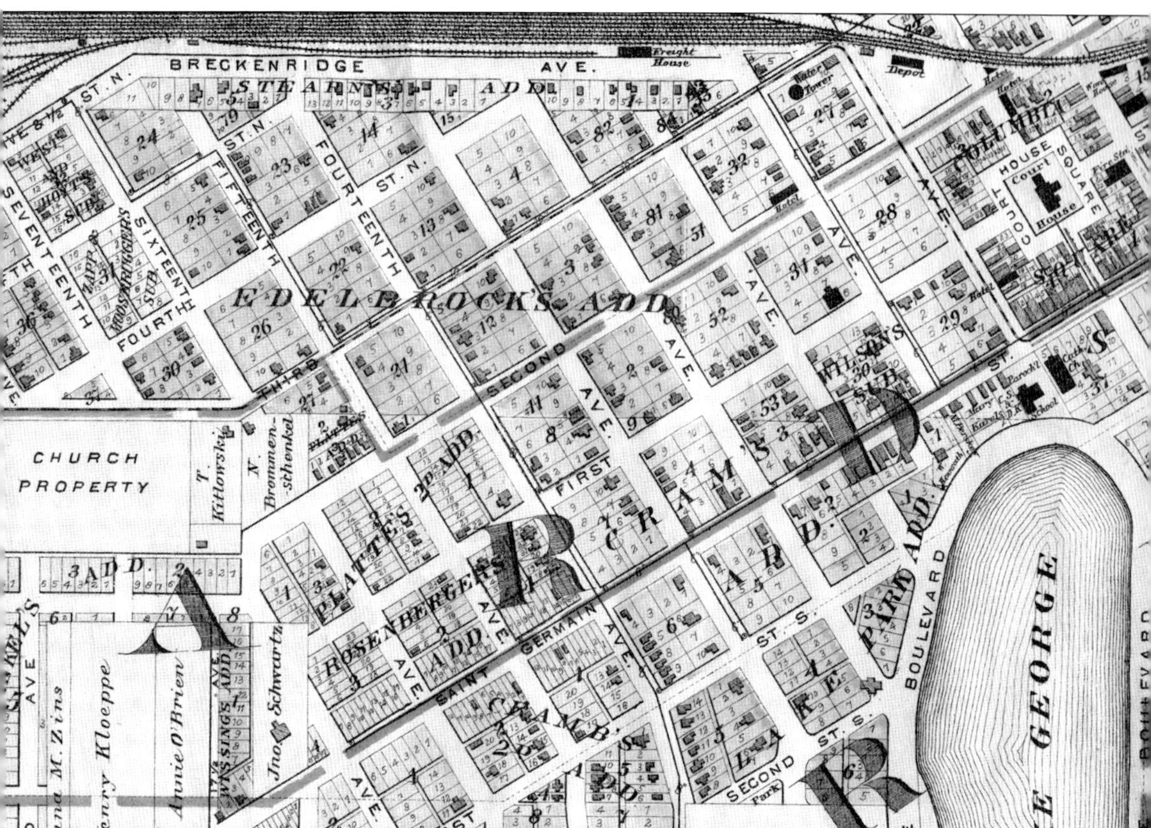

St. John Cantius Neighborhood, 1896. By the 1880s, Polish immigrants began settling northwest of downtown St. Cloud, drawn by jobs on the railroad and in the granite industry as well as affordable housing. Businesses like Janochosky's grocery and Kloskowski's meat market soon served the growing community. In 1890, Polish residents organized St. John Cantius Catholic Church, with parishioners themselves leading its construction. The church became the neighborhood's landmark, anchoring nearly 300 homes and fostering a tight-knit Polish community.

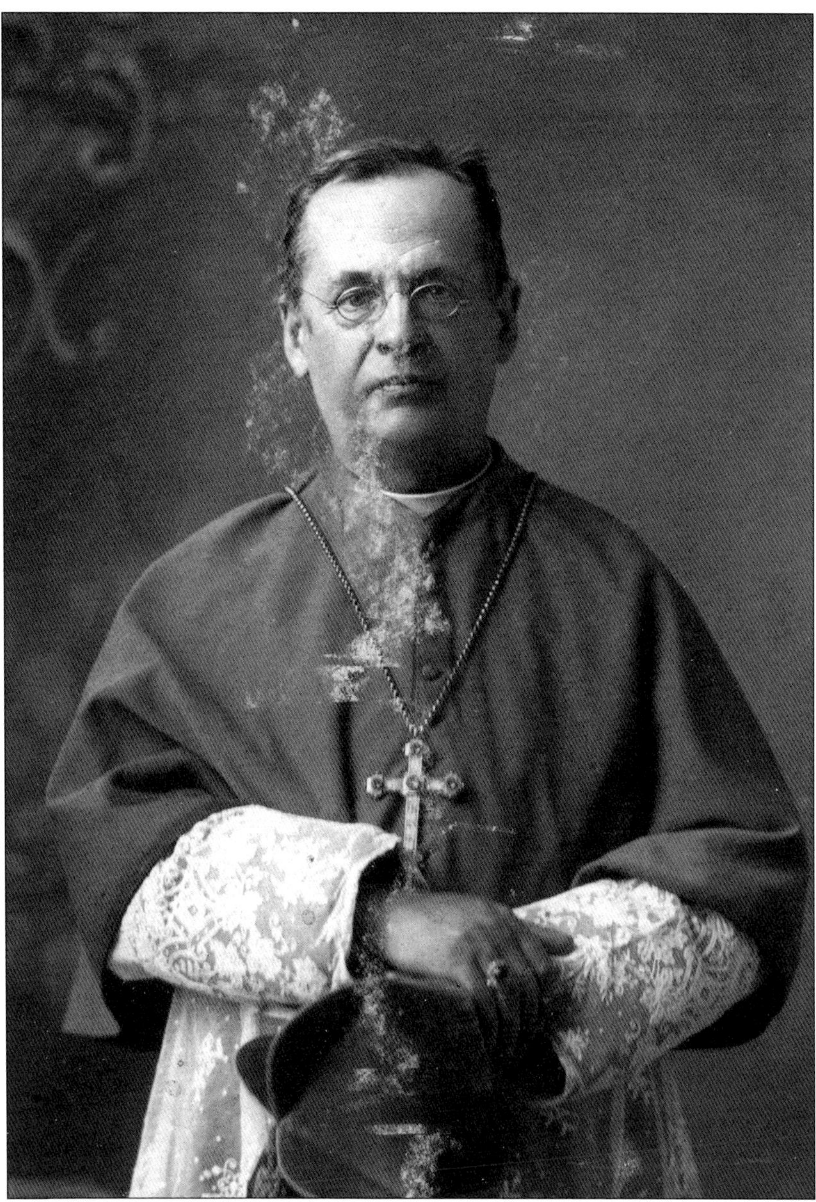

Bishop James Trobec, c. 1900. Bishop James Trobec became the third bishop of the Diocese of St. Cloud in 1897, guiding the region through a transformative era of immigration and growth. A Slovenian immigrant himself, Trobec deeply understood the challenges facing the German, Slovene, Polish, and other Catholic communities who sought to maintain their languages, customs, and devotions in a rapidly Americanizing society. Under his leadership, the number of priests, parishes, and Catholic schoolchildren nearly doubled, reflecting both population growth and a strong commitment to faith formation. He placed special emphasis on education and vocations, supporting parish schools as places where cultural identity and Catholic teaching could coexist. At the same time, he worked to unify a diverse diocese, encouraging mutual respect among groups often divided by ethnicity or language. Balancing heritage and integration, Trobec helped shape a vibrant, inclusive Catholic community that would define central Minnesota for generations. He retired in 1914.

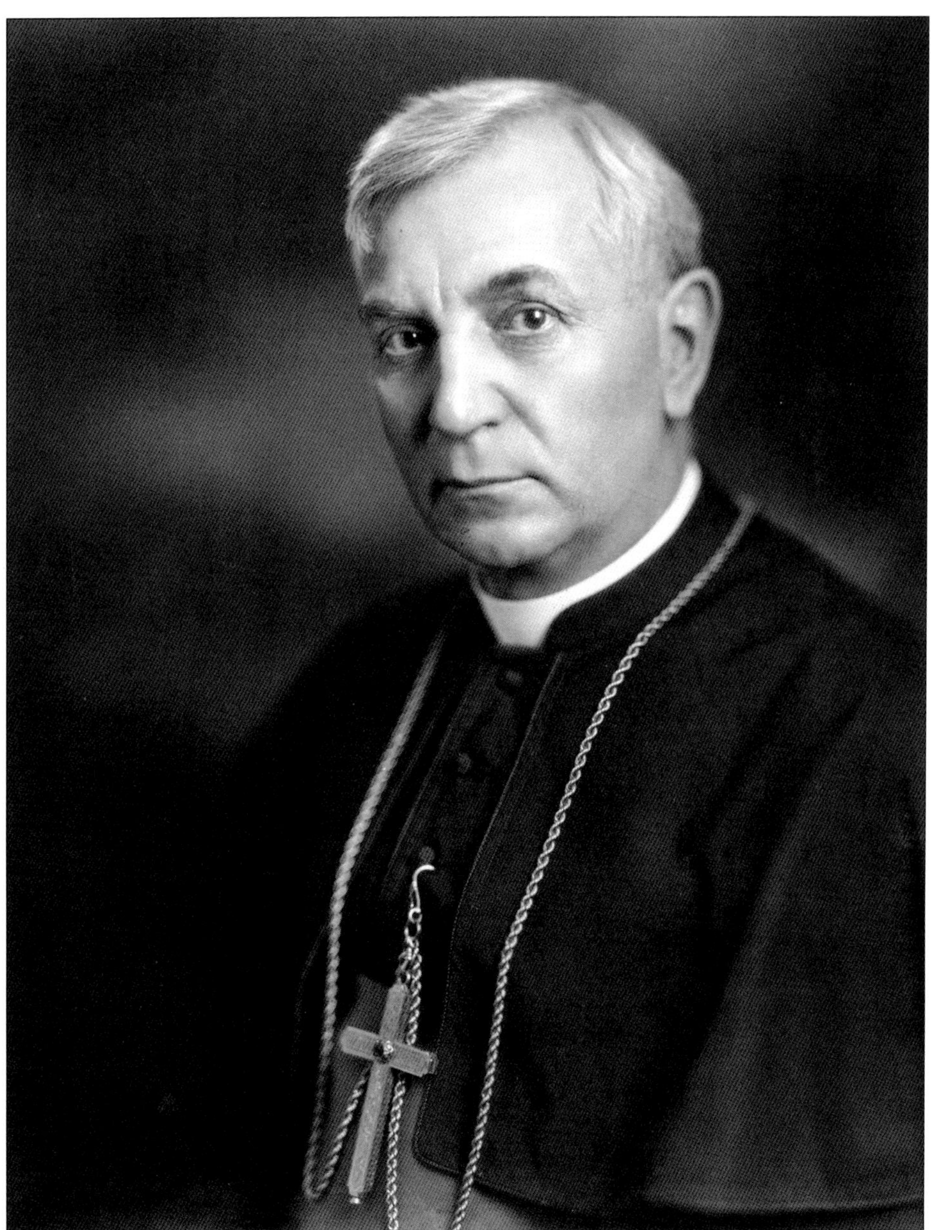

Bishop Joseph Busch, c. 1940. Bishop Joseph F. Busch, the first Minnesota-born bishop of St. Cloud, was appointed in 1915. He led the diocese through a period of profound cultural transition. As German, Slovene, Polish, and Irish families were beginning to establish deeper roots in central Minnesota, Busch recognized the importance of bridging their traditional devotions with the growing desire for unity within an English-speaking church. He encouraged the gradual adoption of English in sermons, confirmations, and pastoral letters, helping diverse parishes find common ground while honoring their cultural heritage. His leadership extended beyond language reform; he promoted lay participation, supported women's organizations, and strengthened Catholic education to serve both long-standing immigrants and their American-born children. During his tenure, he oversaw the construction of the episcopal residence and the current chancery, symbols of stability in a time of change. He served until his death in 1953, making him St. Cloud's longest-serving bishop.

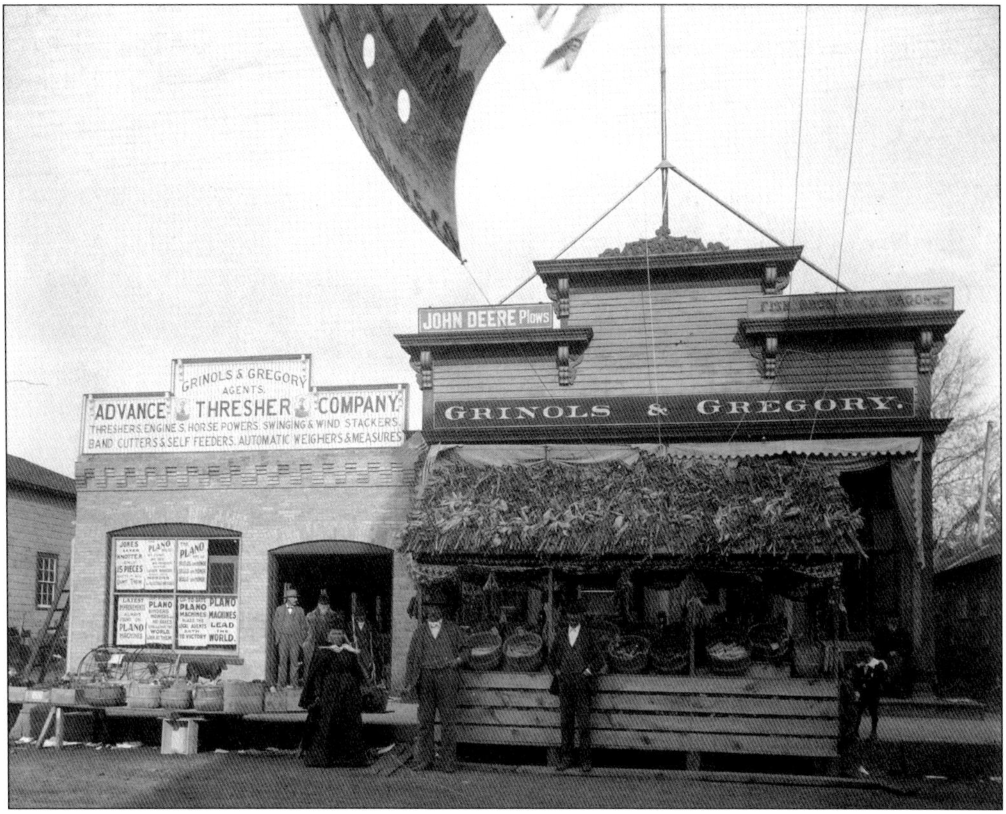

GRINOLS & GREGORY, C. 1898. Clinton Grinols began his career in Fairhaven before becoming a traveling salesman for a farm machinery company in 1891. Moving to St. Cloud in 1893, he cofounded Grinols & Gregory, later reorganized as the Grinols Company, where he served as secretary and treasurer until 1904. After selling most interests, he launched his own threshing machinery business and also served as St. Cloud's postmaster.

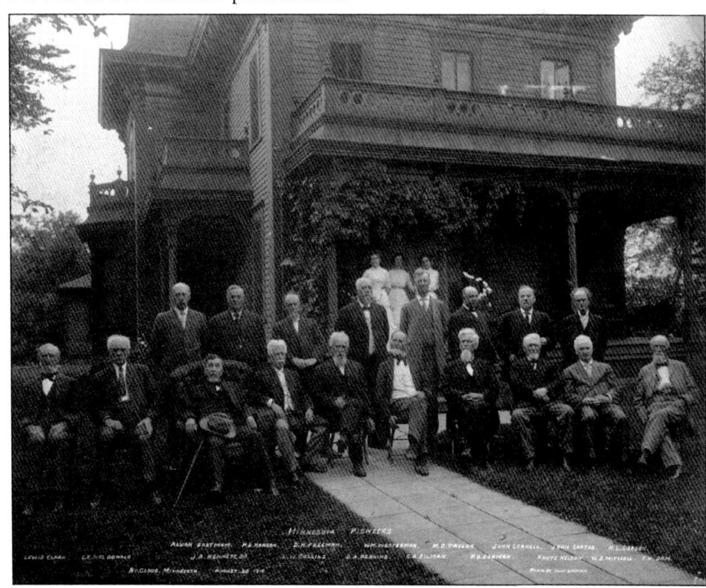

OLD SETTLERS ASSOCIATION, 1910. Old Settlers of Stearns County was organized in 1872 when 30 pioneers met in St. Cloud. John W. Tenvoorde was elected as the president. To be eligible, men must have been residents of Minnesota before January 1, 1859. In 1898, membership expanded to include six of the surrounding counties. In 1905, membership included any person living in Minnesota prior to August 16, 1862.

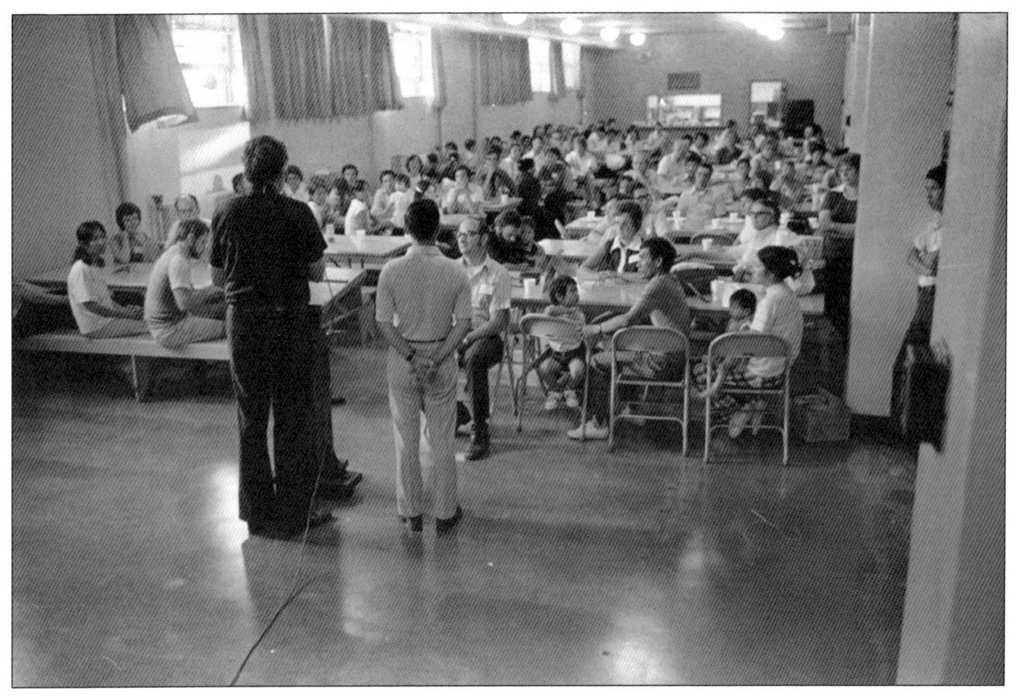

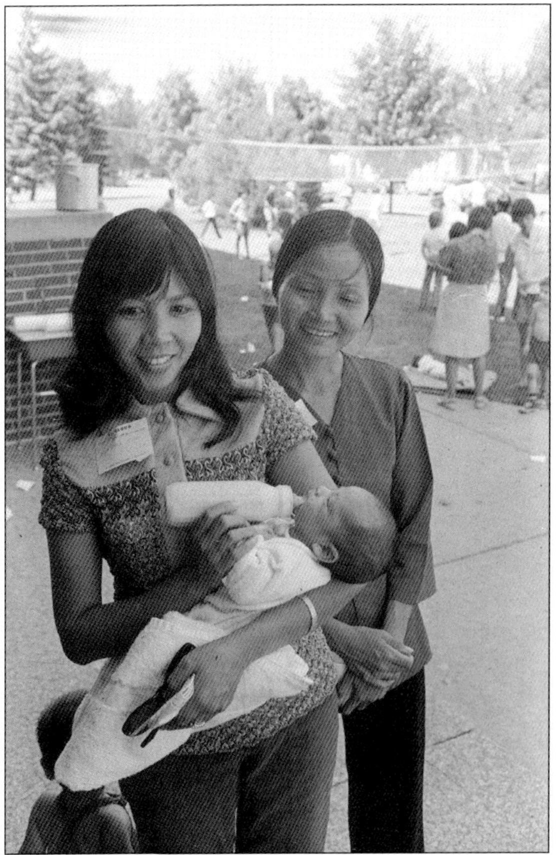

Vietnamese Picnic, 1975. After the United States withdrew from Vietnam in 1975, Rev. Richard Leisen responded to a call from the National Catholic Conference of Bishops, urging assistance for Vietnamese refugees in Guam. Acting swiftly, he traveled to Arkansas for resettlement training before welcoming St. Cloud's first refugee family—Mui and Lan Phan and their children—into his own home while he was away. His efforts continued over the following years, with 1,400 refugees resettled in central Minnesota between 1975 and 1987, including 30 families who found temporary shelter in Leisen's home.

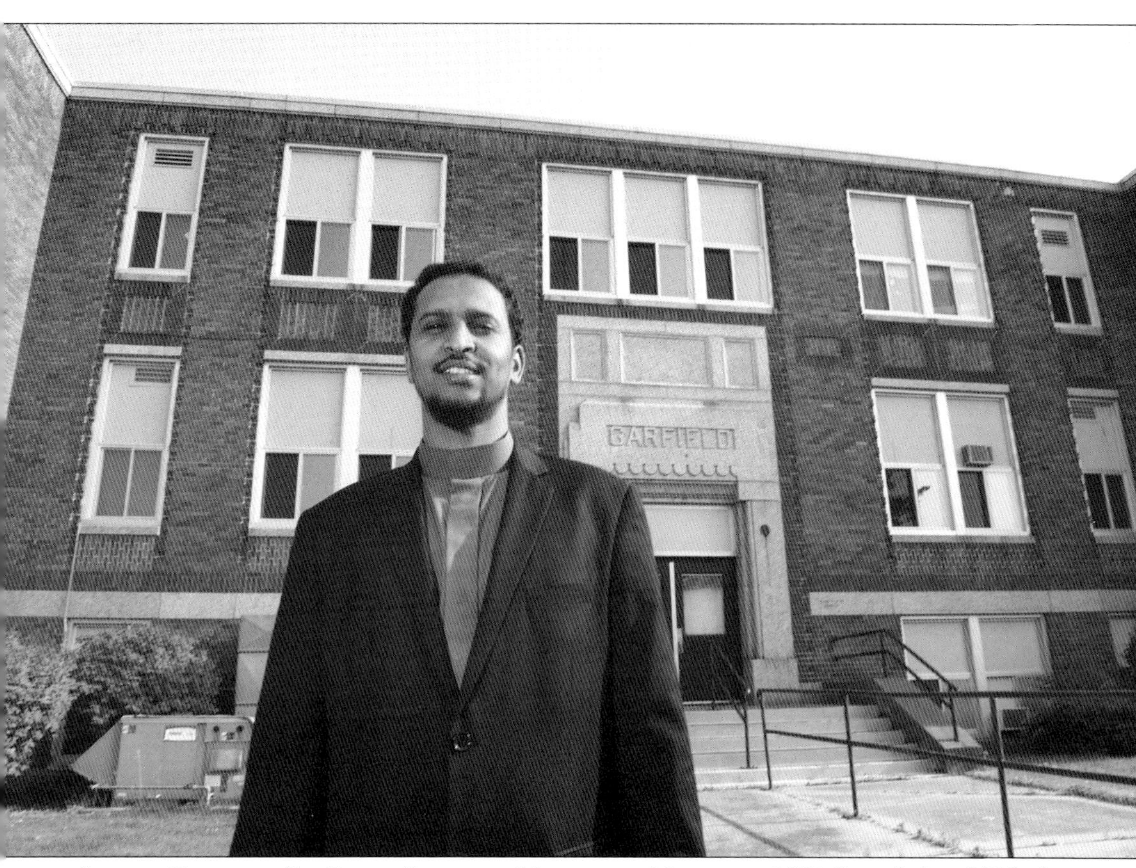

Islamic Center of St. Cloud President Muhayadin Mohamed, 2015. Founded in 2006, the Islamic Center in the former Garfield Elementary School is a welcoming Sunni mosque that serves as a spiritual and community hub. Services are primarily conducted in English, with separate prayer spaces for women and facilities for ablution. The mosque hosts the five daily prayers and Jumu'ah on Fridays, while also offering Nikah (marriage) and Janazah (funeral) services. A weekend school provides religious education for children, helping nurture Islamic values in the younger generation. Through worship, education, and support during life's milestones, the Islamic Center fosters an inclusive space for St. Cloud's Muslim community. (Photograph by Dave Schwarz; courtesy of *St. Cloud Times*.)

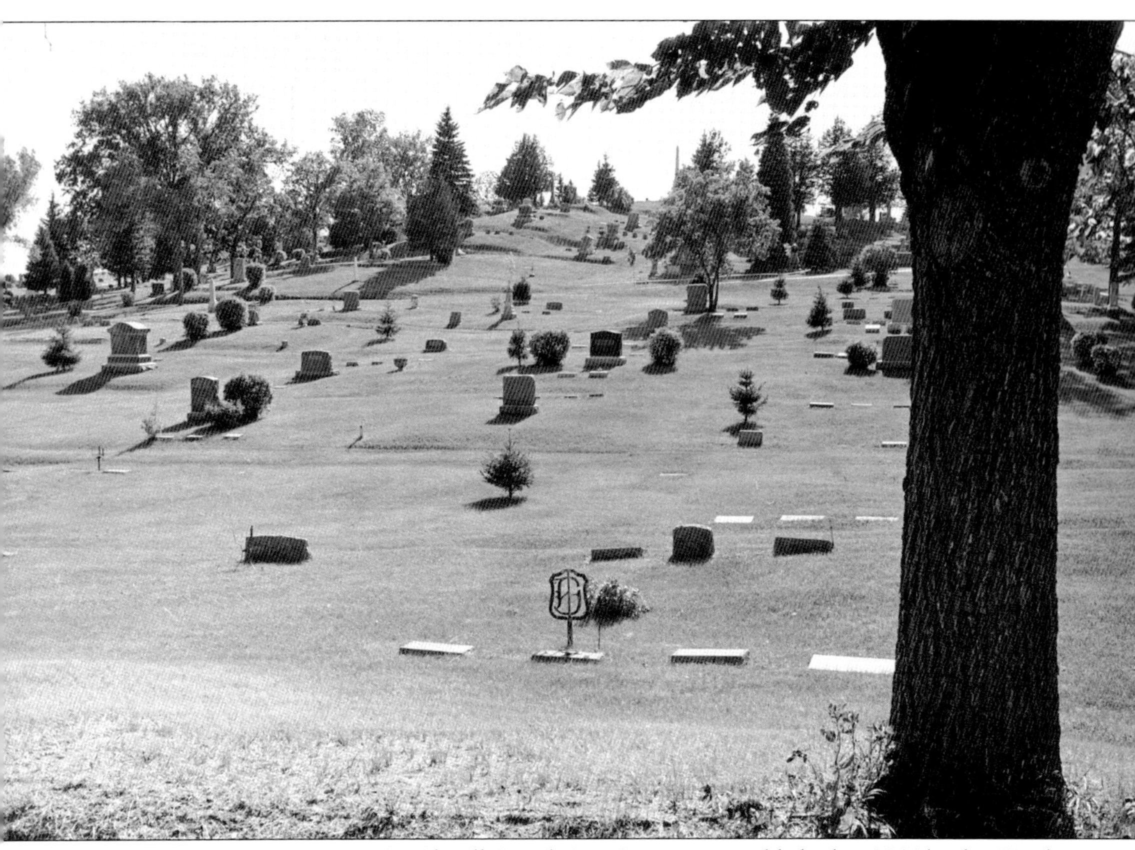

North Star Cemetery, 1954. St. Cloud's North Star Cemetery, established in 1864 by the Watab Lodge of the Masons, is the city's oldest cemetery still in its original location. Once rural, it has evolved alongside the community. In the mid-2000s, the Somali Elders Council, with support from local faith groups, sought a local burial site to serve the growing Muslim population. As Rev. Steve Cook noted in 2008, "When you start burying your dead here, it really marks this as your community." In 2014, a Muslim-only section was formally established at North Star.

Two

Busy, Gritty Granite City

Throughout its history, St. Cloud has been a wellspring of innovators and industry and community leaders. In 1913, a committee chose "St. Cloud—Busy! Gritty! Granite City!" as the city's slogan, reflecting St. Cloud's industrious people and its deep roots in the granite industry. The first successful granite quarry was established in 1868 by Breen and Young at the current location of the Minnesota Correctional Facility–St. Cloud on the east side of the Mississippi River. In the early years of St. Cloud, there was a limited market for structural use of granite for building materials, so St. Cloud granite was mainly used for bridges, foundations, and monuments. Eventually, though, granite sourced from St. Cloud and greater Stearns County would be used to build great structures across the country, including the Cathedral of St. Paul in St. Paul, Minnesota.

St. Cloud's convenient location along the Mississippi River near the Twin Cities made it an ideal location for the logging and lumber industry. Beginning in the 1850s, boats transported logging from northern Minnesota to St. Cloud, where area lumber mills processed the material and sent it farther down the river. Lumber dealers like Matthew Hall, Harkness-Miner, and W.T. Clark supplied the lumber needed to build St. Cloud's homes, businesses, and sidewalks. By 1914, trains replaced the river as the method of transporting logs from the north, but the lumber industry continued to be prevalent in St. Cloud.

A major highlight from the history of the transportation industry in St. Cloud is the Pan Motor Company. In 1917, Samuel Pandolfo chose St. Cloud as the location to manufacture an automobile of his design, the Model A Pan. St. Cloud men sat on the board of directors, were employed by, and invested in the Pan Motor Company. However, the company came to an unceremonious end a few years later when Pandolfo was convicted of mail fraud in Chicago in 1923.

Successful figures in the communications and public utilities industries also had a great influence on St. Cloud in other ways. W.B. Mitchell, Alvah Eastman, and Fred Schilplin were all civic leaders in addition to successful newspaper editors. Albert Whitney shaped the urban development of St. Cloud, while his wife, Alice, was a philanthropist and organizer of community events and organizations. For the past 170 years, St. Cloud has attracted industrious and civically minded men and women.

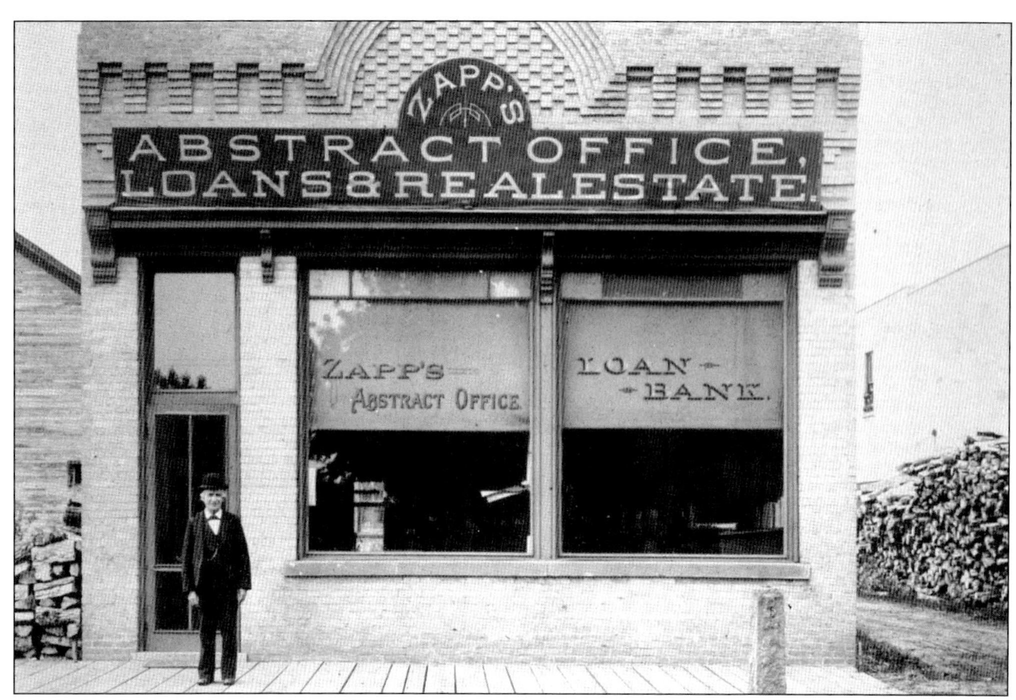

John Zapp, Zapp Abstract Office, c. 1890 (above), and John Zapp, c. 1900 (left). John Zapp arrived in St. Cloud in 1857. In 1861, he was elected register of deeds of Stearns County and became a recognizable and trustworthy citizen in St. Cloud. At a time when confidence in banks had weakened, local residents began depositing their money with Zapp for safekeeping, which he kept in his office safe. In 1870, he opened his own private bank, and in 1907, it was incorporated into Zapp State Bank. In 1998, Zapp Bank was acquired by US Bank, the culmination of a 120-year-old family-run business.

W.B. Mitchell, c. 1930 (right), and St. Cloud Journal-Press and Street Fair Booth, c. 1895 (below). William Bell Mitchell arrived in St. Cloud from Pennsylvania in 1857. He worked in the newspaper office of the *St. Cloud Democrat*, owned by his aunt, Jane Grey Swisshelm. When Swisshelm returned East in 1863, Mitchell purchased the newspaper from his aunt and renamed it the *St. Cloud Journal*. In 1876, he purchased the *St. Cloud Press* and merged the two papers, adopting the name *St. Cloud Journal-Press*. This publication would later combine with other St. Cloud newspapers to become the *St. Cloud Times*. Mitchell is credited with being Stearns County's first historian, publishing the seminal *History of Stearns County* in 1915. The two-volume history provides biographies of Stearns County's earliest residents and businesses and describes events of the county's early history. Mitchell died in 1934 and is buried in St. Cloud's North Star Cemetery.

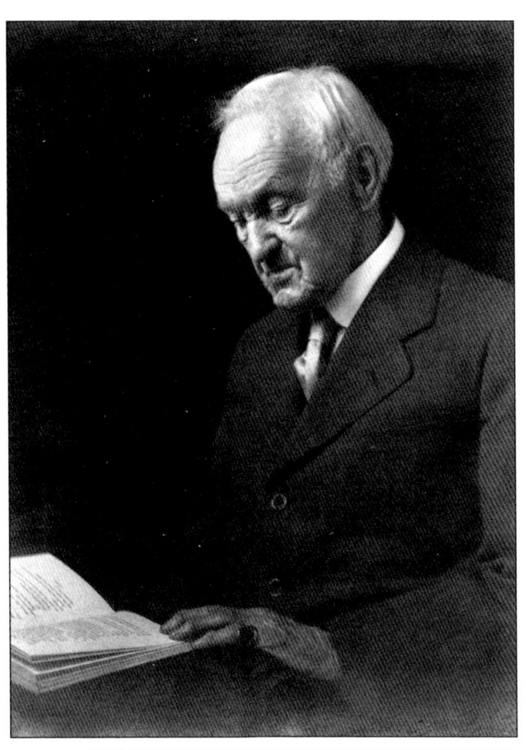

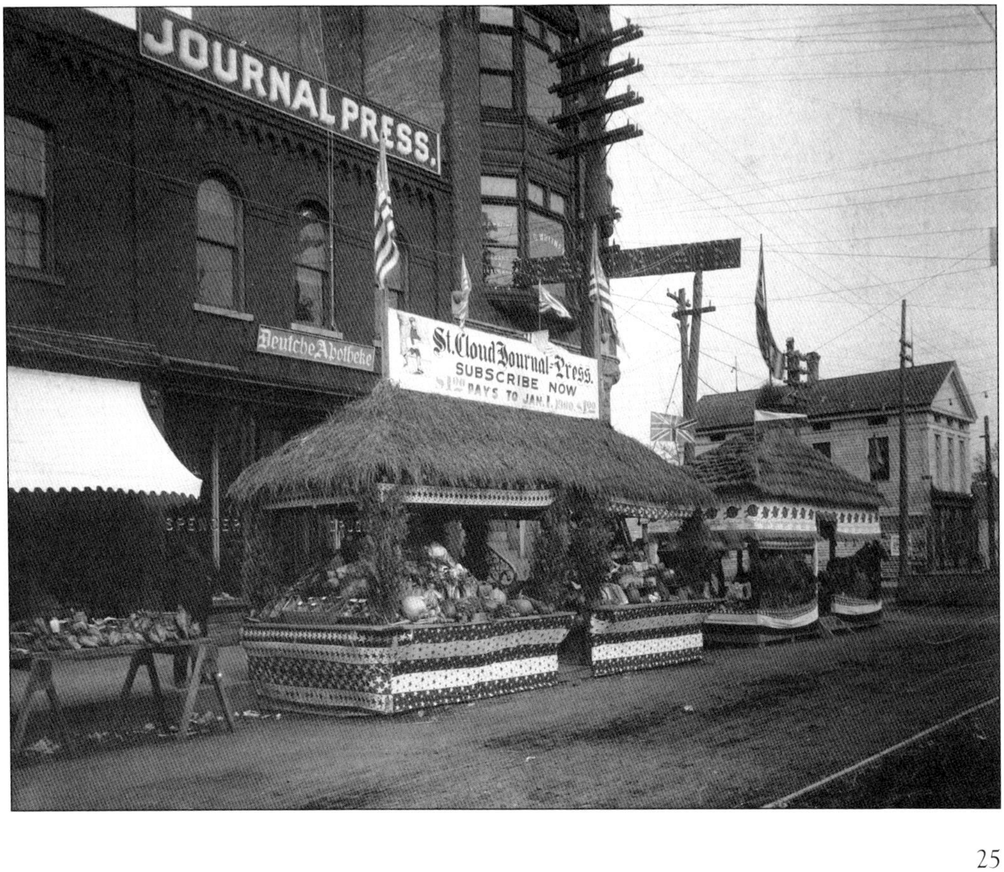

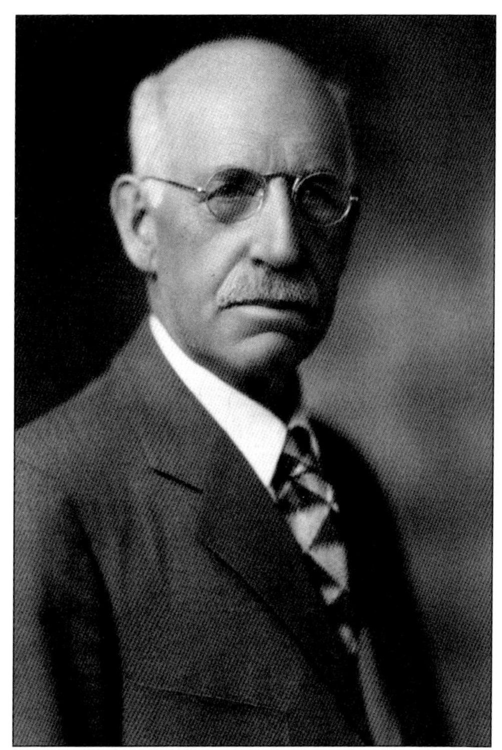

ALVAH EASTMAN, C. 1930 (LEFT), AND HAND PRESSES, THE *ST. CLOUD TIMES*, 1930 (BELOW). Alvah Eastman was a leading citizen of St. Cloud for 47 years. He purchased the *St. Cloud Journal-Press* from W.B. Mitchell in 1892 and became the paper's editor. After the formation of the *St. Cloud Times* in 1929, he remained editor until his death in 1939. Eastman also held a number of notable roles in the St. Cloud community, including president of the St. Cloud park board, receiver of the land office in St. Cloud, resident director of the St. Cloud State Teachers College, founding member of the Stearns County Historical Society, and organizer of the St. Cloud chapter of the Red Cross. He was also known for his generosity, donating land to and establishing scholarships for the Teachers College and providing land to the City of St. Cloud for a city park. After his sudden death on Christmas Eve of 1939, the front page of the *St. Cloud Times* touted the death of "St. Cloud's First Citizen."

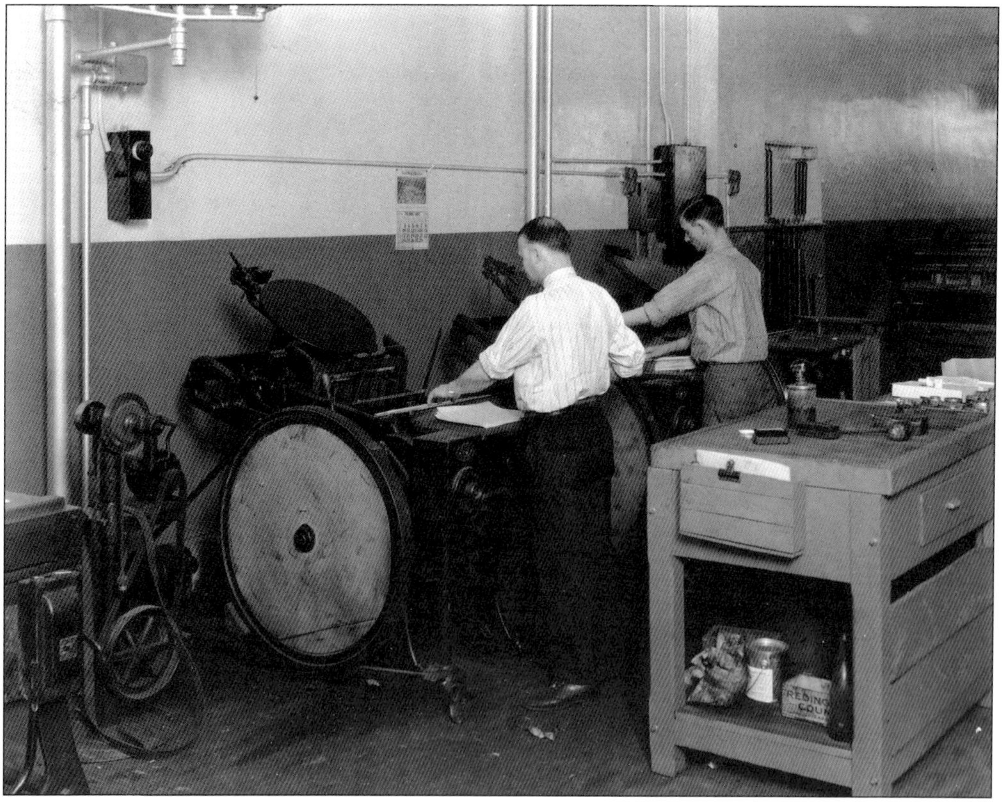

William Campbell, c. 1925 (right), and Carborundum Saw, North Star Granite Plant, c. 1925 (below). Alexander M. Simmers and William Campbell were early pioneers of the granite industry in St. Cloud. In 1898, they formed Simmers & Campbell, which became a leading granite firm in the state of Minnesota. Locally, they provided granite for the St. Cloud Public Library and the Great Northern depot in St. Cloud. In 1919, the partnership dissolved, and each began their own granite companies with their families. Campbell began North Star Granite while Simmers formed A.M. Simmers & Sons. North Star Granite was known nationally for its product, North Star Red, sourced from a quarry near St. Cloud.

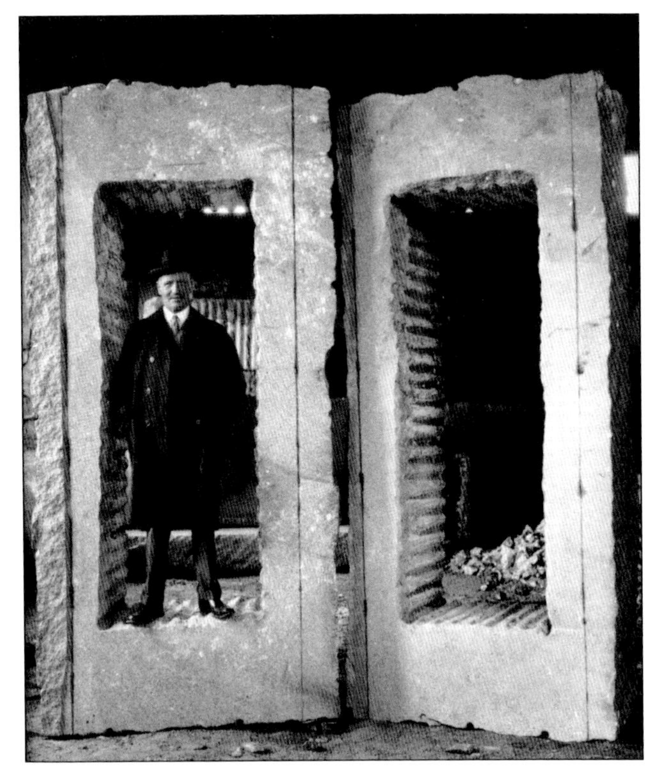

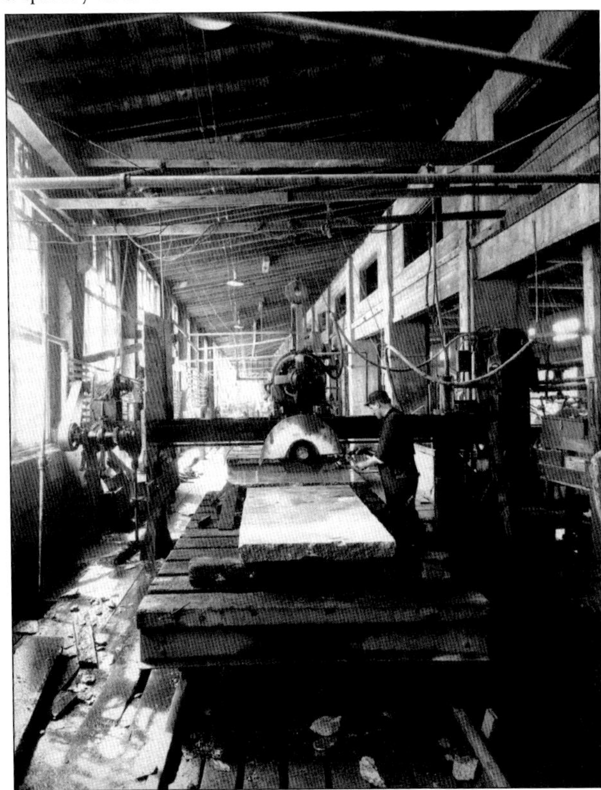

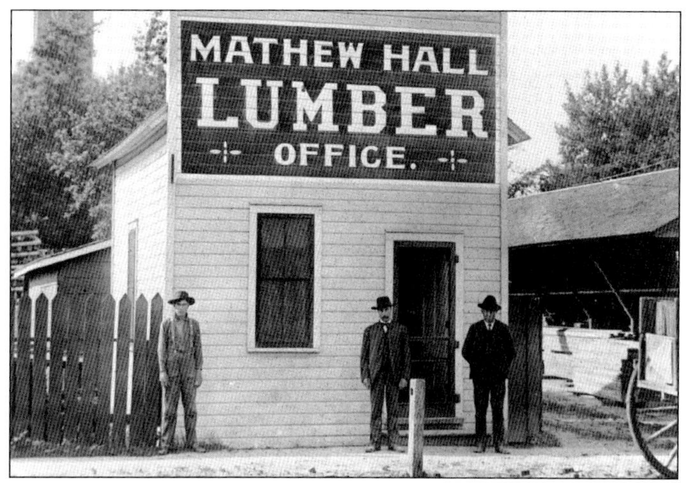

Matthew Hall Lumber Office, c. 1895. After working at C.A. Gilman's sawmills in Benton County, Matthew Hall started his own lumber company in St. Cloud in 1889. Hall was known for his honest treatment of his customers and for extending credit, even during the Great Depression. The business remained in the Hall family for over 100 years until it was acquired by Simonson Lumber in 2019.

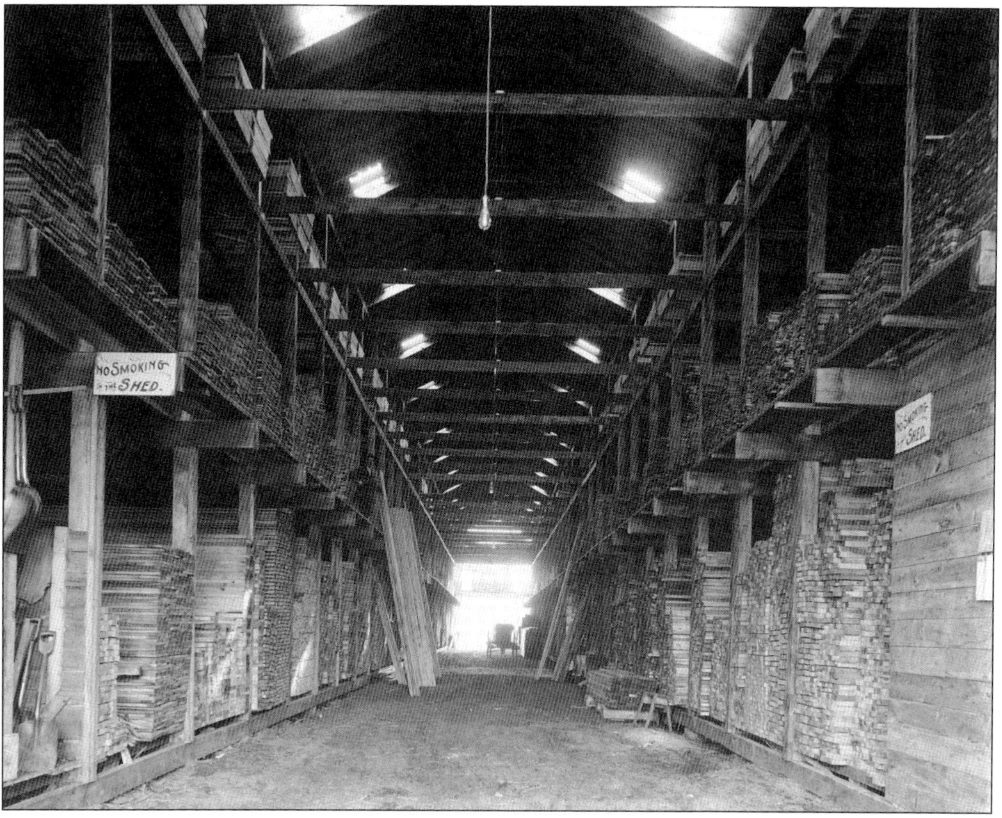

Harkness-Miner Lumber Warehouse, 1903. Business partners C.M. Harkness and George Henry Miner arrived at St. Cloud in 1900. Each had experience working in the lumber industry, Harkness having worked at sawmills in Wisconsin and Washington and Miner working with lumber businesses in Minneapolis. They purchased the lumberyard of W.T. Clark on Eighth Avenue, beginning the Harkness-Miner Lumber Company. This partnership dissolved sometime before 1917.

ALBERT G. WHITNEY, C. 1910 (RIGHT), AND STREET LAMP, ST. GERMAIN STREET, C. 1920 (BELOW). Albert G. Whitney was born near Robbinsdale, Minnesota, in 1860 and lived in several Minnesota towns before settling in St. Cloud in 1887. Whitney was a successful businessman and operated A.G. Land & Loan Company on St. Germain Street. After purchasing the St. Cloud Water and Power Mill Company and St. Cloud Gas and Electric, Whitney organized the St. Cloud Public Service Company in 1904. As the company expanded, it provided electricity for greater Stearns County and parts of Sherburne and Wright Counties. After Whitney's death in 1922, the Northern States Power Company (NSP) acquired St. Cloud Public Service. Whitney's son Wheelock managed the St. Cloud division of NSP.

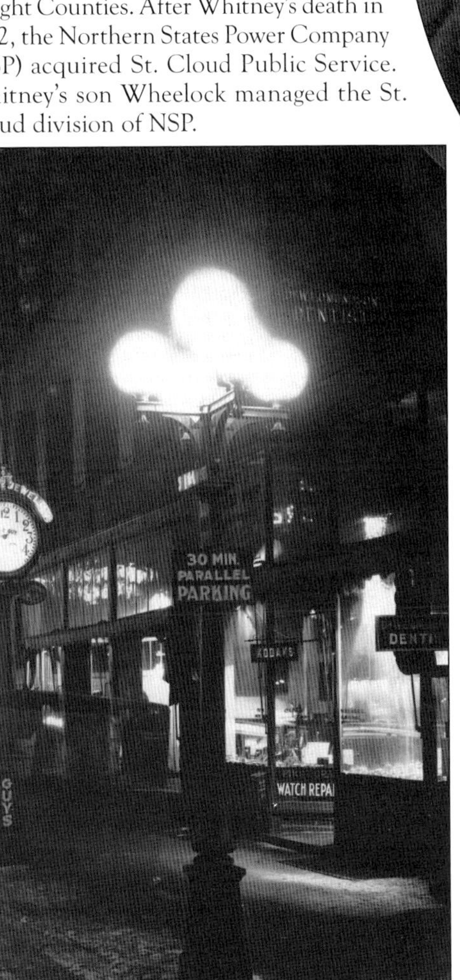

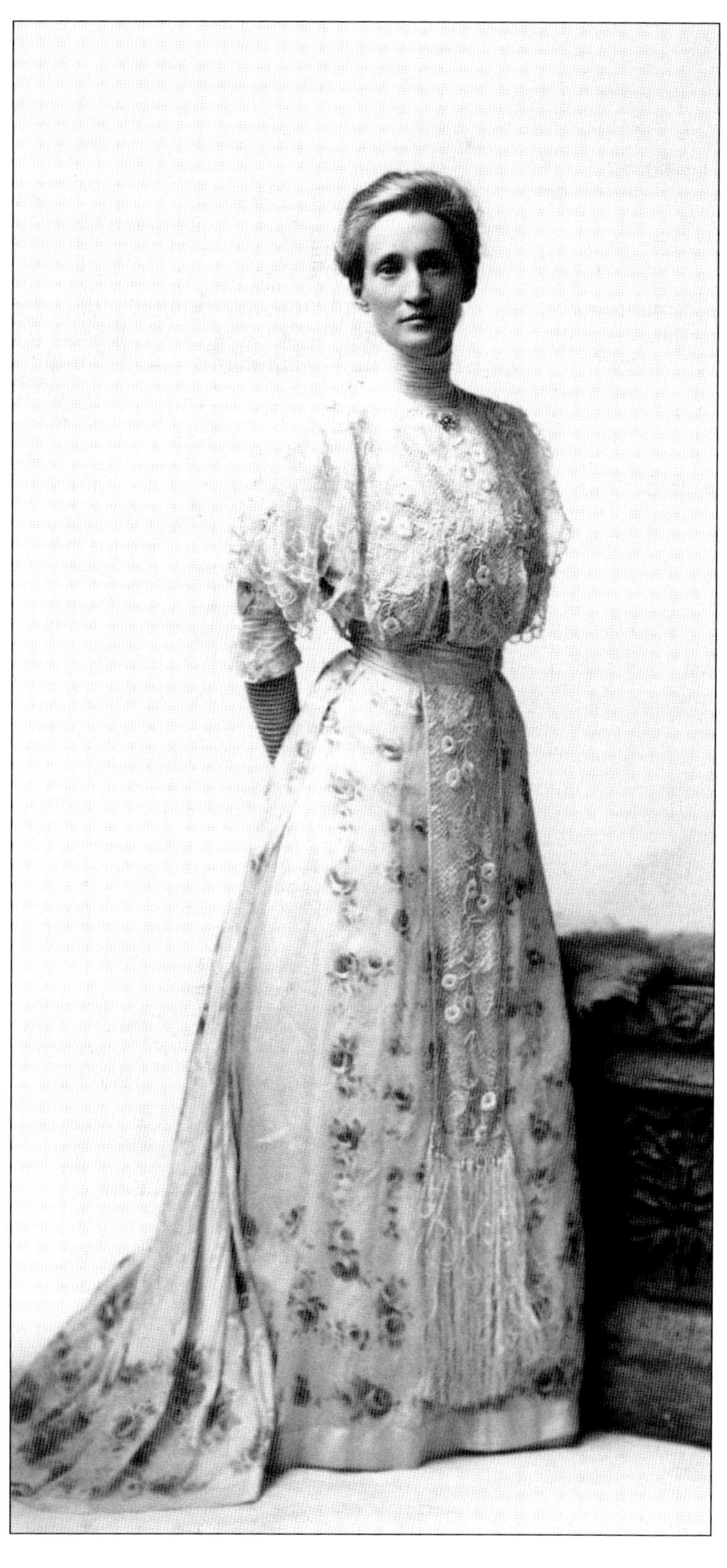

Alice Wheelock Whitney, c. 1890. Alice Wheelock Whitney, the wife of Albert G. Whitney, was an influential and leading citizen of St. Cloud in her own right. She was an active member in several community organizations, including the Reading Room Society, Camp Fire Girls, the Stearns County Historical Society, and the Civic Music Association. She was also on the board of directors of the Minnesota Children's Home. Whitney was a philanthropist and a generous host who opened her home to countless guests. In 1929, she donated 143 acres of land to the City of St. Cloud for the A.G. Whitney Memorial Airport. After it was replaced by another airport built in a different part of town, the land remained in the city's possession and is now Whitney Park.

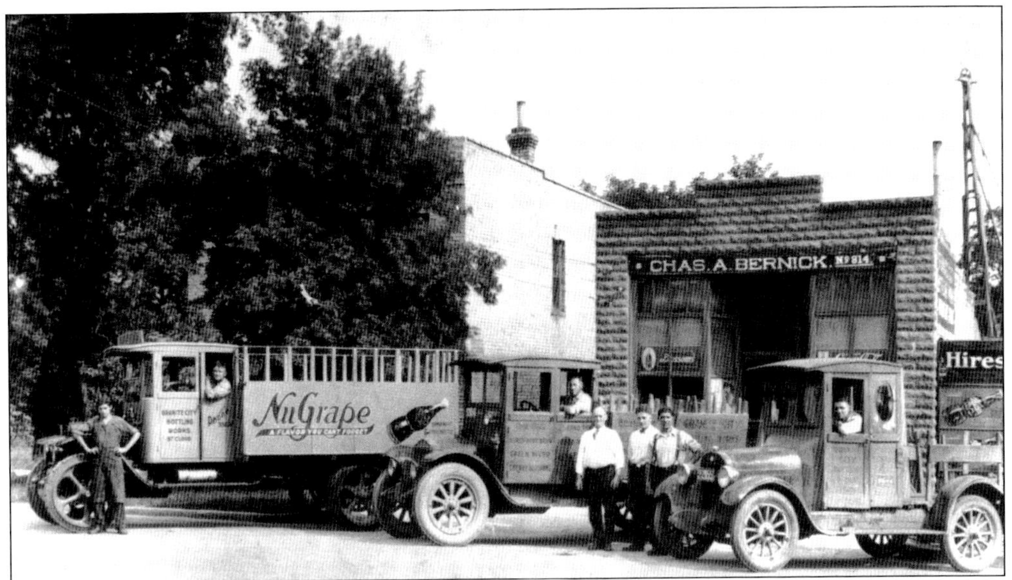

Granite City Bottling Works, c. 1921 (above), and Francis (right) and Richard Bernick at Orange Crush Acquisition, 1956. In 1916, Charles Bernick purchased Granite City Bottling Works. By the 1920s, they were distributing a variety of early soda flavors, including NuGrape and Coca-Cola. After Prohibition ended in 1933, they began distributing Schmidt Beer and remain one of the oldest Schmidt distributors in the country. Shortly following this, they began distributing Dr. Pepper, and in 1952, the company acquired the Pepsi-Cola franchise. Over the following decades, the company continued to grow, and its product line expanded into dozens of varieties of soft drinks and beverages. Now simply known as Bernick's, the over-century-old bottler is still family owned and operated.

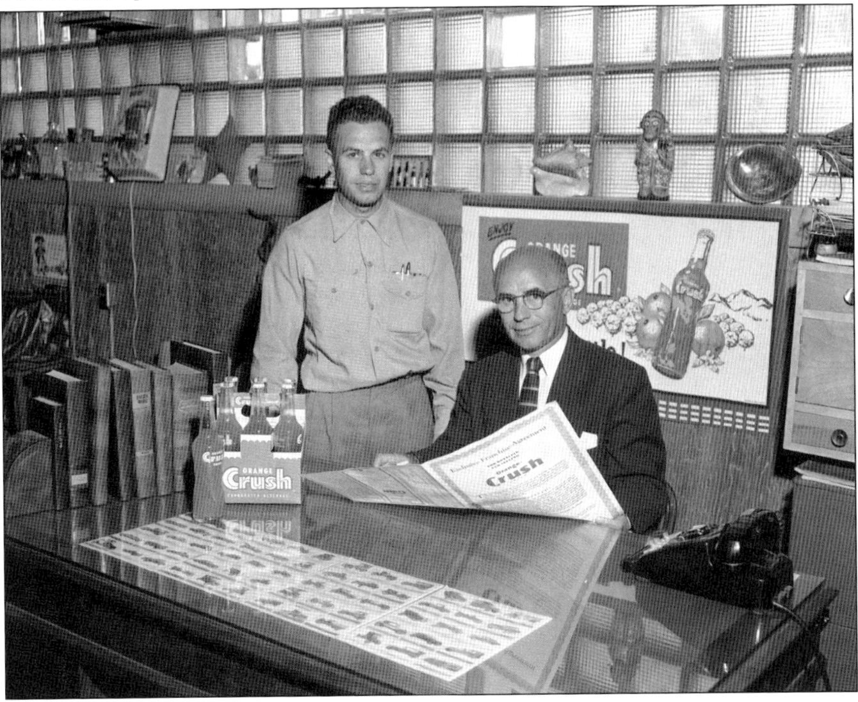

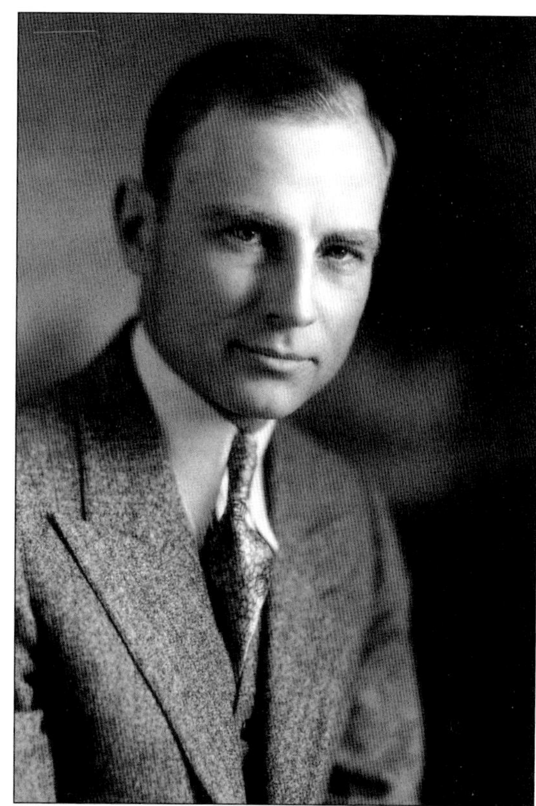

Wilbur Holes, c. 1935 (left), and Holes-Webway Factory, c. 1935 (below). The Holes family arrived in St. Cloud in 1862. Wilbur "Web" Holes, born in 1898 in St. Cloud, developed an innovative form of binding for photo albums, which allowed additional sheets to be added to the album. This style became known as the "Webway" and led to the formation of the Holes-Webway Company. Over the decades, Holes-Webway expanded into stationery and other products. It has survived through a handful of acquisitions and now exists as Creative Memories, based in Sauk Rapids, Minnesota, just across the Mississippi River from St. Cloud.

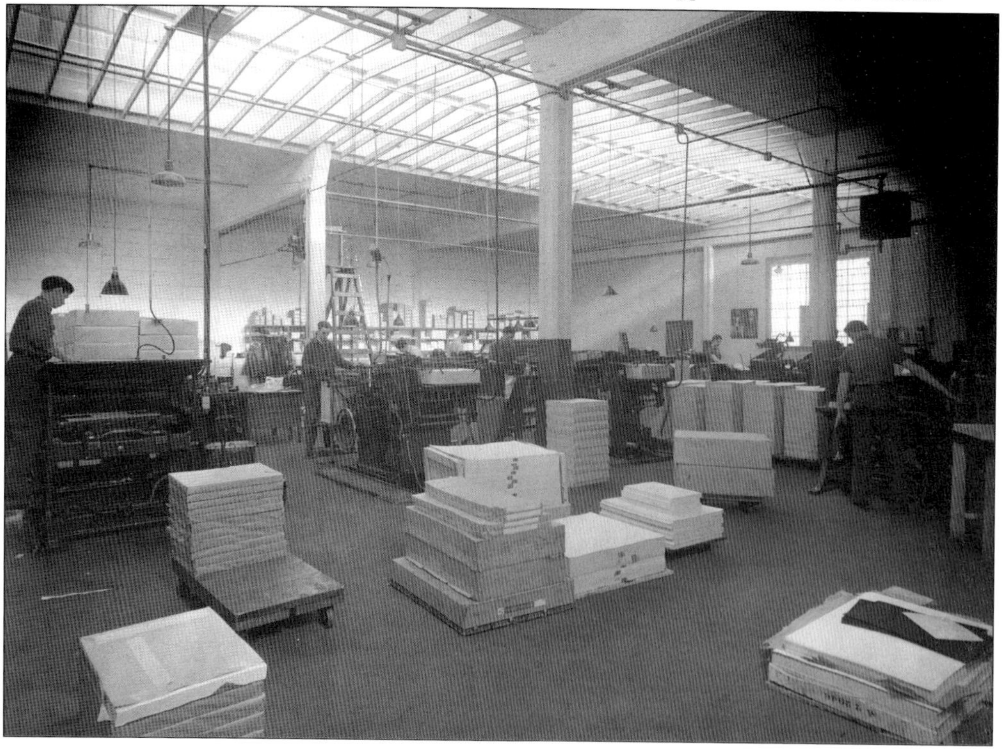

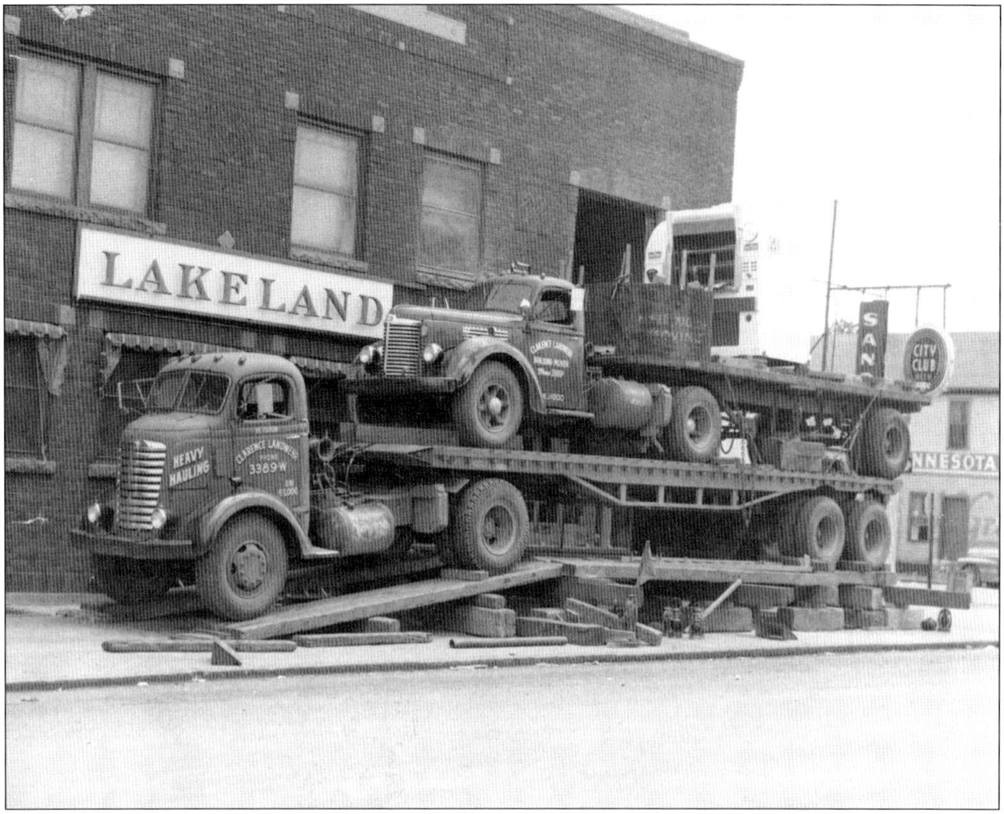

Landwehr Delivers a Dough Mixer to Lakeland Bakery, c. 1950. Landwehr Construction has been in business in St. Cloud for over a century. In 1898, William H. Landwehr acquired a draying business, moving furniture and other household goods in St. Cloud. This aspect of the Landwehr business expanded into moving heavy equipment, bridges, and even entire buildings throughout central Minnesota.

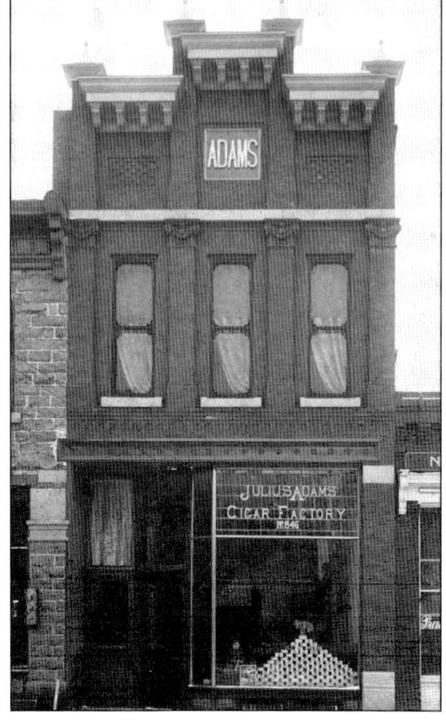

Julius Adams Cigar Factory, c. 1900. In the late 19th and early 20th centuries, tobacco was a major crop in Stearns County. Julius Adams, an immigrant from Germany, started his own cigar factory in St. Cloud in 1895—one of seven that existed in St. Cloud at the turn of the century. Despite the competition, Adams was immensely successful, producing more than one million cigars each year.

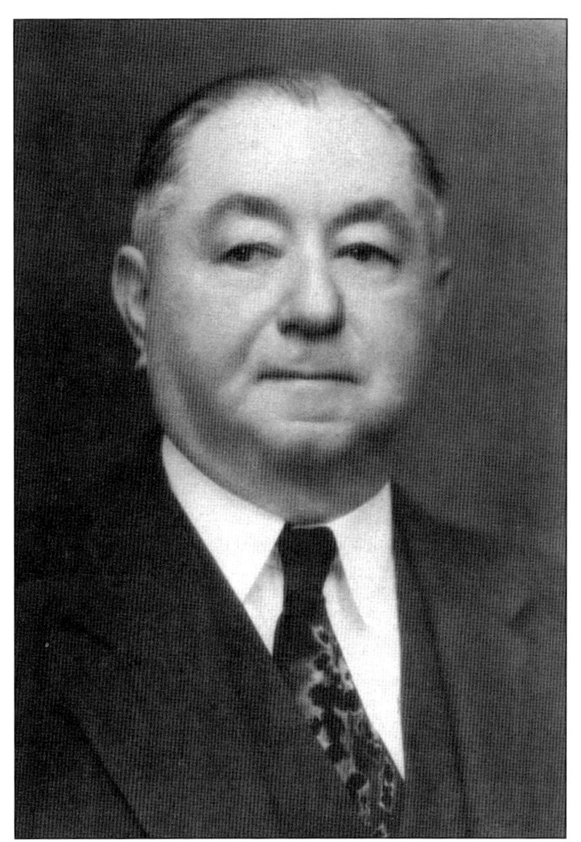

Samuel Pandolfo, c. 1940 (left), and Pan Motor Company, c. 1918 (below). Samuel Pandolfo established the Pan Motor Company in St. Cloud in 1917. Over the next few years, Pandolfo constructed a factory, a hotel, and a residential development for his employees. A charismatic man, Pandolfo was well-loved by the people of St. Cloud, even after he was convicted of mail fraud in 1923. After serving his prison sentence, he returned to St. Cloud to great fanfare and established the Pan Health Food Company in 1928. The company's flagship product was Pan's whole wheat, greaseless donuts. The company dissolved by 1933, and Pandolfo headed west to pursue new ventures. He died in Alaska in 1960. In 2011, his remains were returned to St. Cloud and interred at St. Joseph Cemetery in nearby Waite Park.

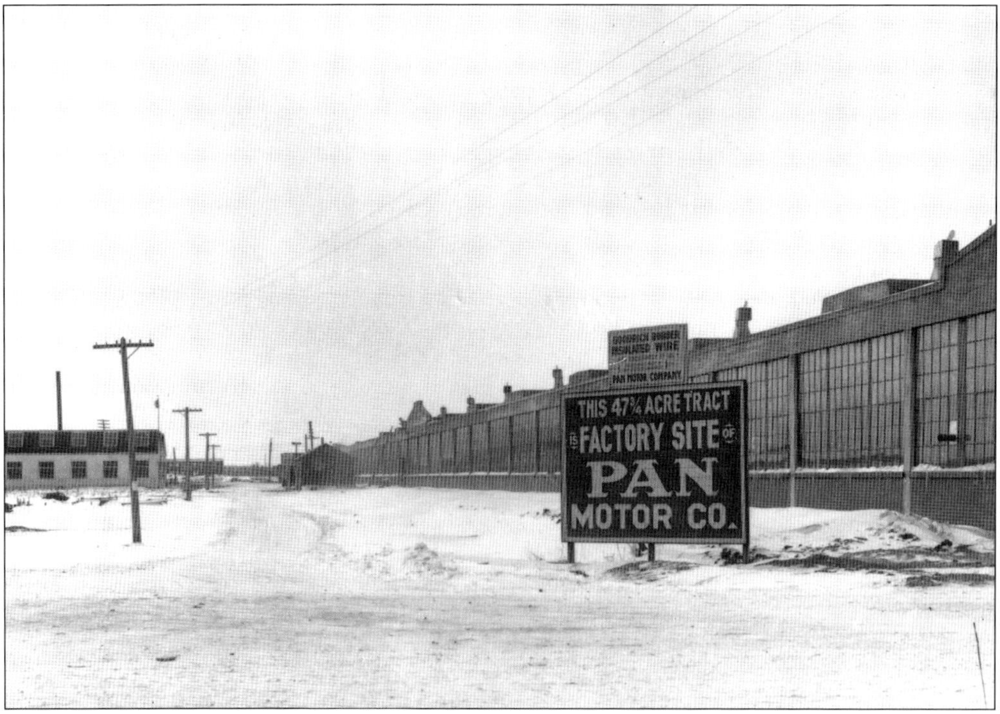

Three

Ora et Educa

Faith and education walked hand-in-hand in the earliest days of St. Cloud. When the first Catholic settlers arrived in St. Cloud in 1853, there were not enough priests present to establish a stable religious life in the new settlement. Missionary priest Fr. Francis Xavier Pierz traveled throughout central Minnesota, celebrating Mass with settler communities whenever there was opportunity, but he appealed to Bishop Joseph Cretin of the Diocese of St. Paul to supply enough clergy to properly minister to the Catholics of the region. In May 1856, five Benedictines arrived in St. Cloud from Pennsylvania and celebrated the first Catholic Mass in the attic of Joseph Edelbrock's home. The ministry of the Benedictines grew from here, and the Diocese of St. Cloud was established by Pope Leo XIII in 1889.

The arrival of the Benedictines in St. Cloud also established the foundation of both Catholic and public education in St. Cloud. In December 1856, Fr. Cornelius Wittmann of St. Cloud began an elementary school in a room of Joseph Edelbrock's residence. He provided free education to Catholic and non-Catholic children of St. Cloud. In 1857, the Protestant families of Lower Town combined enough funds to construct St Cloud's first one-room schoolhouse, the Everett School. The next year, Stearns County commissioners established St. Cloud's first public school district. Founder and pastor of First Presbyterian Church of St. Cloud, Elgy V. Campbell, would later play an instrumental role in expanding the St. Cloud public school system.

St. Cloud buttressed the education of greater Minnesota through the Normal School, now known as St. Cloud State University. The St. Cloud Normal School opened in 1869, providing education for students intending to become educators. These students were incentivized to use their training in Minnesota schools by receiving free tuition if they pledged to teach in Minnesota after their graduation. Over the next 150 years, the school grew into a flourishing state university that dominates the south side of St. Cloud along the high banks of the Mississippi River.

The fulfillment of the spiritual and educational life was as much of a necessity for St. Cloud's early settlers as food and shelter. The Benedictine priests and nuns who arrived in St. Cloud in the 1850s were an answer to the prayers of St. Cloud's Catholic community, and migrants like Elgy V. Campbell ministered to the Protestant communities of St. Cloud. Meanwhile, the Teachers College (later St. Cloud State University) made St. Cloud the educational center of central Minnesota since 1869.

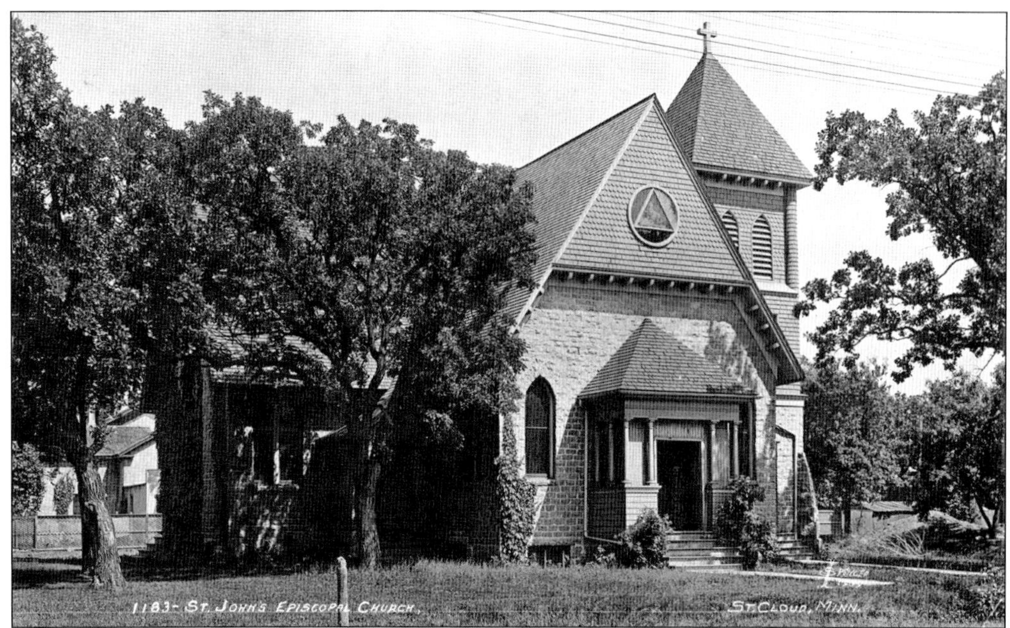

St. John's Episcopal Church, 1908. Organized in 1856, St. John's Episcopal Church is among the earliest churches in St. Cloud. A wood-frame church—the first church building erected in St. Cloud—served the congregants until 1892, when the pictured structure was constructed in its place. In 1969, this granite structure was struck by lightning and destroyed in the resulting fire.

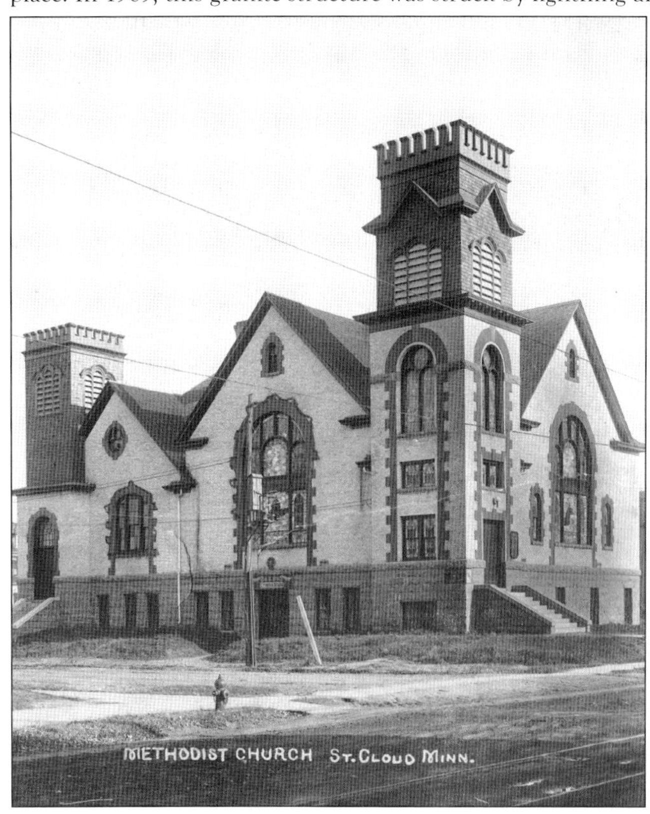

First Methodist Church, c. 1912. The congregation of First Methodist Church is another among the earliest churches of St. Cloud. The first Methodist missionary to come to St. Cloud was Rev. John Pugh in 1857, and the first Methodist congregation of 11 people gathered in 1858. It was not until 1864 that the church had a building to meet in. The pictured structure was dedicated in 1914 when the church's number grew to 277.

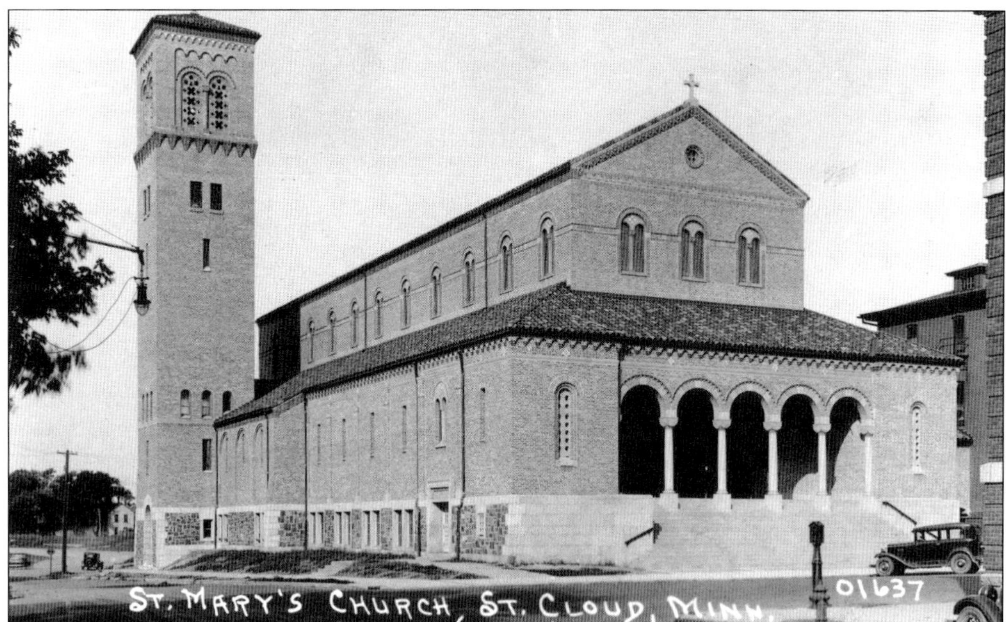

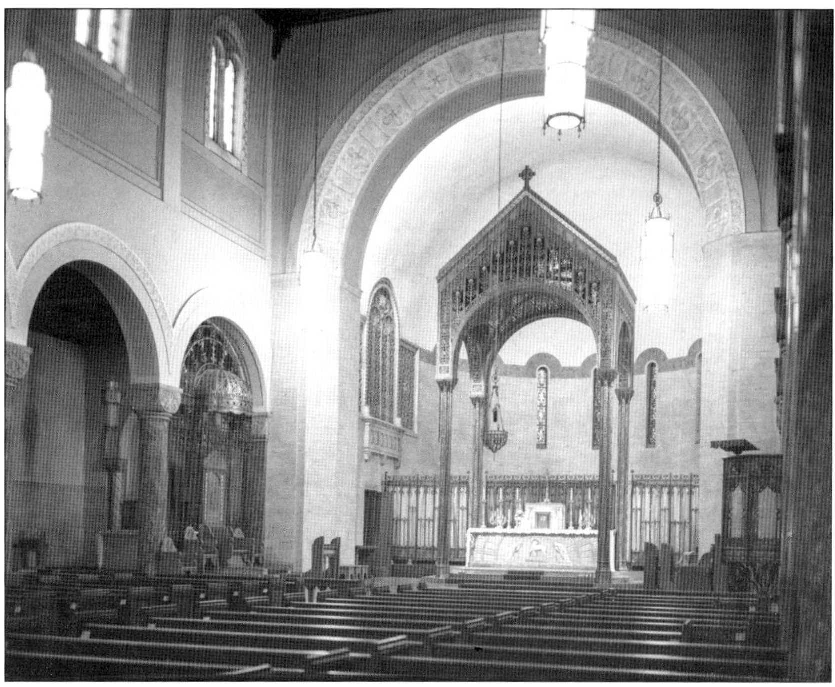

EXTERIOR OF ST. MARY'S CATHEDRAL, C. 1939 (ABOVE), AND INTERIOR OF ST. MARY'S CATHEDRAL, 1944 (BELOW). The Church of St. Mary of the Immaculate Conception—or simply St. Mary's—is firmly rooted in the beginnings of the city of St. Cloud itself. In 1855, J.L. Wilson sold several plots of land to Fr. Francis Xavier, where the first iteration of St. Mary's was constructed. The simple 25-by-35-foot structure was replaced in 1864 by a Gothic-style church. After this second structure burned down in 1920, St. Cloud architect Nairne Fisher designed the basilica church now located on Eighth Avenue, which was constructed in 1931. In 1937, St. Mary's was made the Cathedral Church of the Diocese of St. Cloud.

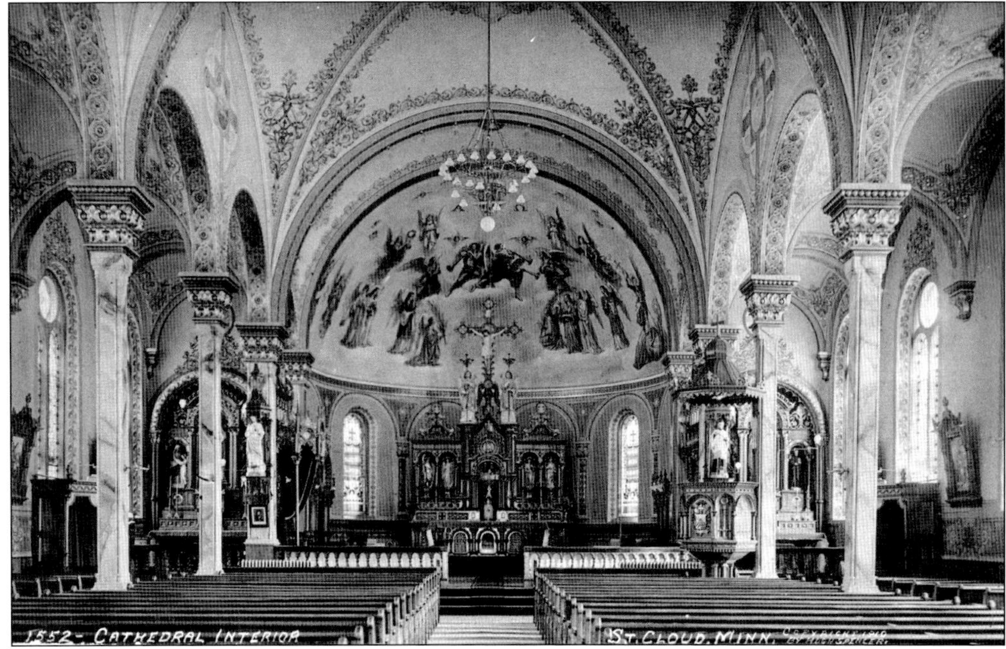

INTERIOR OF HOLY ANGELS PRO-CATHEDRAL, 1893. Holy Angels was the second Catholic parish established in the city of St. Cloud. Founded in 1883, it was established to serve St. Cloud's English-speaking parishioners as an alternative to the German-speaking parish of St. Mary's. It served as the procathedral (or temporary cathedral) of the Diocese of St. Cloud for decades. The church was rebuilt after a devastating fire in 1933. In 1991, due to a priest shortage, the Diocese of St. Cloud merged Holy Angels parish with St. Mary's. Cathedral High School uses the old church as a rehearsal and performance space.

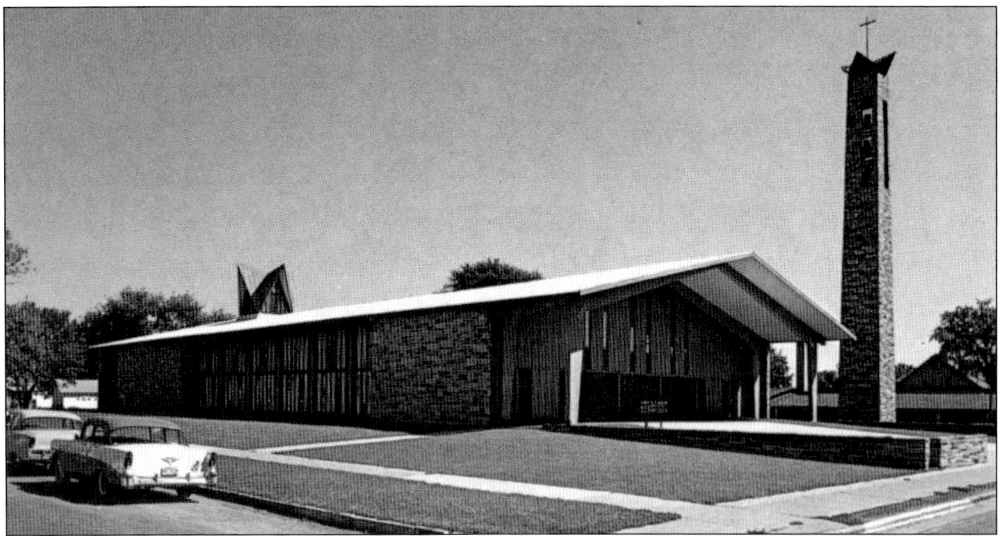

CHURCH OF ST. AUGUSTINE, C. 1963. A native of Albany, Minnesota, Fr. August Preusser served as an Army chaplain during World War I. When he returned to St. Cloud in 1919, Bishop Joseph F. Busch asked him to establish a Catholic parish in east St. Cloud. The parish of St. Augustine was founded that year, and a basement church was completed in 1921. The structure pictured here was built on top of the basement church and dedicated in April 1961.

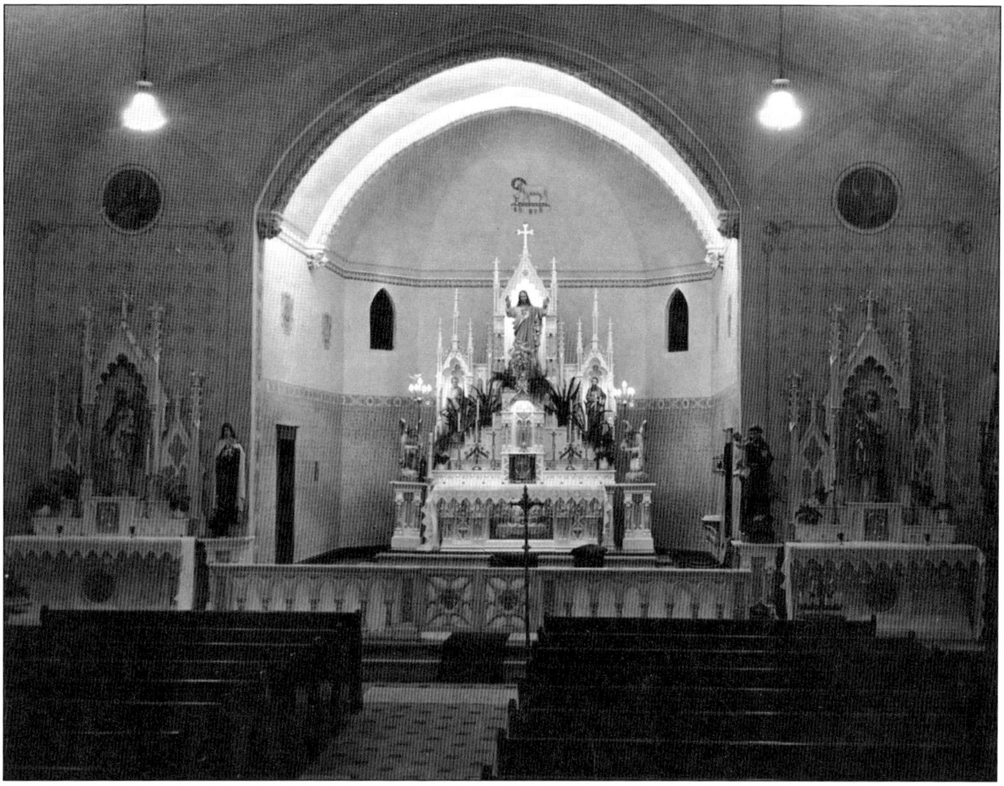

ST. JOHN CANTIUS INTERIOR, C. 1950 (ABOVE), FIRST COMMUNION CERTIFICATE, 1928 (BELOW). For almost 30 years, the Polish Catholics of St. Cloud did not have their own parish where services could be conducted in their own language. After a number of years, Fr. John Kitowski of Opole began holding services with Polish Catholics in the basement of Holy Angels. Finally, in 1893, Bishop Otto Zardetti permitted Father Kitowski to organize a Polish parish in St. Cloud. The parish was fittingly named after a Polish saint, John Cantius. A social hall was constructed where the congregants met and worshiped until the Church of St. John Cantius was built in 1901, the interior of which is pictured above. Below is Meinard Sakry's First Communion certificate in the Polish language from St. John Cantius.

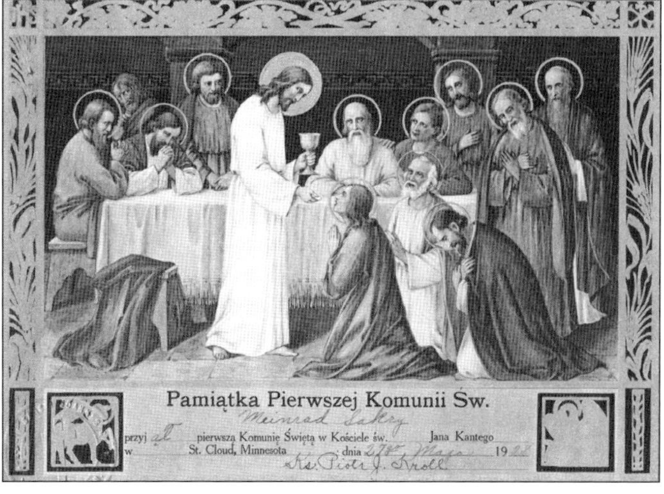

Pamiątka Pierwszej Komunii Św.

Meinrad Sakry

przyj ął pierwszą Komunię Świętą w Kościele św. Jana Kantego

w St. Cloud, Minnesota dnia 27th Maja 1928

Ks. Piotr J. Kroll

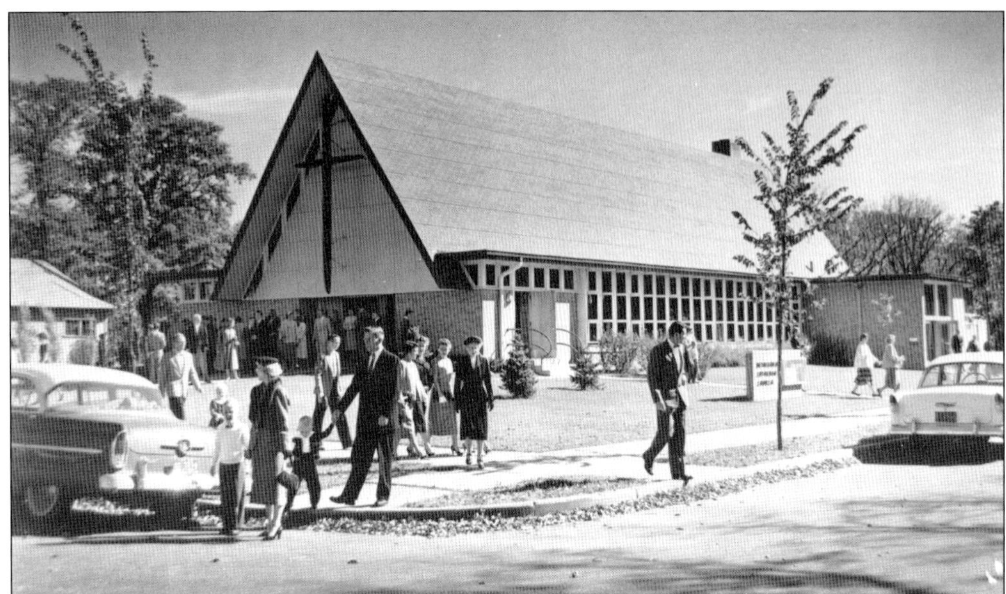

BETHLEHEM LUTHERAN CHURCH, C. 1955. The congregation of Bethlehem Lutheran was founded in 1908 by Lutherans of Norwegian heritage. Until they purchased a building in 1909, they gathered each Sunday in the church of their German brethren at Holy Cross Lutheran. The building pictured was constructed on Fourth Avenue in 1953 when the congregation's number had reached 900.

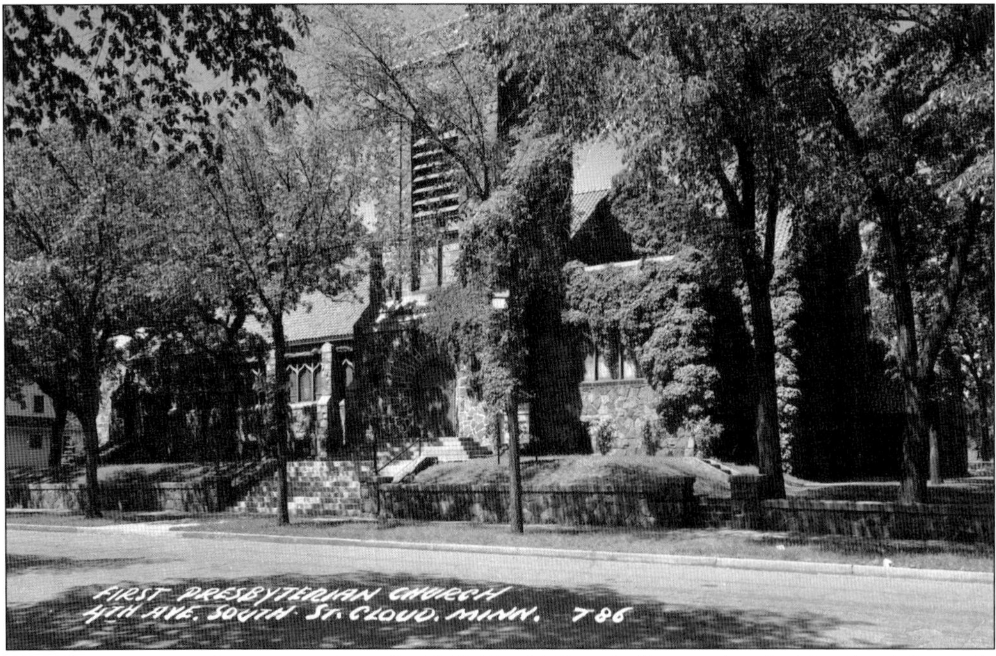

FIRST PRESBYTERIAN CHURCH, C. 1930. In 1864, Elgy V. Campbell arrived in St. Cloud with his wife, Mary Shane. He soon organized a Presbyterian congregation with a total membership of 10 people. A building was constructed in 1865 for the congregation to meet in, so simple in its appearance that it was nicknamed the "Presbyterian warehouse." By 1916, however, the congregation had grown to such a number that they were able to construct a new church building at a cost of $70,000. It was completed in 1917 and remains in use to this day.

E.V. Campbell, c. 1915. After organizing the First Presbyterian Church in St. Cloud, Campbell was hired as the church's first pastor in 1871. Besides his flock, he was committed to the greater education of St. Cloud. He served on St. Cloud's school board and is credited as a founder of the St. Cloud public school system, being the driving force behind the funding and building of Union School. After pastoring for 57 years, he retired in 1922 at the age of 86.

Union School, c. 1877. Union School was the first public schoolhouse constructed with St. Cloud tax dollars after the student population outgrew the Everett School. It was constructed in 1869, and in 1898, two wings were added to the building to accommodate the growing student population. In 1930, Central Junior High School was constructed and attached to the old Union School. In 1961, the Union School portion was finally demolished, and Central Junior High was later converted into the St. Cloud City Hall in 1984.

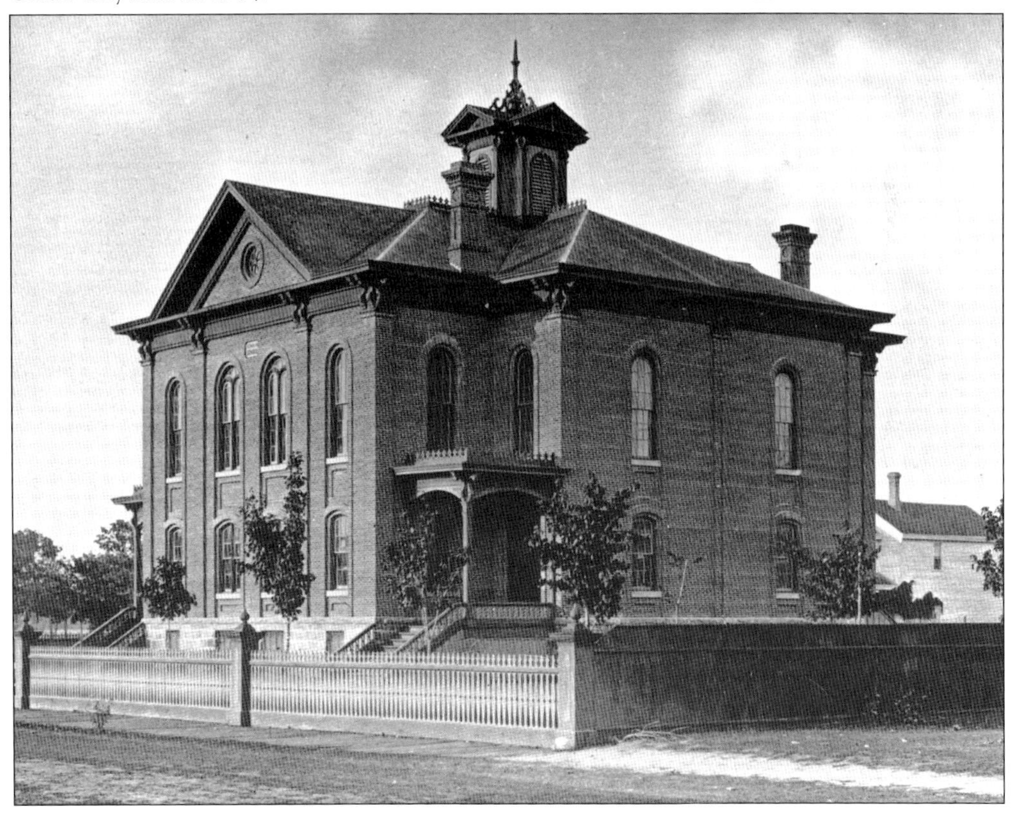

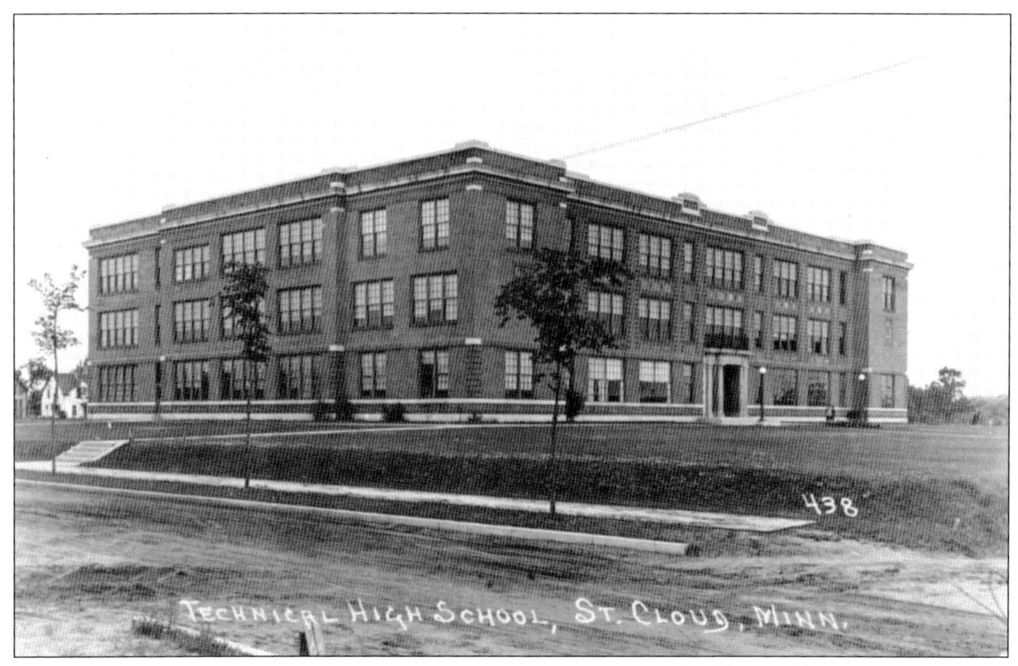

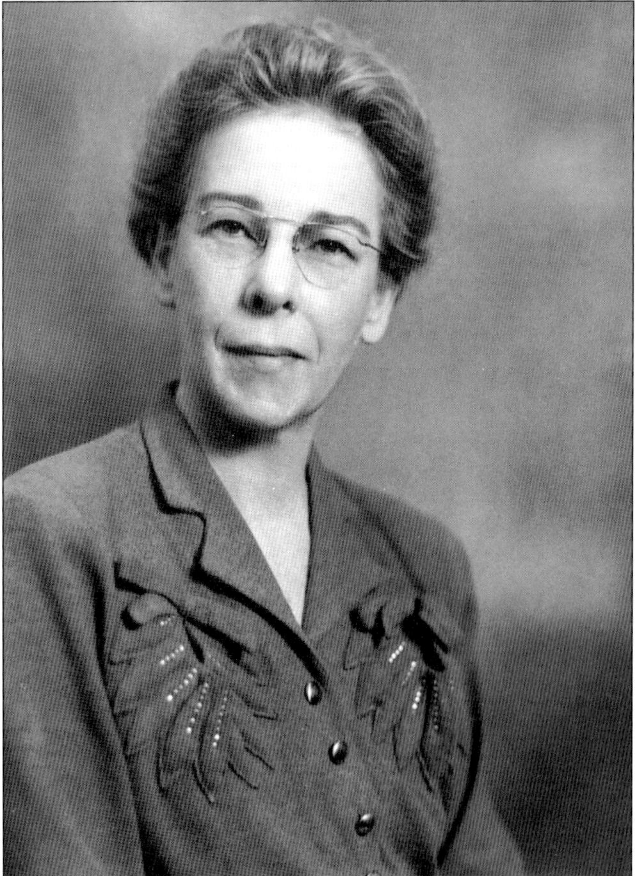

St. Cloud Technical High School, c. 1920. The construction of Technical High School was completed in January 1917, accommodating the growing student population of St. Cloud. The school was given its name due to the technical skills taught to students, including printing, typewriting, and accounting. The 1917 building was in use until a new Tech High building was completed in 2019. The original building was renovated and converted into the new St. Cloud City Hall in 2022.

Helen Carter, 1946. A graduate of St. Cloud Normal School, Helen Carter taught English, Latin, and music at Technical High School. After 10 years of teaching, in 1929, Carter resigned in protest when several teachers were let go due to high salaries. She returned to Tech High in 1946 and continued teaching until her retirement in 1965 at the age of 65.

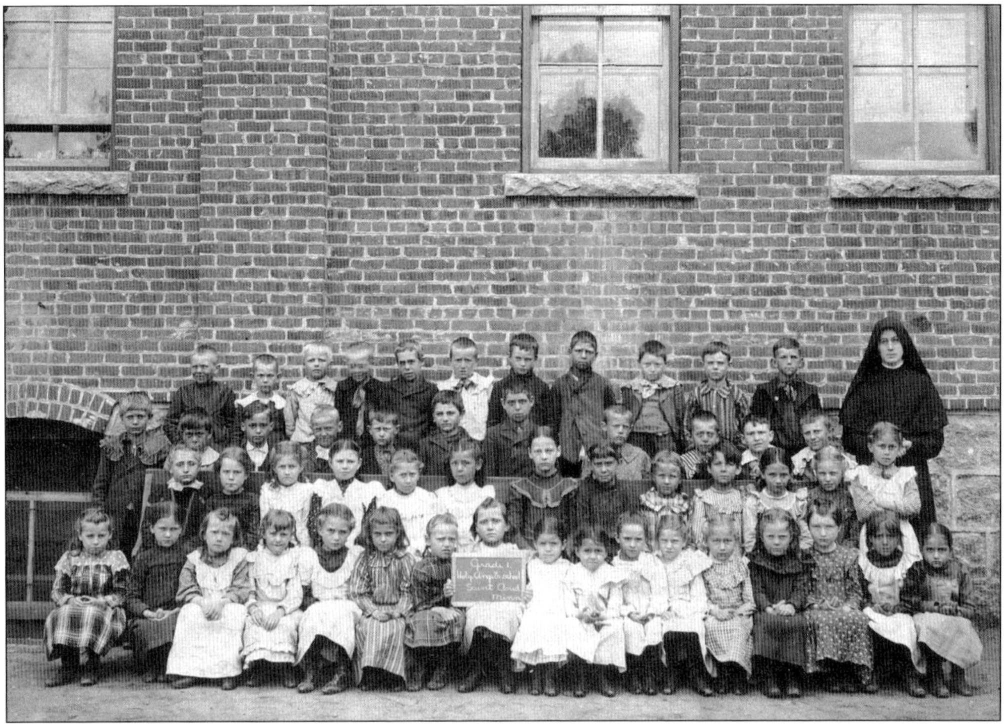

Holy Angels School First-Grade Class, c. 1910. Shortly after the establishment of the Holy Angels parish, parish children received education in a one-room schoolhouse. But in 1887, Holy Angels Grade School officially began with the construction of a three-story brick building and an enrollment of 160 students. When St. Cloud's first bishop, Otto Zardetti, arrived in 1889, he charged the parish clergy to establish Holy Angels Grade School as an exemplary center of education for both Catholic and public schools. The grade school dissolved in 1967, and its students were transferred to other parish schools in the city.

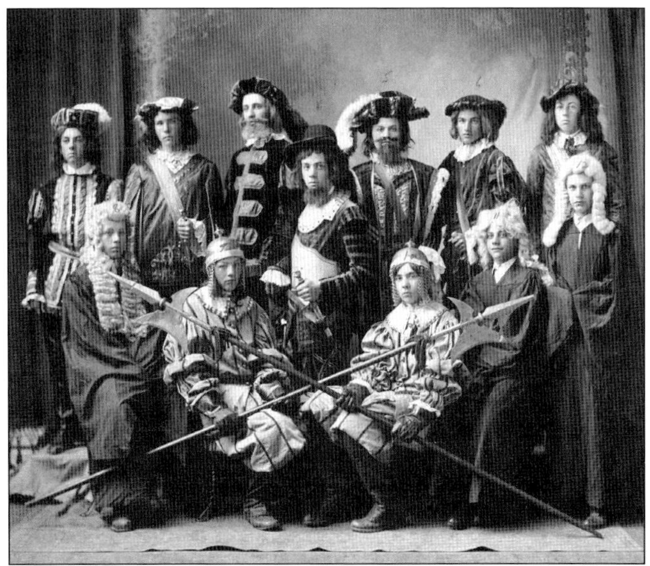

Cathedral High School Cast of Sir Thomas More, 1912. Cathedral High School began in 1902 when Holy Angels Grade School principal Sr. Eleanor Irving added a ninth-grade class to the school. The school expanded significantly in the 20th century, with building additions constructed in 1914, 1938, and 1956 and a gymnasium built in 1965. Cathedral High School's enrollment reached its peak in 1964 with 1,621 students. Although St. Mary's became the cathedral of the St. Cloud Diocese in 1937, the school retained the Cathedral name.

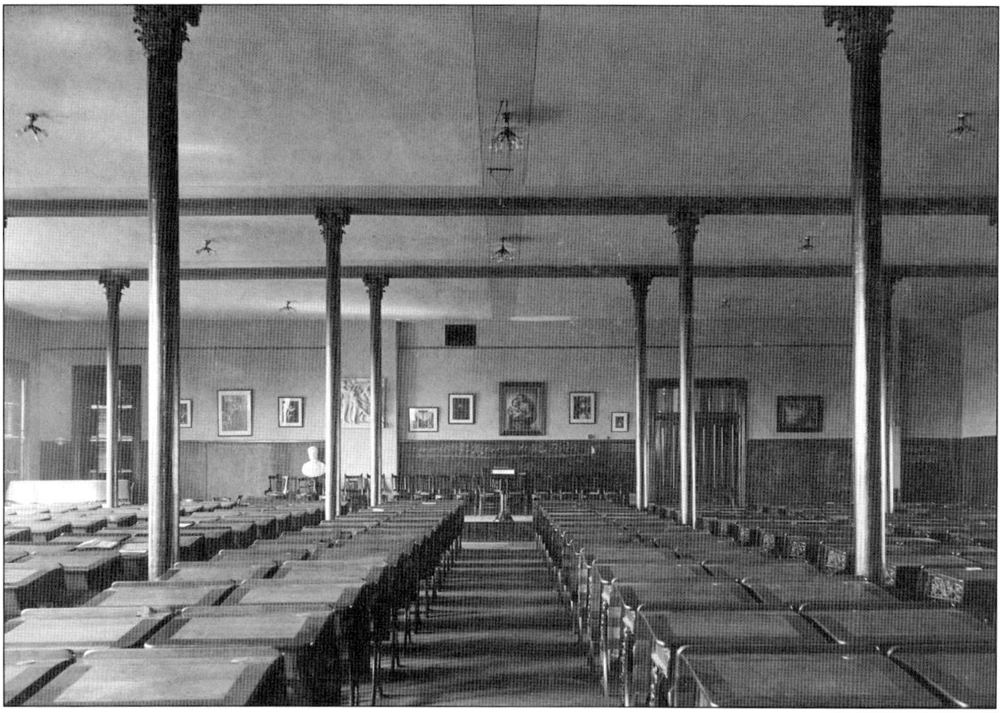

Normal School Assembly Hall, 1901 (above), and Kindergarten Model Class, 1897 (below). St. Cloud State University began as the St. Cloud Normal School in 1869 with 50 students. The Normal School educated and trained students to be future teachers, and tuition was free for those who pledged to teach in Minnesota schools. Instruction included model classes where Normal School students could practice teaching with local children. In 1921, the Normal School changed its name to the Teachers College, and the school awarded its first bachelor's degree in 1928. After a series of name changes over the years, the school officially became St. Cloud State University in 1975. (Both, courtesy of St. Cloud State University Archives.)

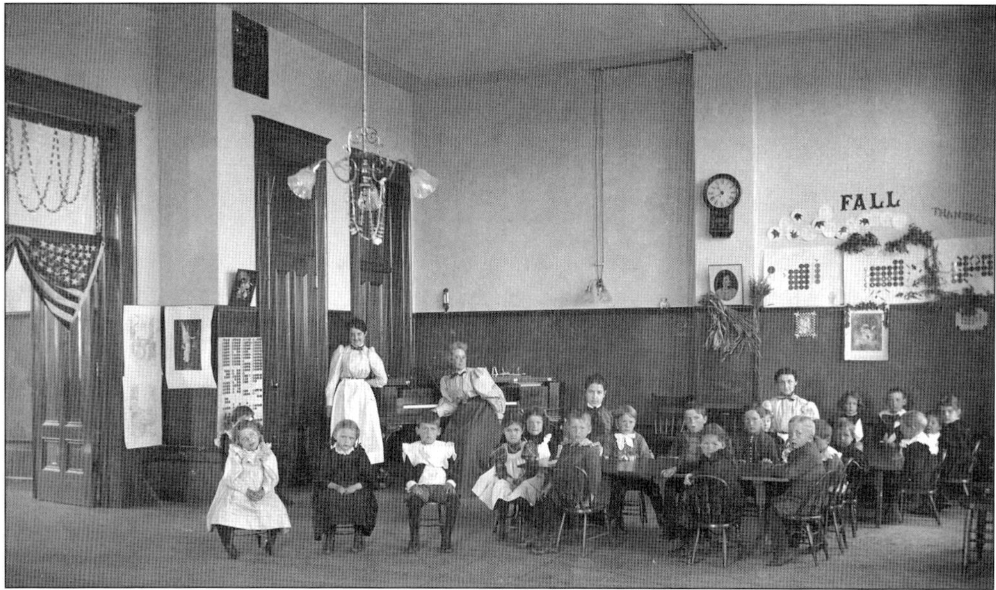

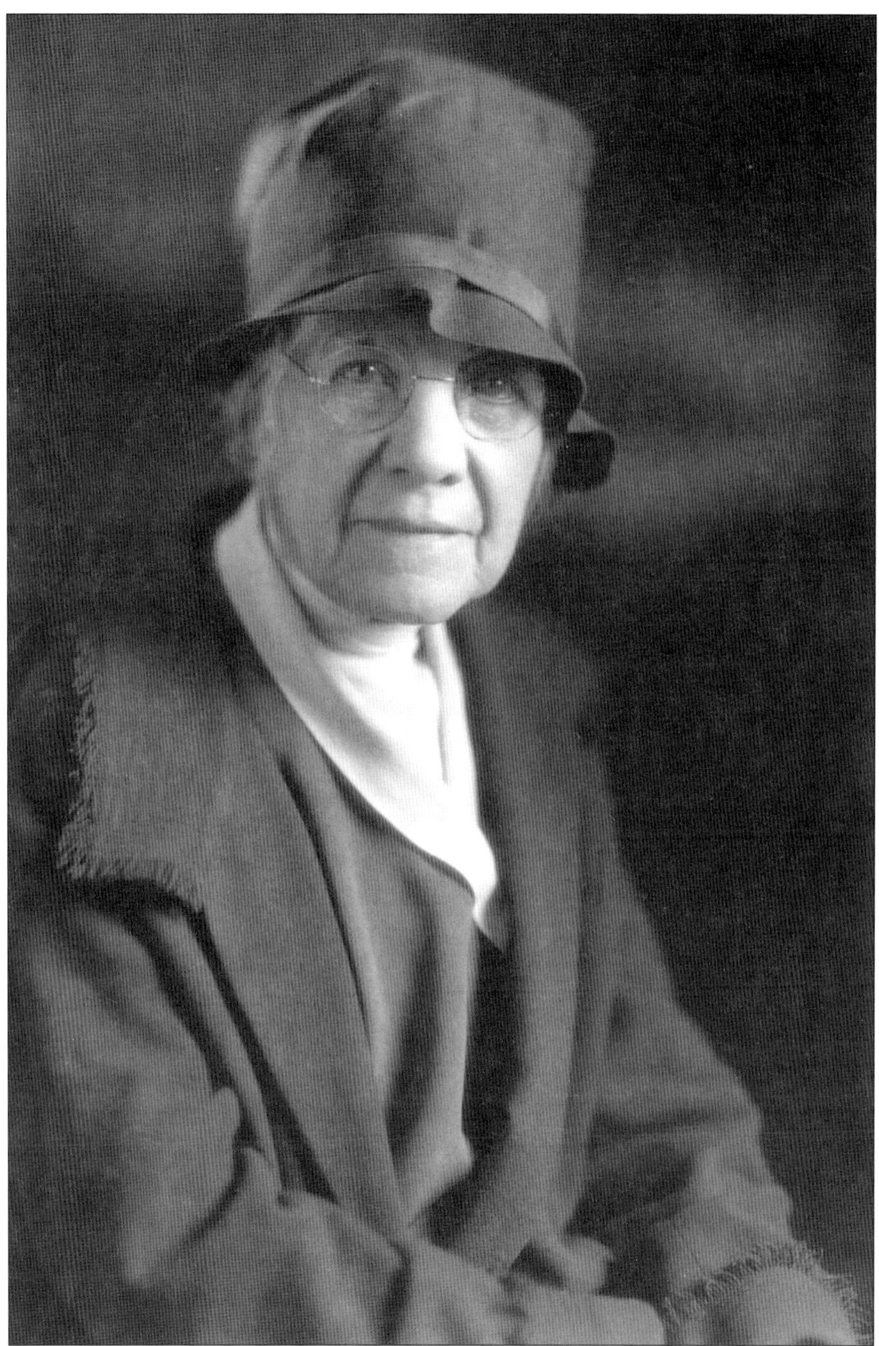

Isabel Lawrence, c. 1935. Isabel Lawrence is a major figure in the history of St. Cloud State University. When she arrived in St. Cloud in 1879, St. Cloud State was a school for training future teachers, and Lawrence was made director of the practice school. Between 1914 and 1916, Lawrence served as St. Cloud State's acting president, the first woman to hold that position in the school's history. She remained at the school for over 40 years, and the school dormitory Lawrence Hall is named in her honor. In addition to her vital role in education, she was also an active member of the League of Women Voters and is listed in their National Honor Roll.

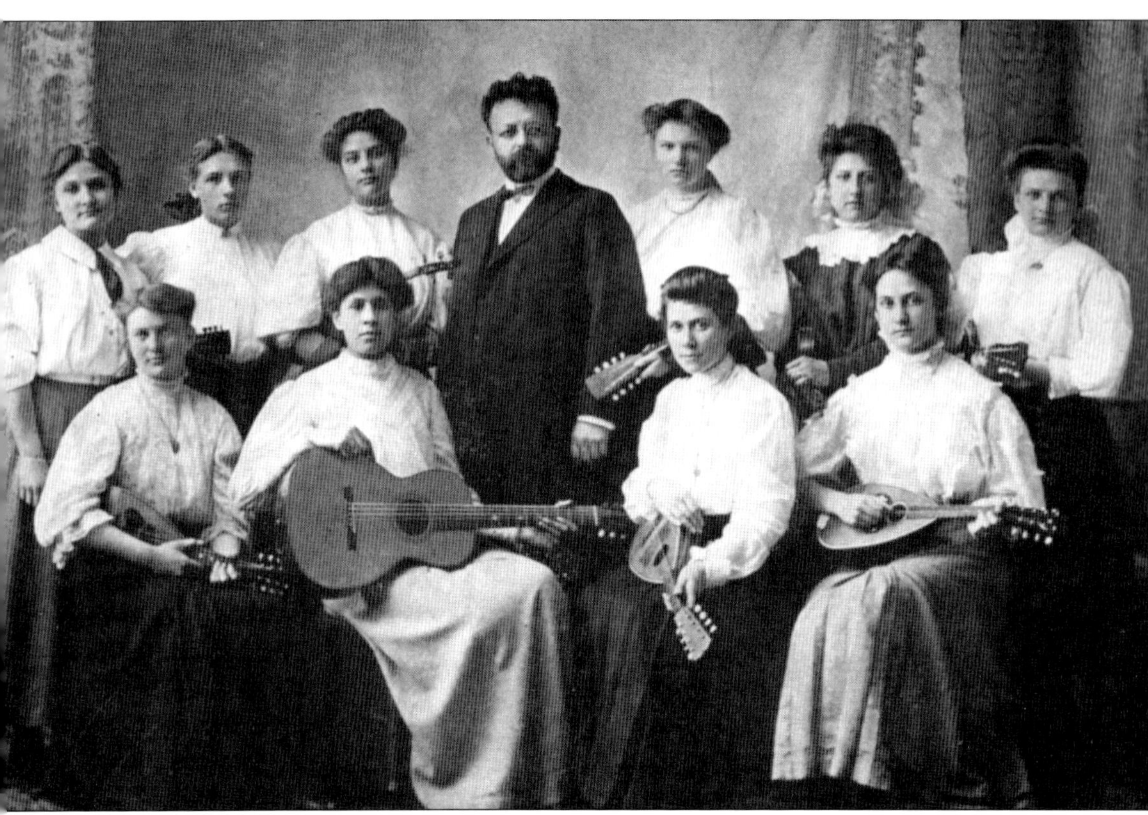

St. Cloud High School Orchestra, 1906. Ruby Cora Webster (first row, second from the left, holding a guitar) was born in 1889 to former slaves John and Lizzie Webster in Delphos, Ohio. Webster and her three siblings moved with her parents to St. Cloud sometime between 1888 and 1893. She attended St. Cloud High School, graduating in 1908. She enrolled in St. Cloud Normal School later that year and was the school's first Black graduate. After graduating, she worked as a teacher in Kansas City, Missouri, then spent the rest of her life in Canada. In 2018, St. Cloud State University's 51 Building was named the Ruby Cora Webster Hall in her honor. Her parents are buried in North Star Cemetery in St. Cloud.

Four

Hands that Built St. Cloud

St. Cloud has long been a hub of labor and agricultural productivity, with its location along the Mississippi and Sauk Rivers shaping its economy. The hardworking individuals in quarries, fields, and factories laid the foundation for the city's growth and prosperity.

The discovery of rich granite deposits in the 1850s made the city a cornerstone of the American stone industry. Quarrymen, many skilled immigrants from Scotland, Ireland, and Scandinavia, extracted and shaped stone used in monuments and infrastructure nationwide. Working with hand tools and steam-powered machinery in challenging conditions, these laborers demonstrated strength, precision, and resilience, leaving a lasting legacy in the city.

Before railroads, the Mississippi River served as a vital transportation route. Steamboat crews, including pilots, deckhands, and engineers, moved agricultural products, timber, and manufactured goods while navigating dangerous currents and unpredictable weather. Their labor connected St. Cloud to broader markets and facilitated regional commerce.

Farming has long been central to the area's economy. Early settlers cultivated wheat, corn, and oats, while dairy farming became a staple. Farmhands and migrant workers planted, harvested, and maintained livestock, ensuring a steady supply of food and raw materials for local use and export. Dairy operations and food processing, including companies like Heim Milling, employed laborers in milking, milling, packaging, and distribution, sustaining the region's agricultural reputation.

Industrial labor also became significant as the city modernized. The Frigidaire freezer plant, active in the mid-20th century, employed hundreds on assembly lines, quality control, and production of appliances for nationwide distribution. Their work exemplified the city's shift from agrarian to industrial labor.

Labor movements in St. Cloud reflected national trends. Workers organized for better wages, safer conditions, and improved rights. Unions in the granite industry, for example, strengthened safety protocols and labor standards. Across farming, quarrying, and manufacturing, these efforts shaped the city's workforce and left a lasting impact on its labor landscape.

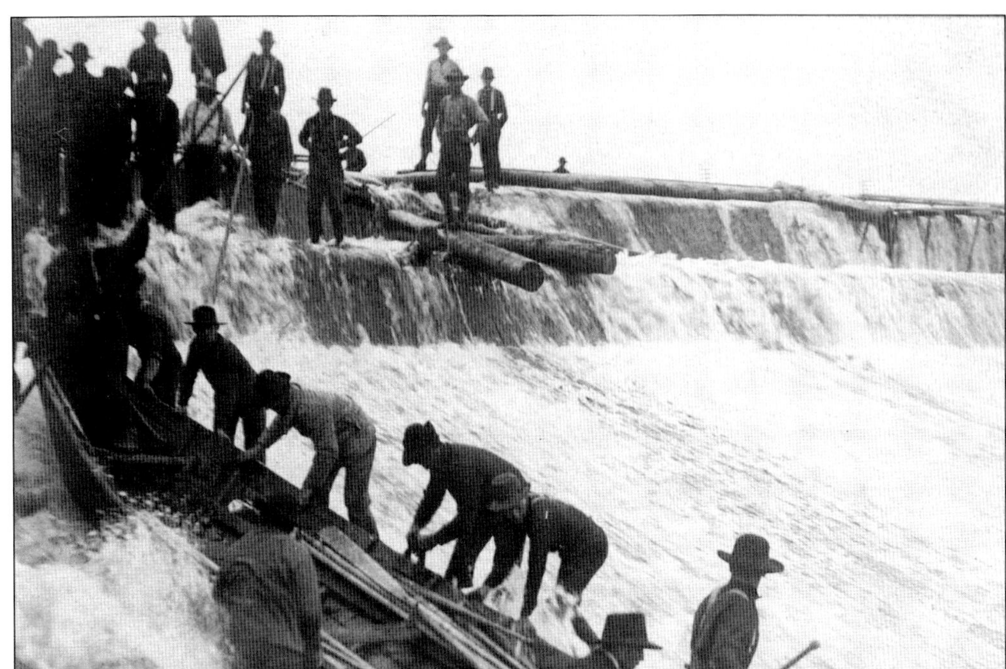

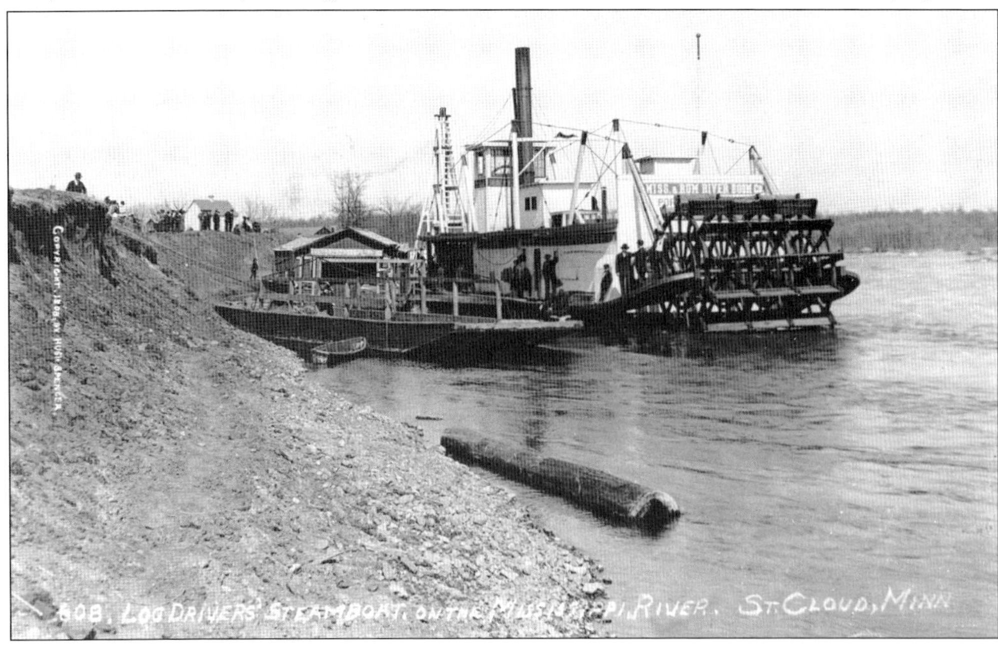

LOGGERS ON THE MISSISSIPPI DAM, 1908 (ABOVE), AND LOG DRIVERS ON A STEAMBOAT ON THE MISSISSIPPI RIVER, 1908 (BELOW). Logging in the 19th century was grueling and complex. Entire crews, teams of oxen, sleds, and supplies, had to be gathered from hundreds of miles away, roads had to be cut through the timber, and everything had to be ready to start before winter set in. It required careful planning, hard physical labor, and endurance just to get started. Once the logging crew arrived, the work was backbreaking. Men felled massive trees with axes and saws, hauled logs over rough terrain using oxen and sleds, and endured freezing winter conditions. Each day required strength, skill, and coordination, as a single mistake could ruin hours of effort or risk serious injury.

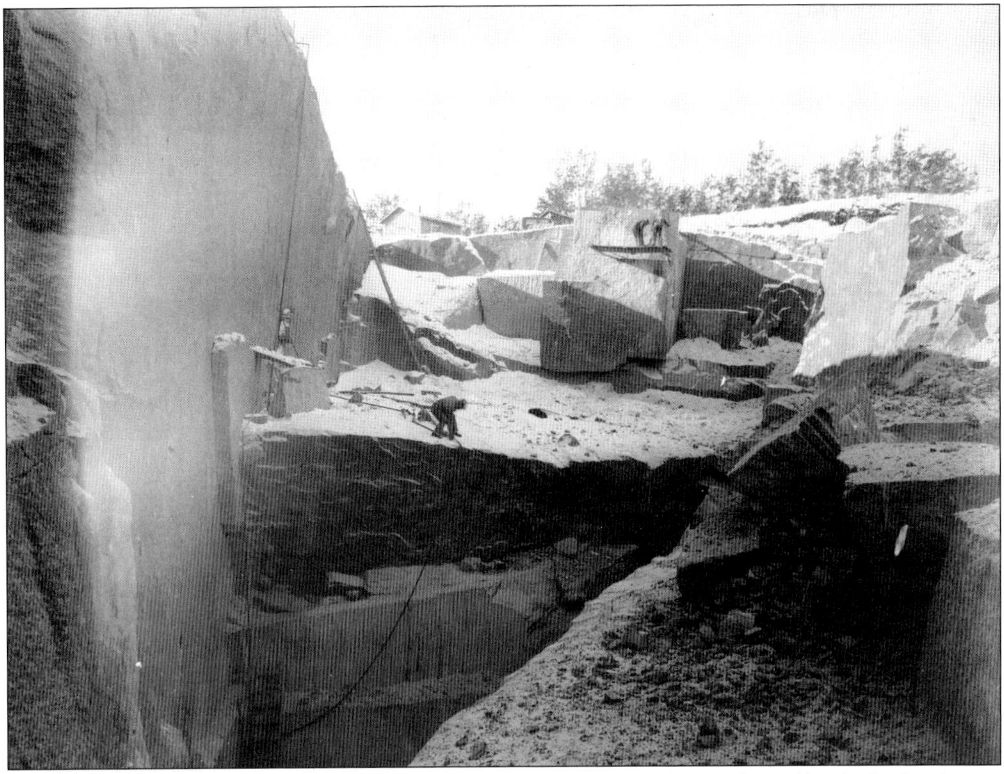

North Star Granite Quarries, c. 1925. St. Cloud's granite industry shaped both the landscape and the people who worked it. The granite's unique consistency within a single quarry allowed builders to match stone perfectly across large projects, while the variety of colors, from soft grays to deep pinks, came from multiple ancient magma formations beneath the region. Extracting this high-quality stone required intense manual labor; quarrymen used drills, chisels, and sheer strength to cut and haul massive blocks before the days of mechanization. Their skill and endurance turned local stone into monuments, churches, and buildings recognized around the world.

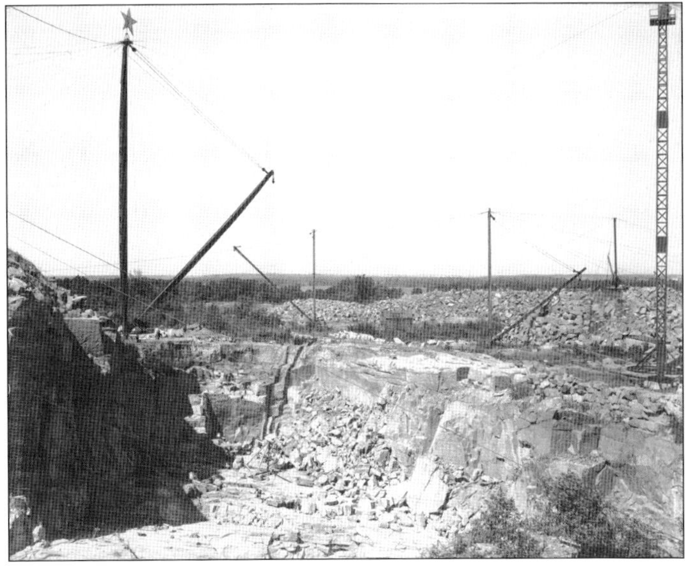

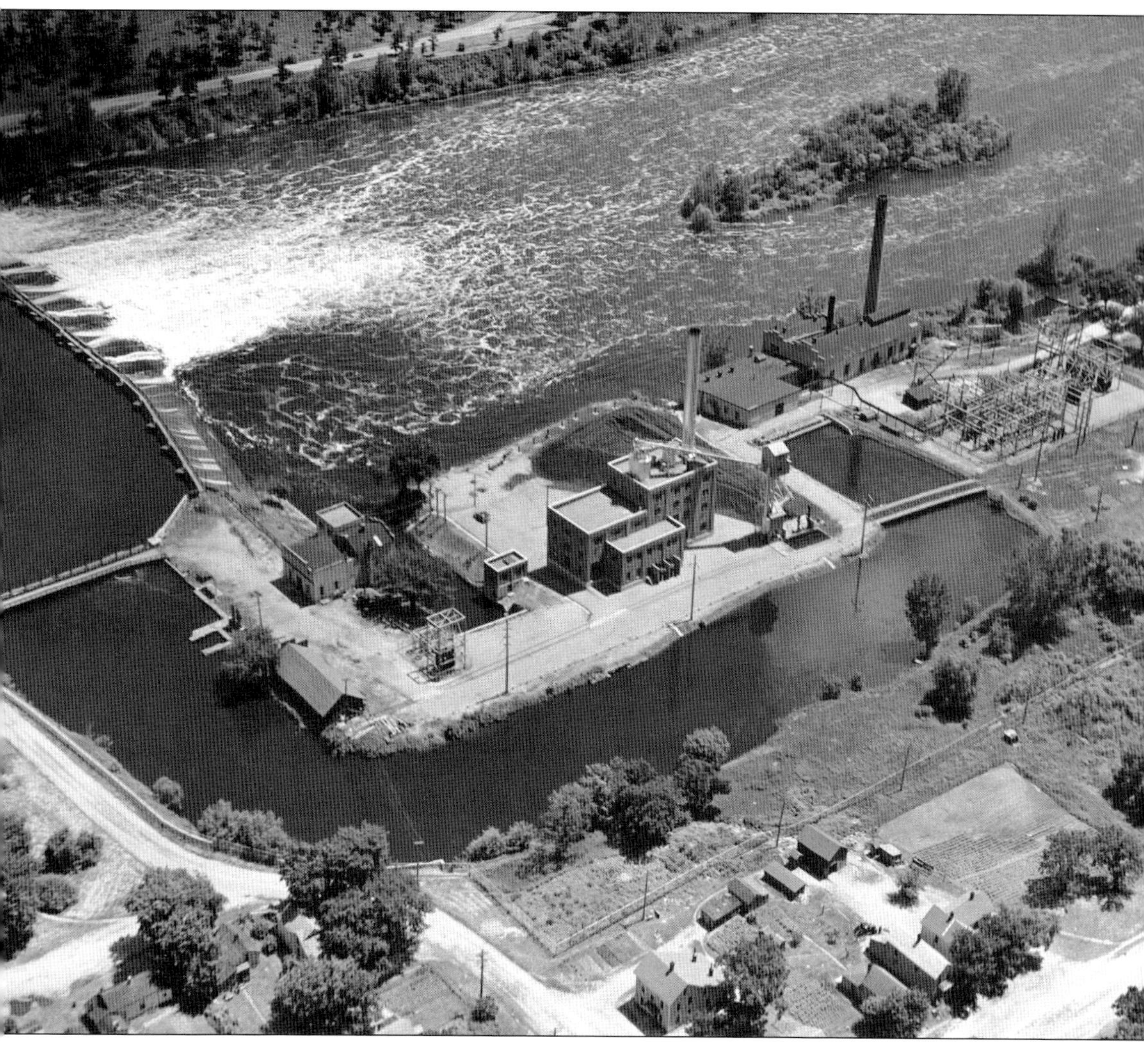

NORTHERN STATES POWER DAM AND PLANT, C. 1950. Set along the Mississippi River, the St. Cloud Dam has powered progress and preservation for more than a century. Built in 1887, the structure began as a Northern States Power project before being transferred to the City of St. Cloud in 1967, marking a new era of local stewardship. With a generating capacity of 8.5 megawatts, it stands as the largest municipally owned hydroelectric plant in Minnesota. Beyond its role in energy production, the dam supports recreational use and environmental balance along the river, connecting the city's industrial past with its renewable energy future.

St. Cloud Iron Works, c. 1900. In 1893, J.B. Rosenberger acquired a half interest in a local foundry business, which soon became known as St. Cloud Iron Works. The company evolved into a multifaceted operation with three primary divisions: the foundry, which produced industrial castings; the machine shop, specializing in the repair of industrial machinery; and the supply division, which provided parts and equipment to support machine operations.

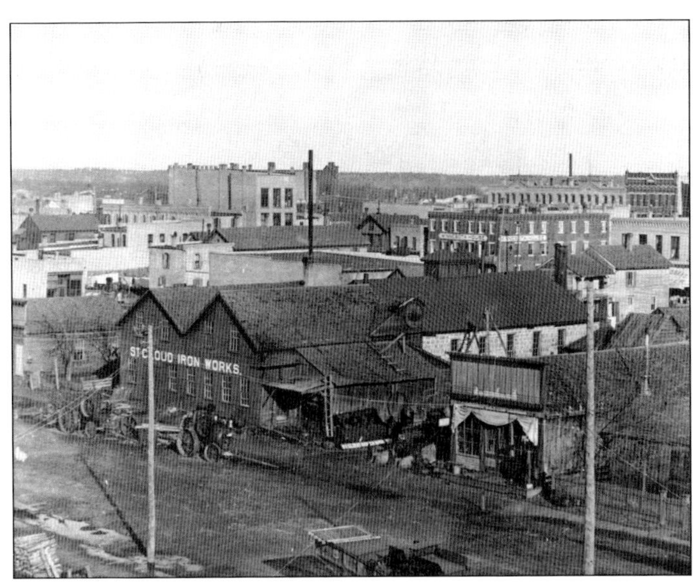

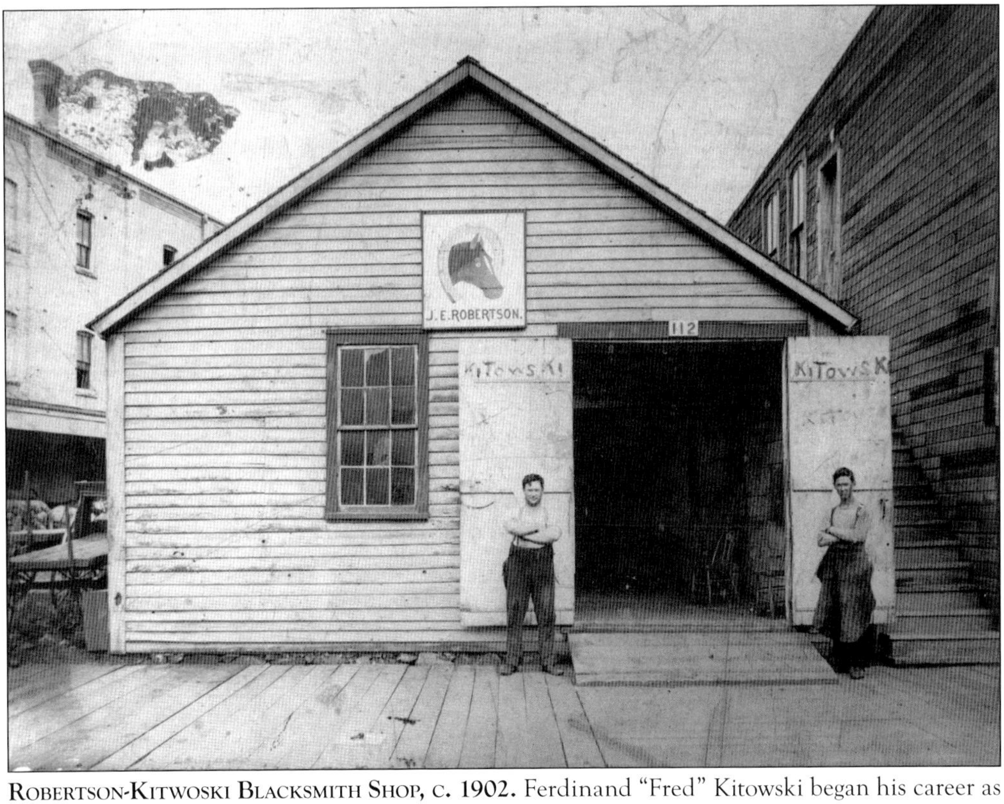

Robertson-Kitwoski Blacksmith Shop, c. 1902. Ferdinand "Fred" Kitowski began his career as a blacksmith and millwright, and by 1909, he owned a blacksmith shop on Courthouse Square. With the rise of automobiles, Kitowski invented a spring-turning machine, patented in 1918, which could form eyes on car springs in seconds, a process once done by hand. His invention led to the formation of the Kitowski Manufacturing Company in 1921, evolving from his original horseshoeing business.

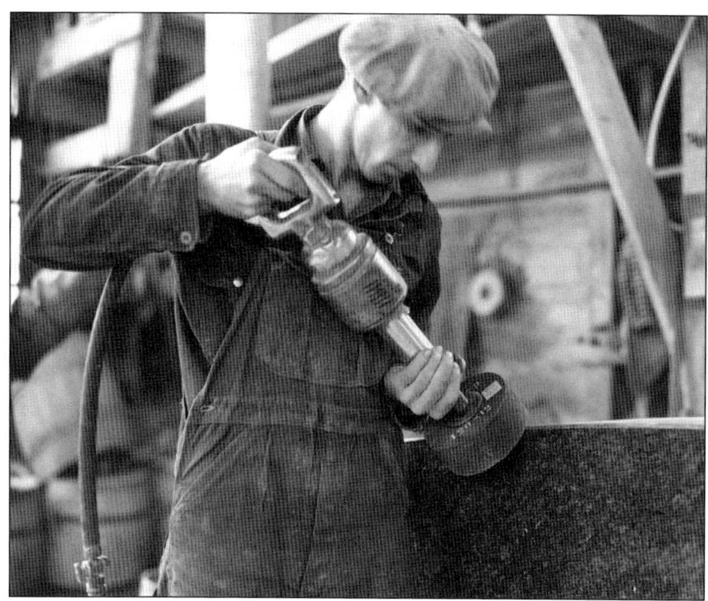

Worker Hand Polishing Granite, c. 1960. In the 1960s, hand-polishing granite was grueling, skilled work. Workers spent long hours using sandpaper, grinders, and polishing stones to smooth and shine each slab by hand. The process required strength, precision, and endurance, as even small mistakes could ruin hours of labor. Polishing large pieces could take days, reflecting both the physical demands and craftsmanship needed in the granite industry.

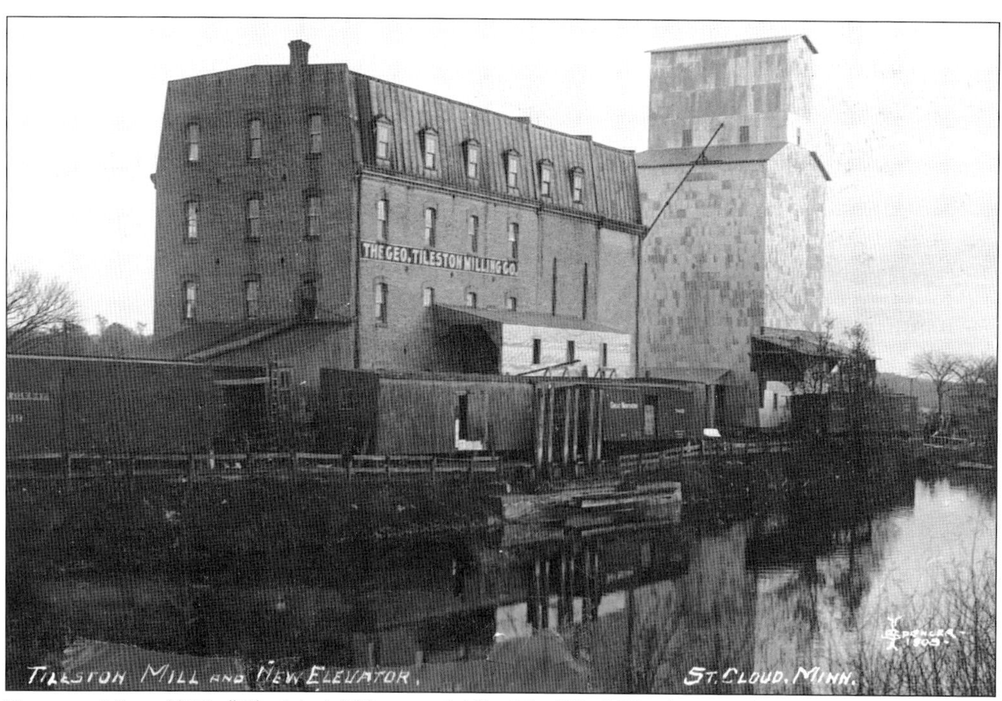

Tileston Mill, 1908. "The Model Flouring Mill of the World," Tileston Flour Mill was built south of the Tenth Street (University) Bridge in 1888. It was four stories and had the capacity for 1,000 barrels a day. A fire broke out in 1915, and workers recalled the need to jump into the canal to escape. The loss was valued at $120,000.

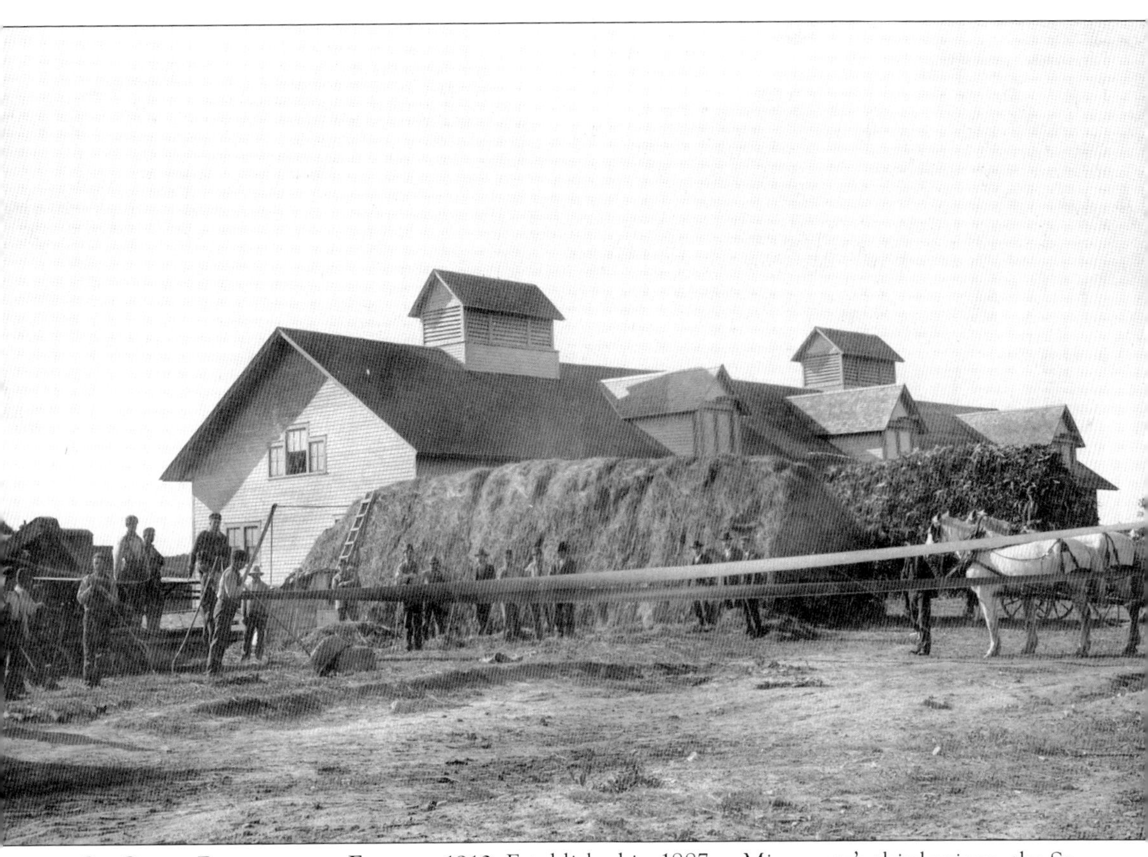

St. Cloud Reformatory Farm, c. 1910. Established in 1887 as Minnesota's third prison, the St. Cloud State Reformatory opened in 1889 with 77 inmates transferred from the Stillwater State Prison. Built on 240 acres to utilize the region's granite quarries, the reformatory quickly became a place where labor shaped both the land and the lives within it. Inmate labor was central to its growth, most notably in creating the monumental granite perimeter wall, the second largest in the world, standing as a testament to skill, discipline, and endurance. By the early 20th century, vocational programs expanded beyond quarry work to include construction, clothing and shoe manufacturing, printing, greenhouse operations, and farming. Between 1923 and 1956, inmates operated a productive farm that fed the institution, while their highly regarded livestock program and herd were nationally recognized as one of the best-managed in its class.

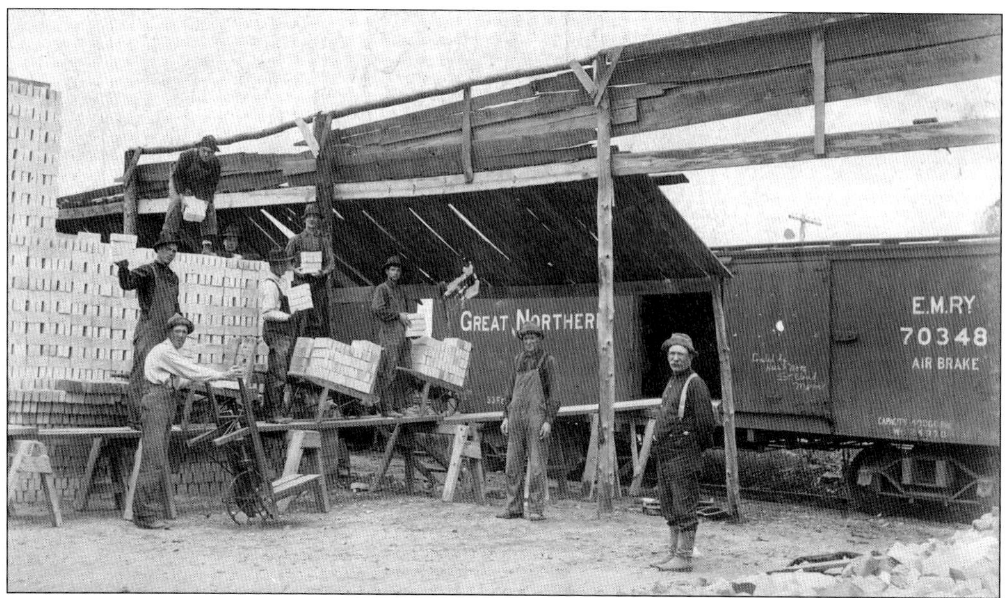

Hess Brick Workers Load Bricks onto Train, c. 1915. Henry Hess turned a clay deposit south of St. Cloud into a thriving brickmaking operation. At its peak, Hess employed 20 men and produced up to 30,000 bricks a day, with all his children helping in the factory as they grew. The labor-intensive process, from molding and firing to shipping in 6,000-brick boxcars, left a lasting mark, with Hess bricks still featured in many St. Cloud buildings today.

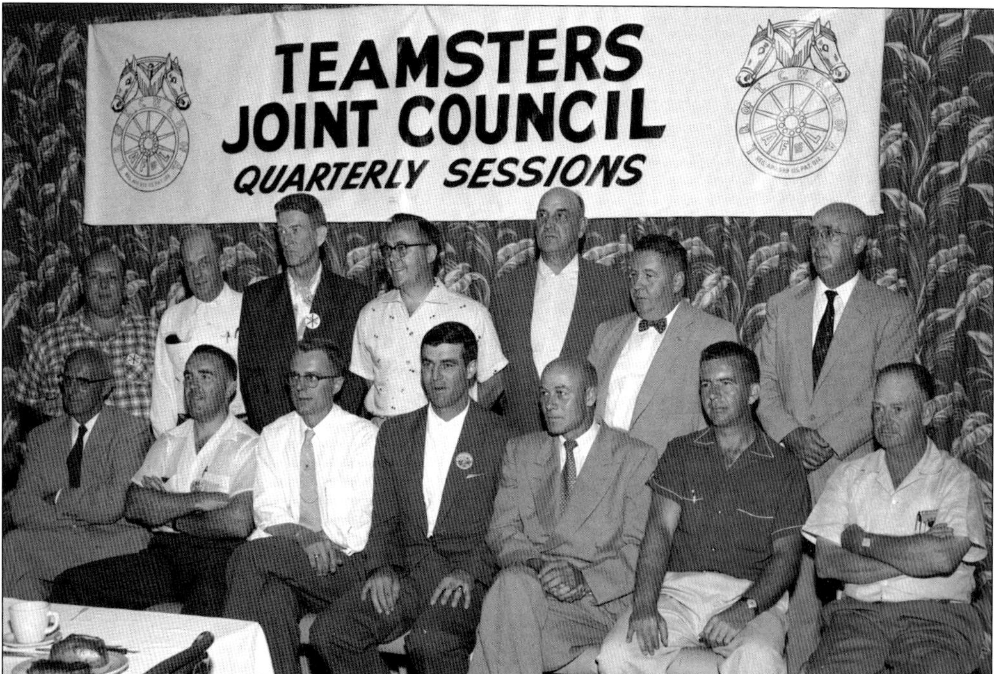

Teamsters Joint Council Luncheon, 1955. In the early 20th century, local unions formed in St. Cloud and regularly met at Puff's Hall. In 1913, the Minnesota State Federation of Labor's convention was held in St. Cloud, and Paul Sherer, president of the local council, was elected as vice president of District 6.

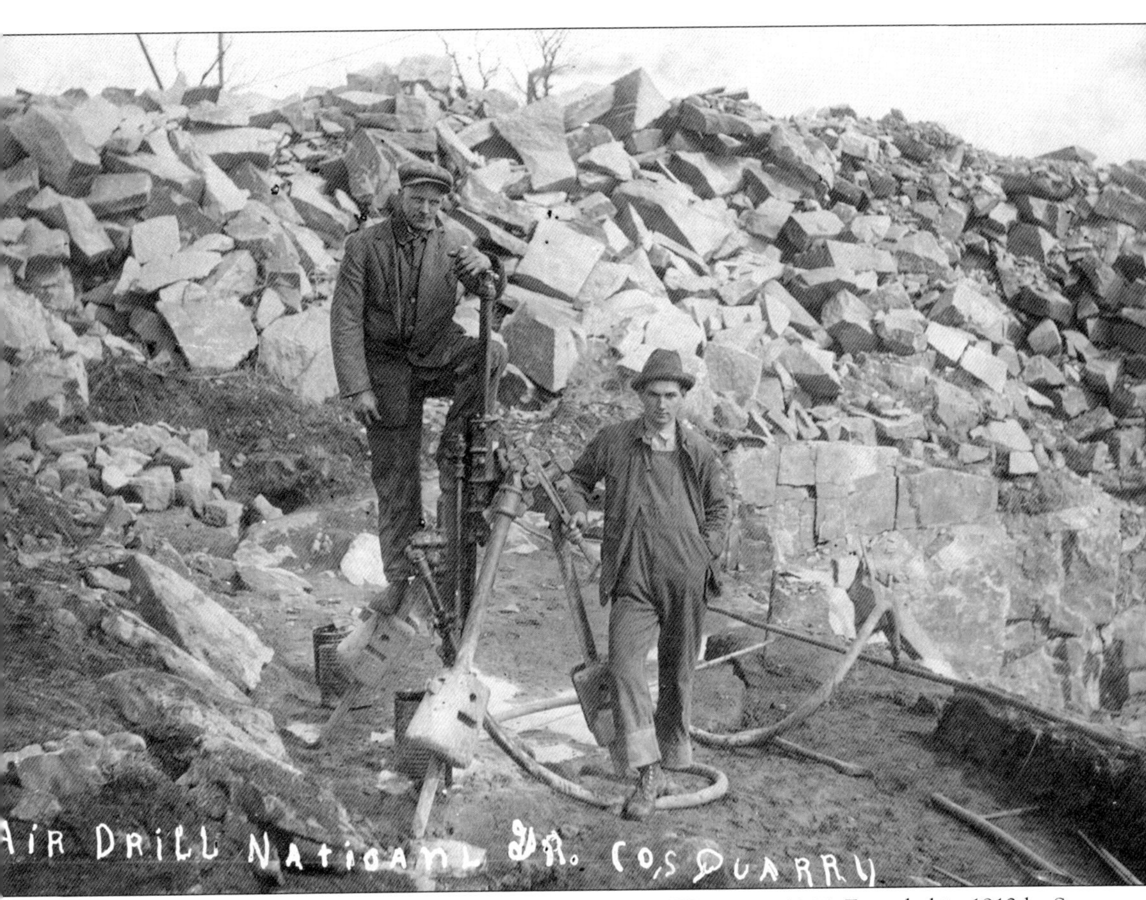

Two Employees with an Air Drill, National Granite Works, c. 1915. Founded in 1912 by St. Cloud producer Louis Brown, National Granite Works quickly established itself as a cornerstone of the granite industry and became known for its distinctive "Mahogany Red" granite. The company operated at maximum capacity for many years, and its success rested heavily on the skill and perseverance of its laborers, who faced the demanding and often dangerous realities of quarry work. Extracting and shaping massive granite blocks required precision, stamina, and teamwork under harsh conditions. As technology evolved, labor adapted in step. The introduction of the air drill revolutionized production, replacing the slow, hand-driven and steam-powered drilling methods that once dominated the quarries. Powered by compressed air, these pneumatic tools dramatically increased output while easing some of the physical burden on workers. Yet, despite technological advances, granite work remained a craft rooted in human effort, where every cut, polish, and finish carried the mark of those whose labor built St. Cloud's enduring reputation for stonework.

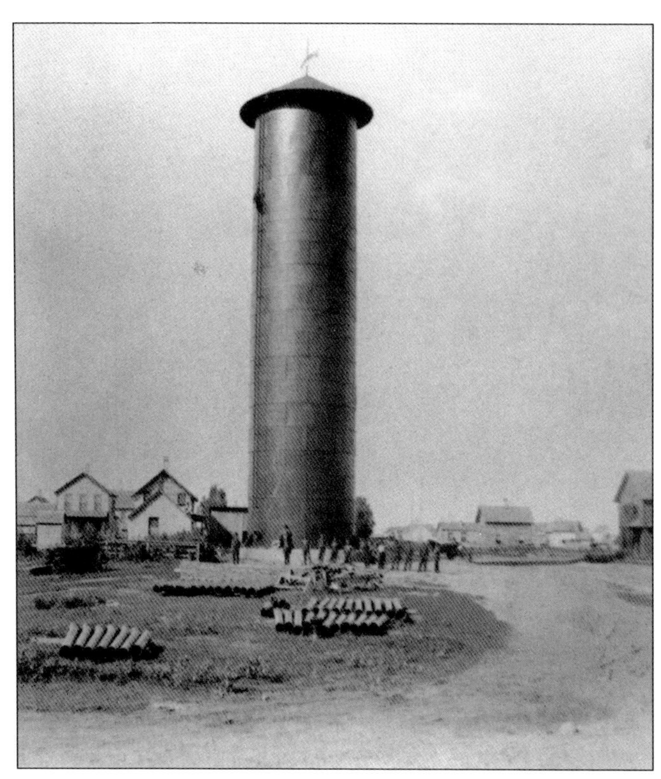

Water Tower Construction, 1888 (left), and Water Tower Demolition, c. 1930 (below). St. Cloud's first water tower was built in 1888 on Third Street North. They soon realized the location had many issues: spring would thaw and burst pipes, and sometimes it would flow into nearby streets. It was constructed on a concrete base, and crews riveted steel plates together by hand, a tough, rhythmic job that earned $1 a day for heating rivets. The tower stood 125 feet tall, 25 feet across and held 365,000 gallons of water. The tower was dismantled plate by plate in 1931.

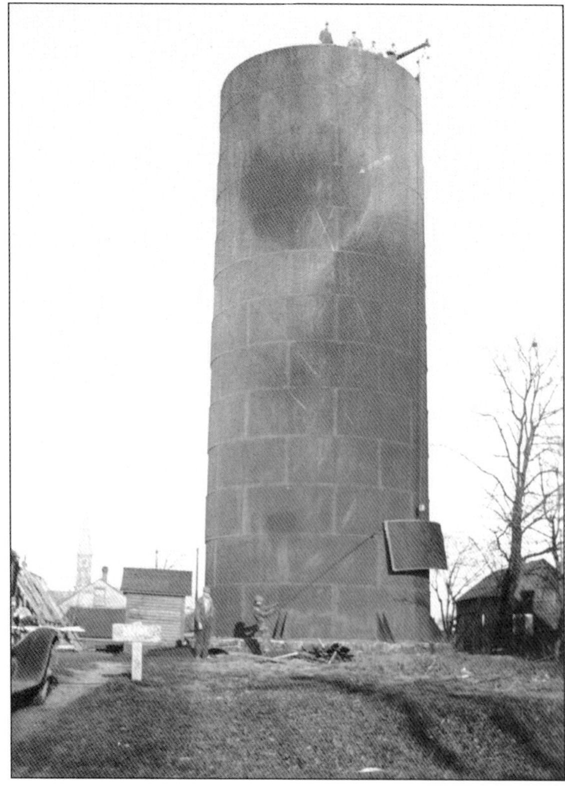

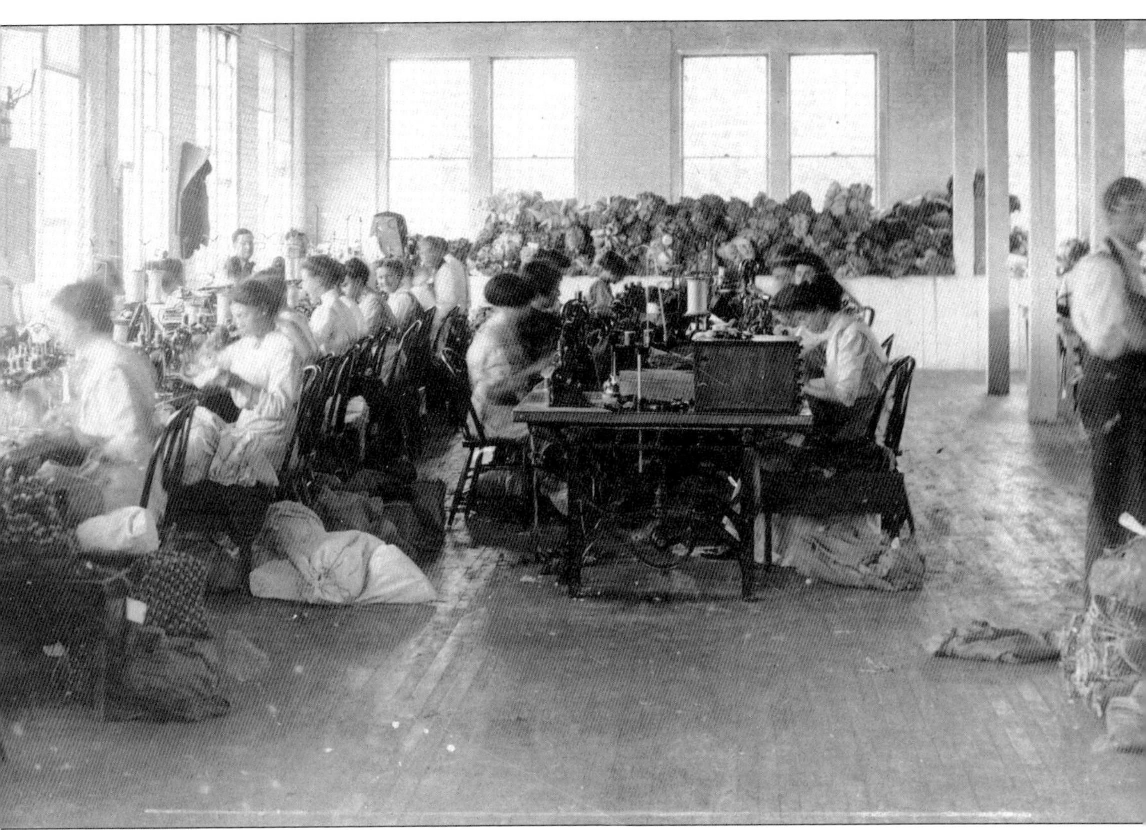

Workers at the Gordon-Ferguson Glove Factory, c. 1913. The Gordon & Ferguson Cap and Glove Factory began in St. Paul in 1871 and expanded to St. Cloud in 1910. Upon its opening in St. Cloud, the factory employed 120 workers, producing between 300 and 400 pairs of gloves per week, along with lightweight caps. It was anticipated that production would increase significantly as the workforce gained more experience and skill in manufacturing processes.

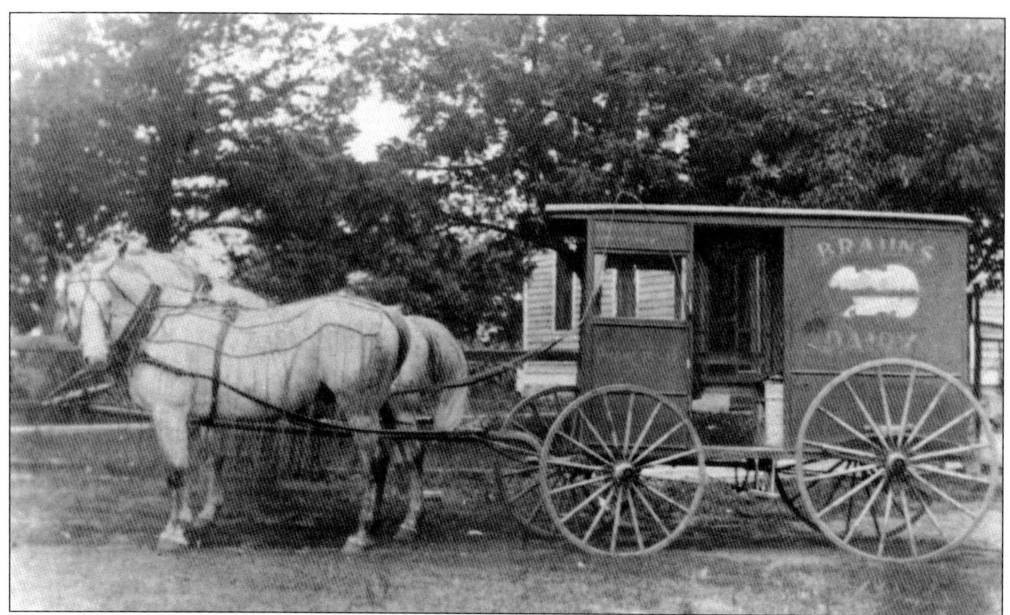

BRAUN'S DAIRY HORSE-DRAWN CARRIAGE, 1915 (ABOVE), AND BRAUN'S DAIRY TRUCK, C. 1930 (BELOW). In 1904, John P. Braun bought the "Old Braun Homestead" in St. Cloud Township. Known for his progressive, scientific approach, he outfitted the farm with everything needed for successful farming and dairying. The Braun family operated well-known milk routes in St. Cloud, recognized for the quality of their products. John Braun began delivering milk by horse and wagon in the early 1900s. When he retired in 1913, his son Alphonse and stepson Bernard took over the dairy farm. In 1929, Alphonse modernized the business by introducing a bottling machine and delivery truck, making Braun's Dairy deliveries faster and more efficient.

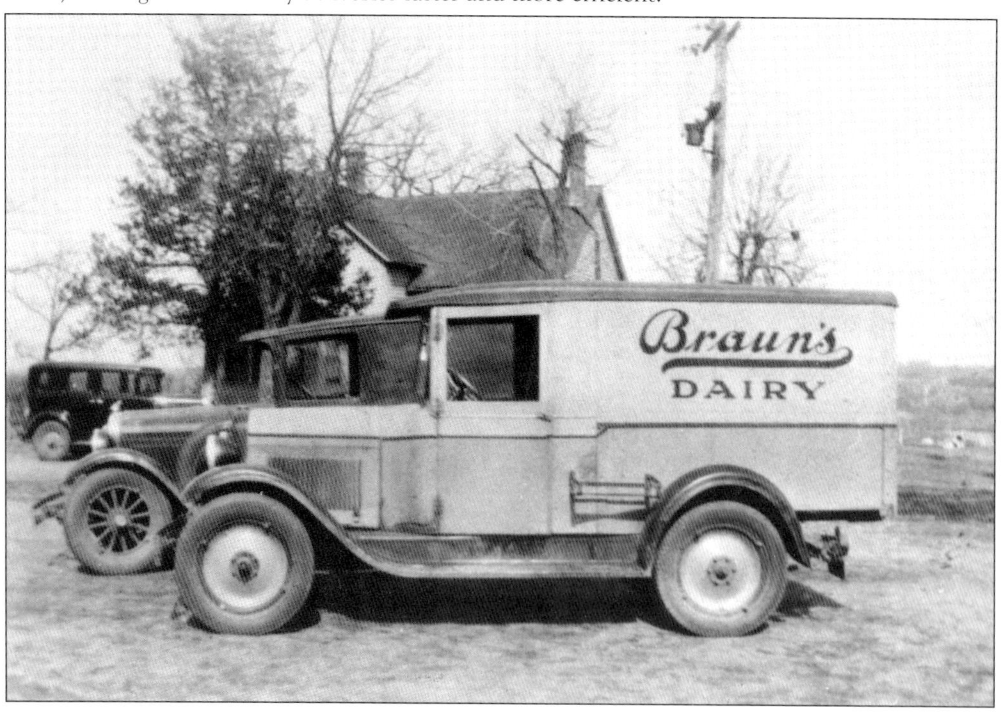

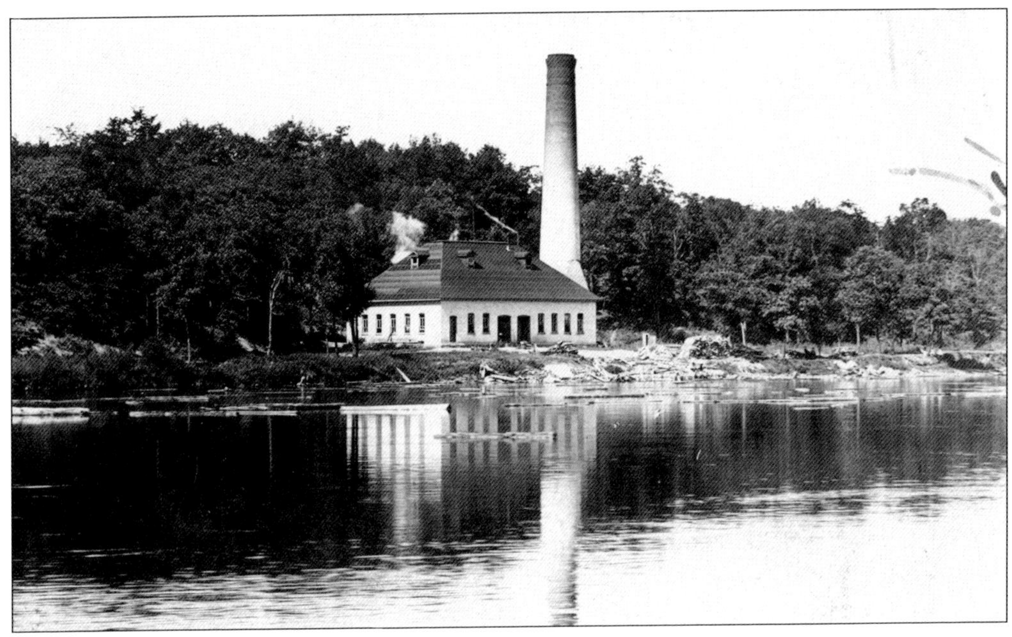

WATER TREATMENT PLANT, C. 1912 (ABOVE) AND 1978 (BELOW). St. Cloud's water system has a long history of hard work and development. The Drinking Water Treatment Facility, first built in 1954 to replace an inadequate 1907 system, has been expanded multiple times, most recently in 2016, to handle 24 million gallons per day. Similarly, the Wastewater Treatment Facility evolved from an untreated discharge in 1956 to a federally funded resource recovery center, reflecting decades of labor and dedication to providing safe water for the community.

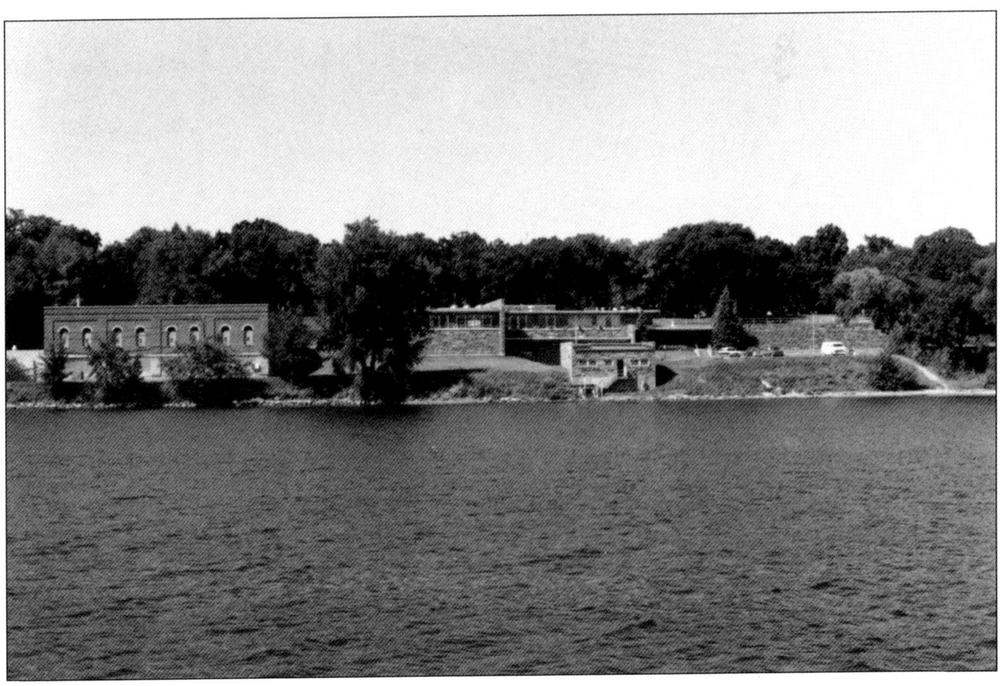

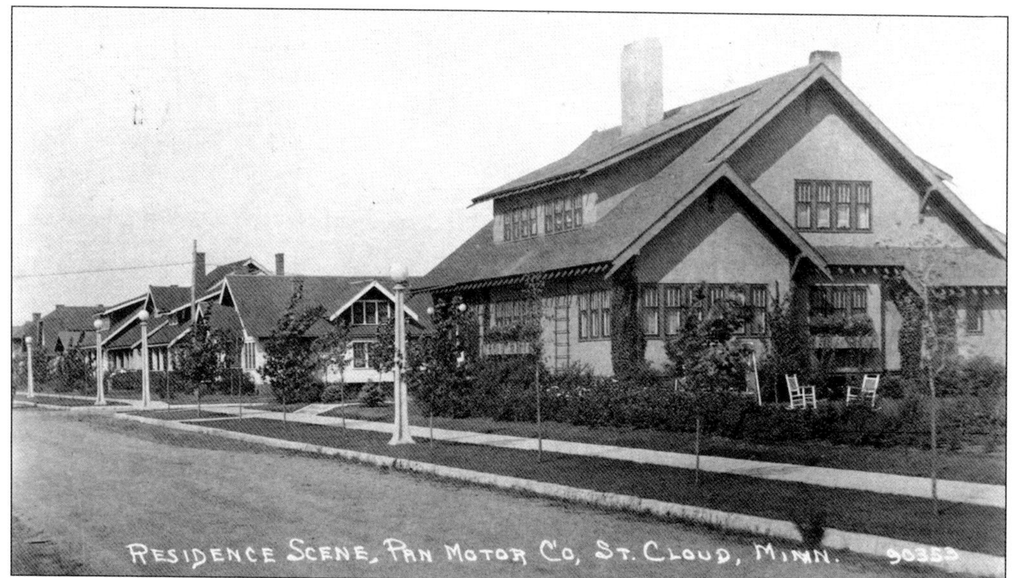

PANTOWN, C. 1920 (ABOVE), AND POWERHOUSE BUILDING AND WATER TOWER, PAN MOTOR COMPANY, 1919 (BELOW). Pantown was built in 1917 to house workers for Samuel Pandolfo's Pan Motor Company. Employees moved to the area and contributed their labor to both the factory and the development of the neighborhood, which included Craftsman-style homes, a hotel, and a fire department. Although the company closed in 1922 due to financial and legal troubles, the workers' efforts left a lasting mark.

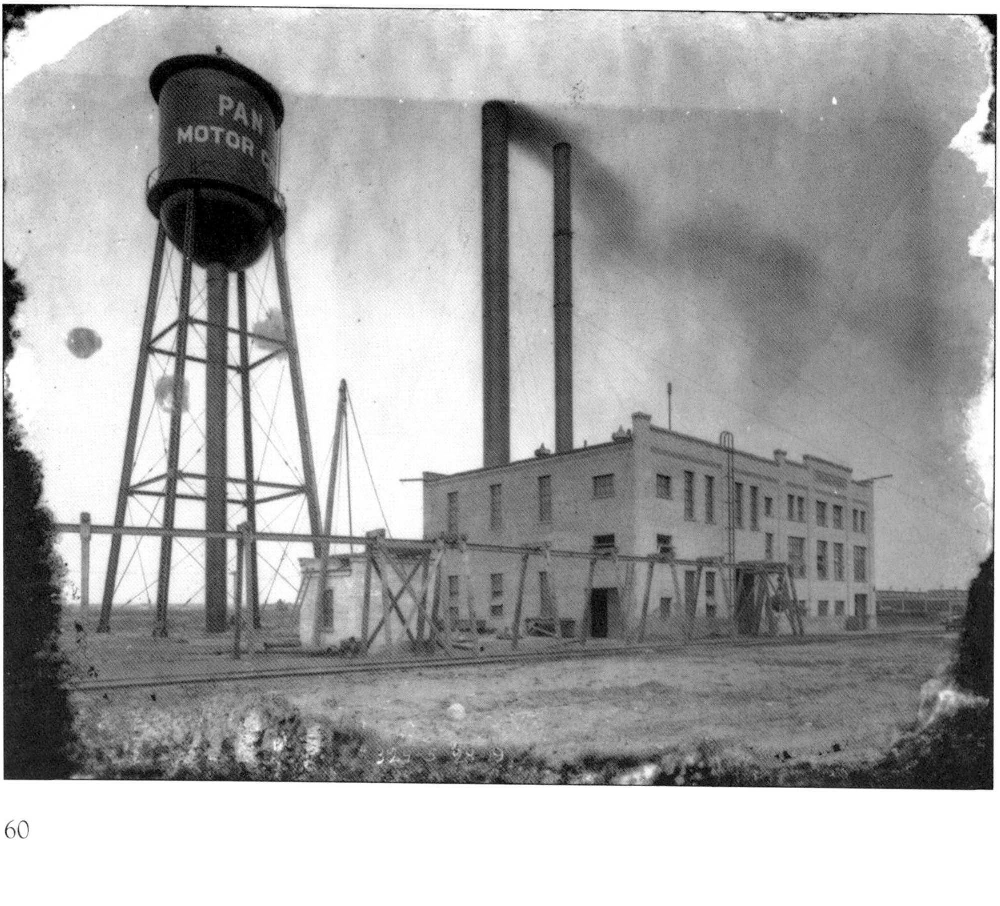

Five

The Places that Made Us

St. Cloud's neighborhoods tell the story of a city shaped by the people who built, lived in, and cared for them. From its earliest days, when three small settlements along the Mississippi merged in 1856, St. Cloud has reflected the diverse communities that made their homes here. Southerners, New Englanders, German immigrants, and later generations of workers and families each left their imprint on the city's culture, institutions, and built environment.

Neighborhoods grew around gathering spaces, schools, churches, parks, and commercial buildings, where daily life played out. On the city's west side, families settling along the railroad helped create the Seberger neighborhood, with Seberger Park as its centerpiece. More than just green space, the park became a place where neighbors met, children played, and civic identity was strengthened. Downtown, St. Germain Street developed into the city's commercial spine, its storefronts and offices reflecting decades of local enterprise and resilience.

On the South Side, one of the oldest parts of the city, generations of residents built homes, businesses, and institutions that anchored community life. Within the South Side lie streets like Highbanks Place, once the site of the McClure mansion, which was later subdivided into single-family lots, built out by the 1930s with period revival houses that still exhibit architectural unity and mature landscaping. Its surviving houses and historic blocks still echo the experiences of those who first laid down roots there.

Public spaces, too, reveal how residents shaped the city: Barden Park, the oldest park in St. Cloud, became a hub for music, picnics, and civic gatherings; the Paramount Theatre hosted everything from Broadway productions to local celebrations; and the municipal pool drew thousands of children and families each summer, offering affordable recreation and a shared sense of belonging. The riverfront gardens, first envisioned by parks superintendent Joseph Munsinger and later expanded by Bill and Virginia Clemens, show how civic vision and personal passion can create lasting spaces of beauty and reflection. Even buildings like the Breen Hotel, the Stearns County Courthouse, and Fandel's department store speak to the ambitions of entrepreneurs, leaders, and everyday workers who invested in their community.

St. Cloud's neighborhoods are more than physical spaces or architectural landmarks; they are living records of the people who shaped them. Each street, park, and building tells a story of how residents worked, gathered, celebrated, and adapted. Together, they reveal a city culture rooted in community life, where neighborhoods were not simply places to live but expressions of shared identity and enduring connection.

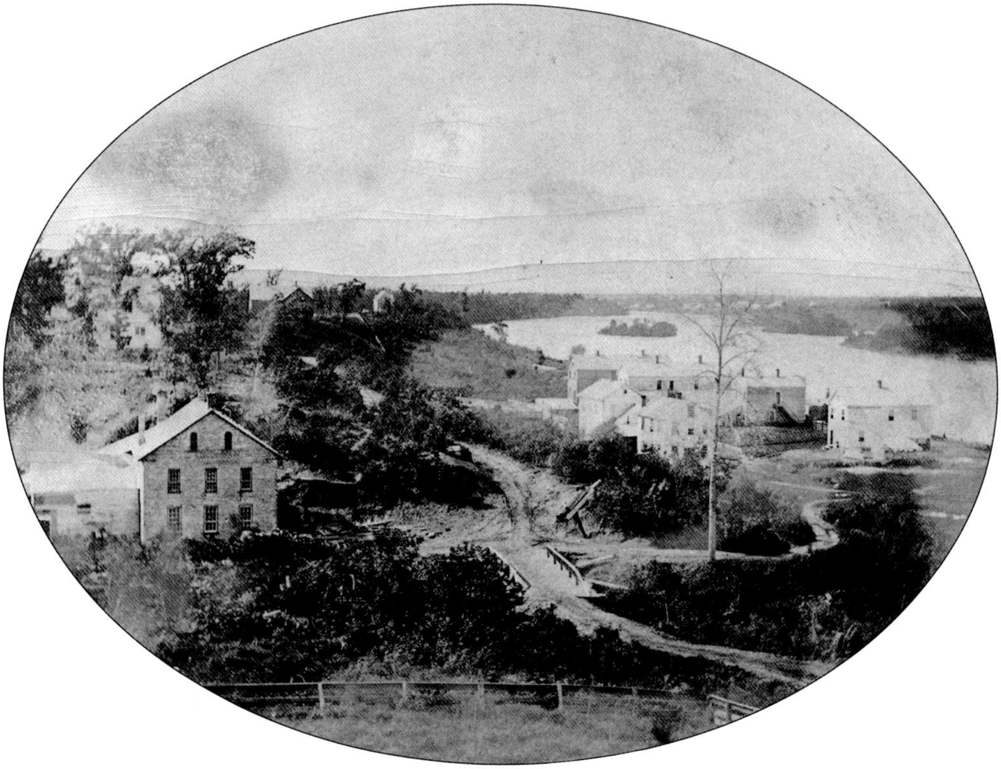

LOWER TOWN, 1877 (ABOVE), AND UPPER TOWN, 1858 (BELOW). St. Cloud was incorporated in 1856, uniting three early settlements: Upper Town, Middle Town, and Lower Town. Upper Town, near the Mississippi ravines, was settled by Southerners led by Gen. Sylvanus Lowry, Middle Town featured many German Catholic immigrants, and Lower Town held New Englanders.

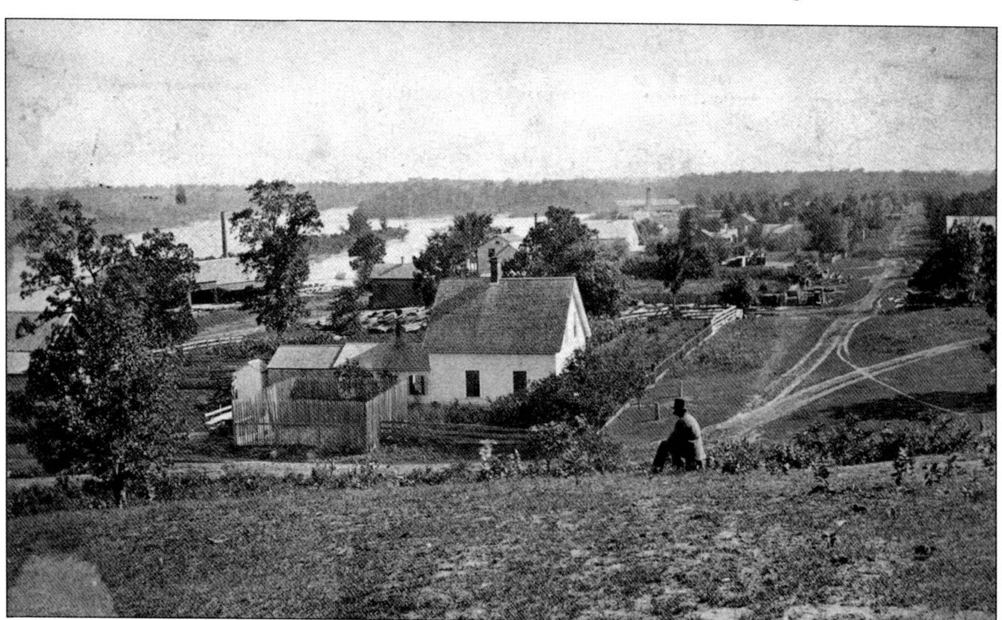

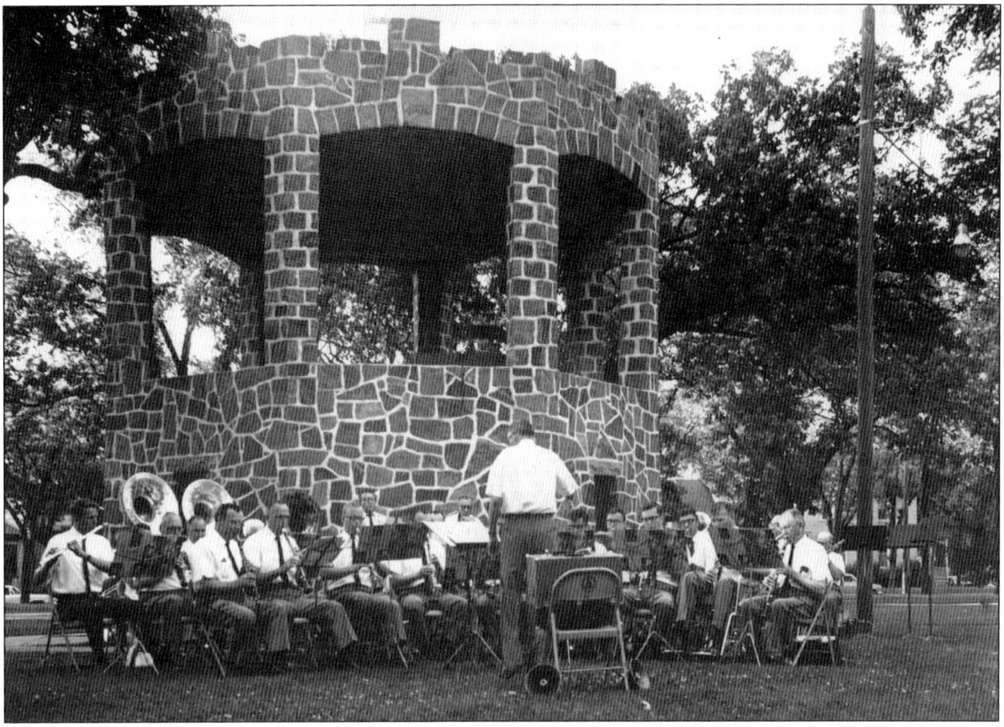

BARDEN PARK, 1928 (ABOVE) AND 1966 (BELOW). Barden Park, originally known as Central Park, is the oldest park in St. Cloud. The 2.5-acre site was gifted to the city by John L. Wilson and marked as a park on the 1855 plat map. Its most iconic feature is the octagonal granite bandstand at the center, built in 1925 to replace an earlier wooden structure. For over a century, the St. Cloud Municipal Band has performed there, making the park a long-standing hub for music and community gatherings. Barden Park has also featured a fountain and lily pond donated by Clarence L. Atwood, which was later converted into a wading pool. A Spanish-American War cannon, once displayed in the park's northeast corner, was eventually salvaged for the war effort during World War II.

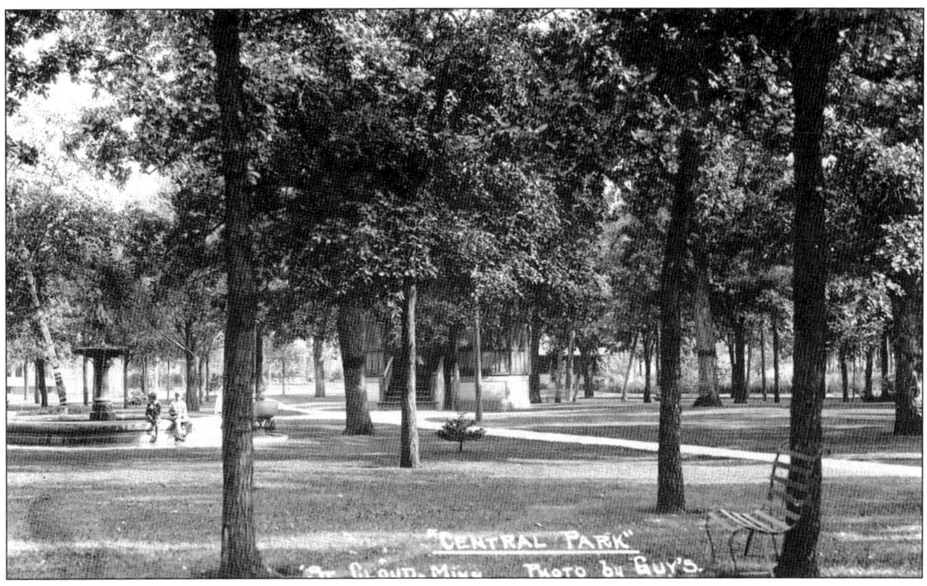

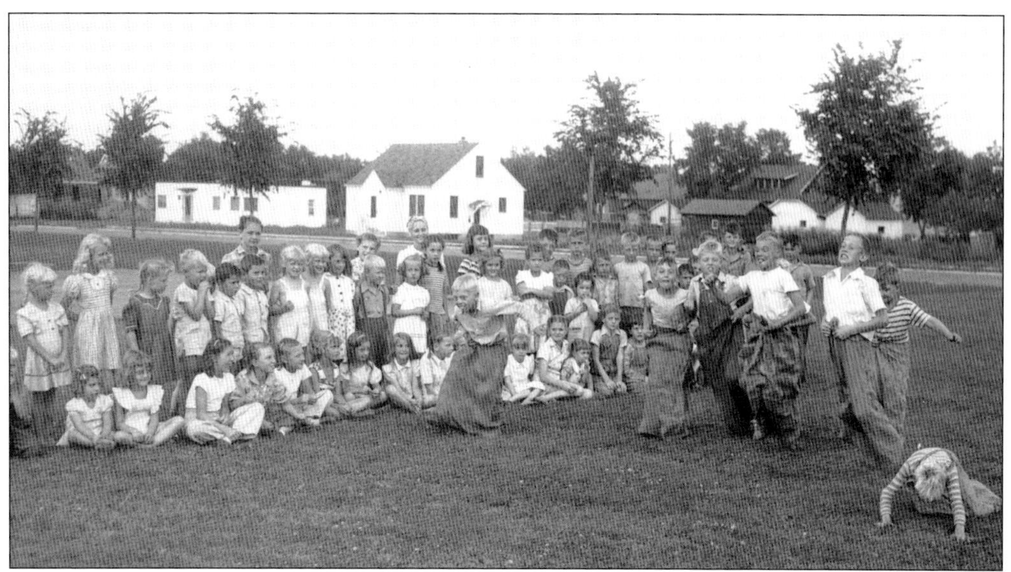

Sack Race at Seberger Park, c. 1950. Developed in the early 1900s as the city expanded westward along the railroad corridor, the Seberger neighborhood takes its name from Seberger Park, a central landmark within the community. The park offers expansive green space, a pool, and various amenities, serving as a vibrant gathering place for residents and a hub for recreation.

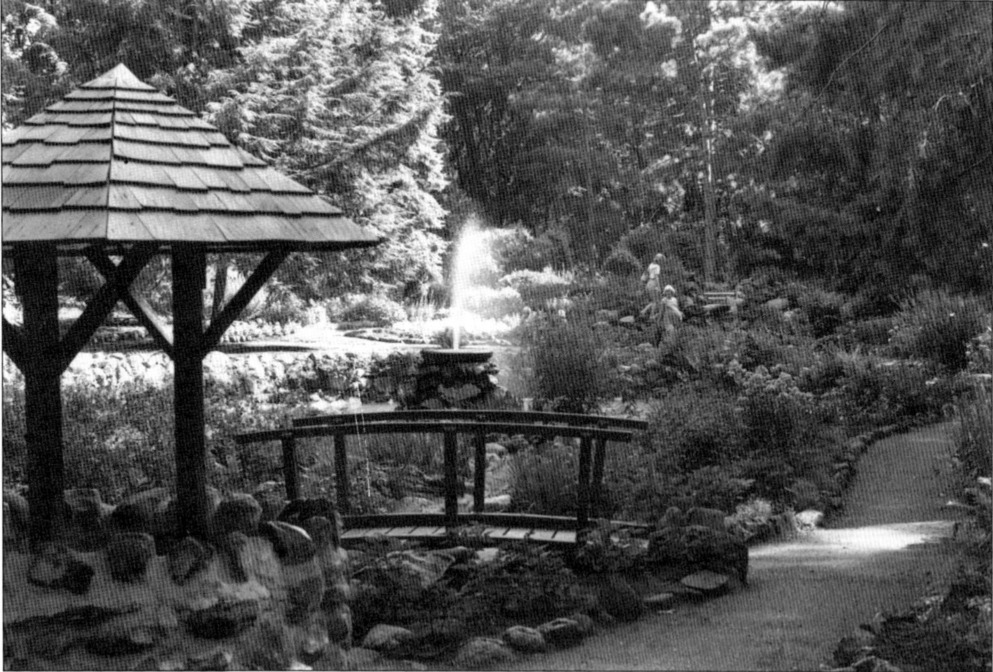

Munsinger Clemens Gardens, 1975. Munsinger Gardens began along the Mississippi River in 1890 as a sawmill site, under parks superintendent Joseph Munsinger. WPA and CCC labor transformed the area in the 1930s with flower beds, paths, a lily pond, a greenhouse, and other features. Bill and Virginia Clemens later donated land across the boulevard, and in 1990, Bill funded the Rose Garden in her honor. Today, a memorial statue of the Clemenses stands beside the Rose Garden they cherished.

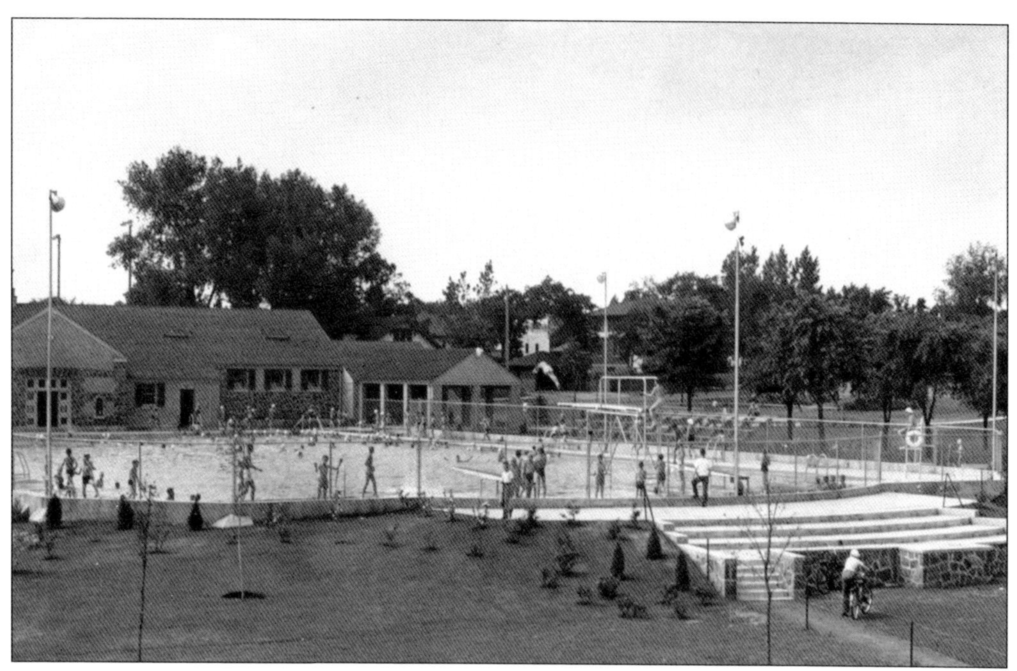

MUNICIPAL SWIMMING POOL, C. 1950 (ABOVE), AND ST. CLOUD SYNCHRONIZED SWIMMERS, 1957 (BELOW). The municipal pool, dedicated in 1947, quickly became a hub of community life. As the first outdoor Olympic-size pool, it welcomed thousands of residents each summer for swimming lessons, recreation, and neighborhood gatherings. Affordable admission made it accessible to families, and by 1955, attendance topped 50,000 in a single season. Although the pool closed in 2002 and was later demolished, the bathhouse was preserved and transformed into a community center in 2006, continuing its role as a gathering place for residents.

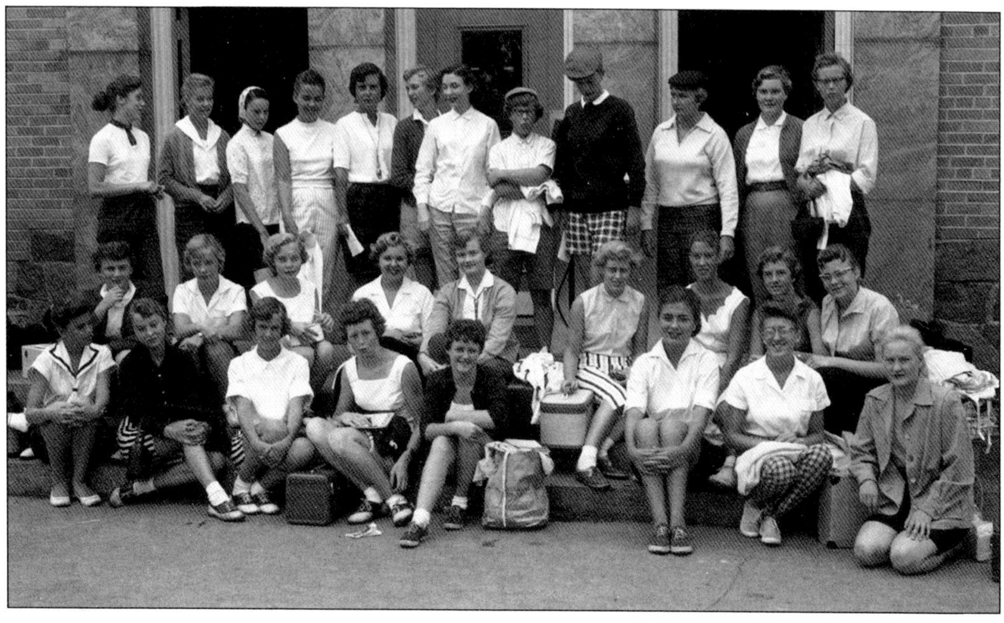

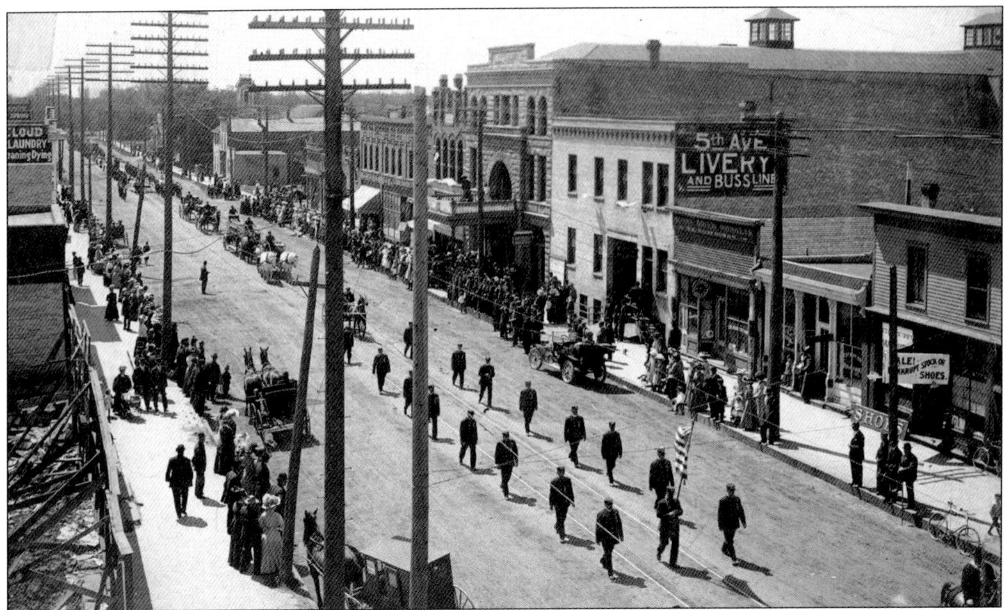

Parade on Fifth Avenue South, c. 1910. The South Side neighborhood spans land once part of two of St. Cloud's original towns, Middle Town and Lower Town. In the early 20th century, it was a strong center of community life and was home to some of the city's oldest surviving structures.

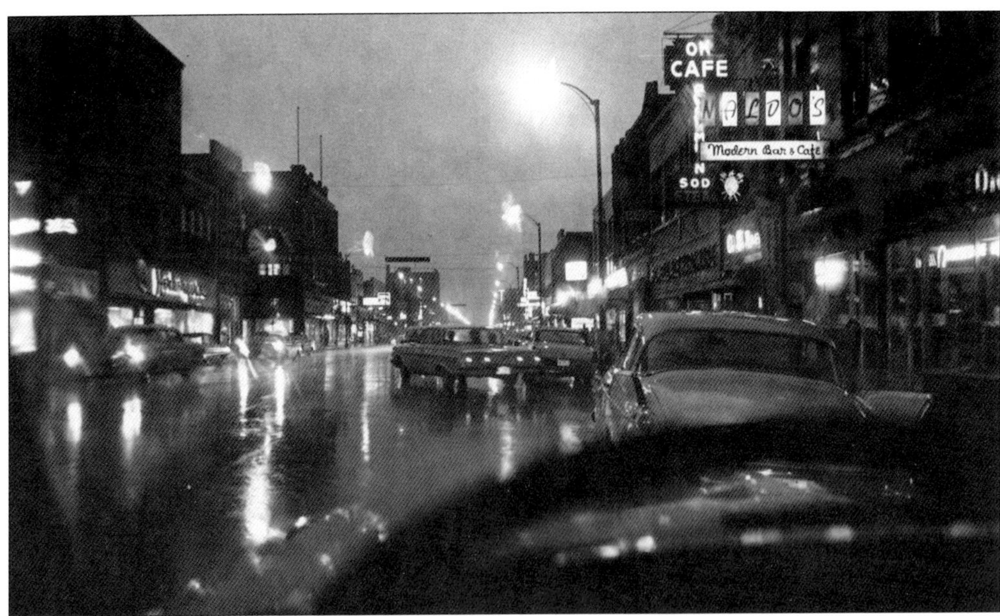

St. Germain Street at Night, c. 1960. St. Germain Street is a key historical landmark in St. Cloud, Minnesota, serving as the city's main commercial route since its early days. Originally called the St. Cloud to Maine Prairie Road, it played a vital role in the city's growth and commerce. Today, St. Germain Street remains central to downtown, with many historic buildings still standing, adding to the city's architectural heritage.

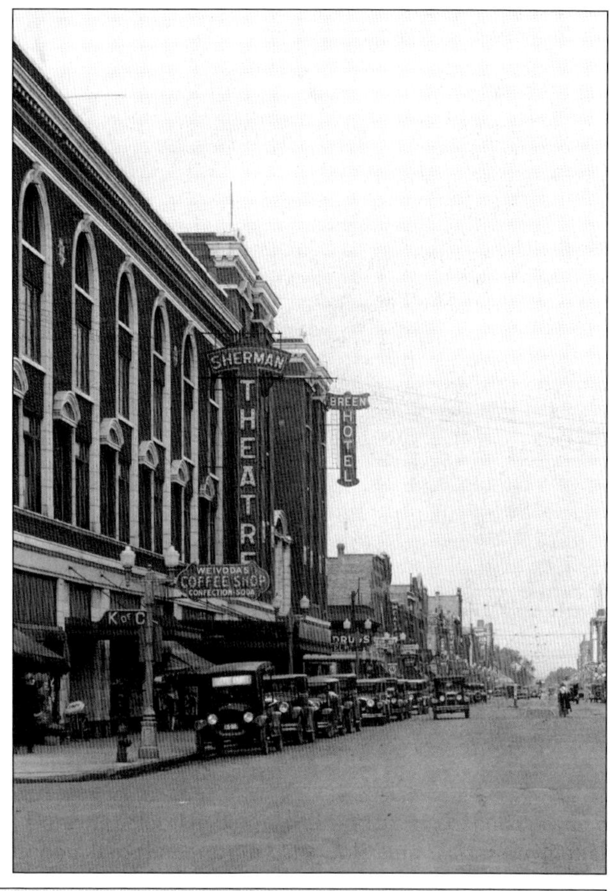

Sherman Theatre, c. 1925. On a chilly Christmas Eve in 1921, the Sherman Theatre opened its doors. A decade later, it was renamed the Paramount, a name it still holds today. For over a century, it has welcomed audiences for civic events, Broadway productions, live theater, films, and concerts.

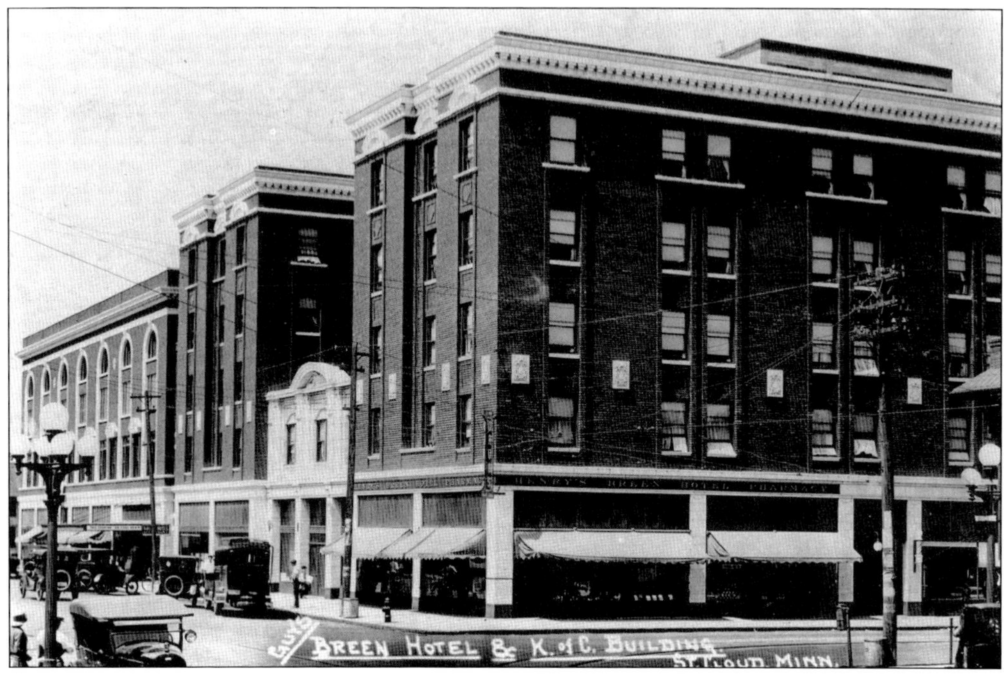

Breen Hotel, c. 1921. Breen Hotel opened on Easter Monday in March 1921. Over 450 people attended the banquet that celebrated the hotel's completion. Constructed by Henry Breen, the hotel was lauded as the nicest hotel in the state outside of the Twin Cities. The H-shape design of the building permitted natural light to reach every room in the five-story hotel. Since its opening over a century ago, it has gone through extensive renovations and two name changes. Now known as Germain Towers, it is still home to St. Cloud residents.

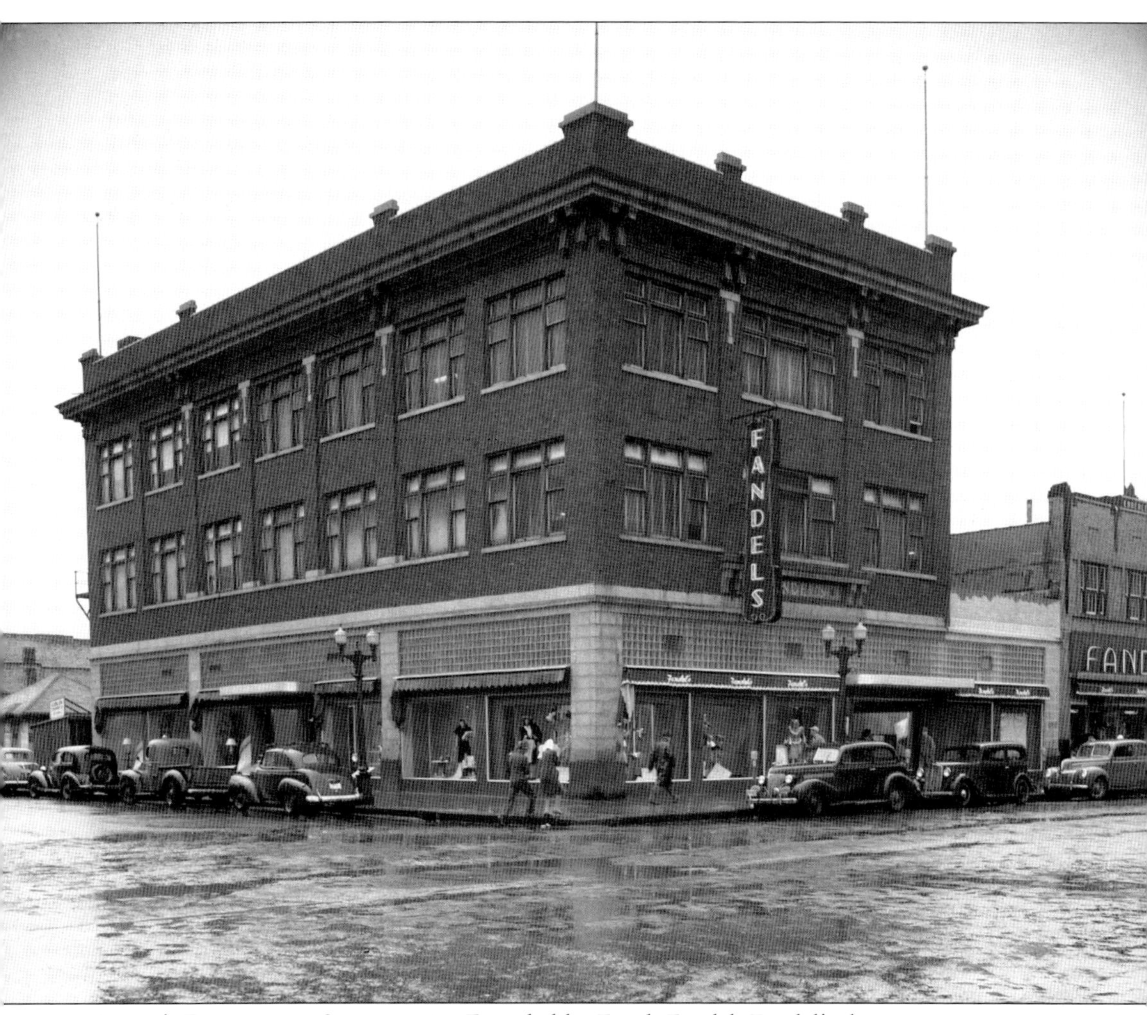

Fandel's Department Store, 1946. Founded by Frank Fandel, Fandel's department store was a mainstay in St. Cloud for a century. Fandel began the Empire Store with business partner Michael Nugent in 1882. When Fandel bought out Nugent in 1895, the store became known as Fandel's. Fandel's adapted to the changing cultural landscape in St. Cloud at the turn of the century, providing ready-to-wear women's clothing, greeting cards, drapery, and carpeting. In 1914, a three-story building was constructed on the corner of Sixth Avenue and St. Germain Street to accommodate the growing business. Fandel's remained a family business until it was sold to Herberger's in 1985. The three-story building, which stood stalwart on St. Germain Street for 70 years, was demolished the same year.

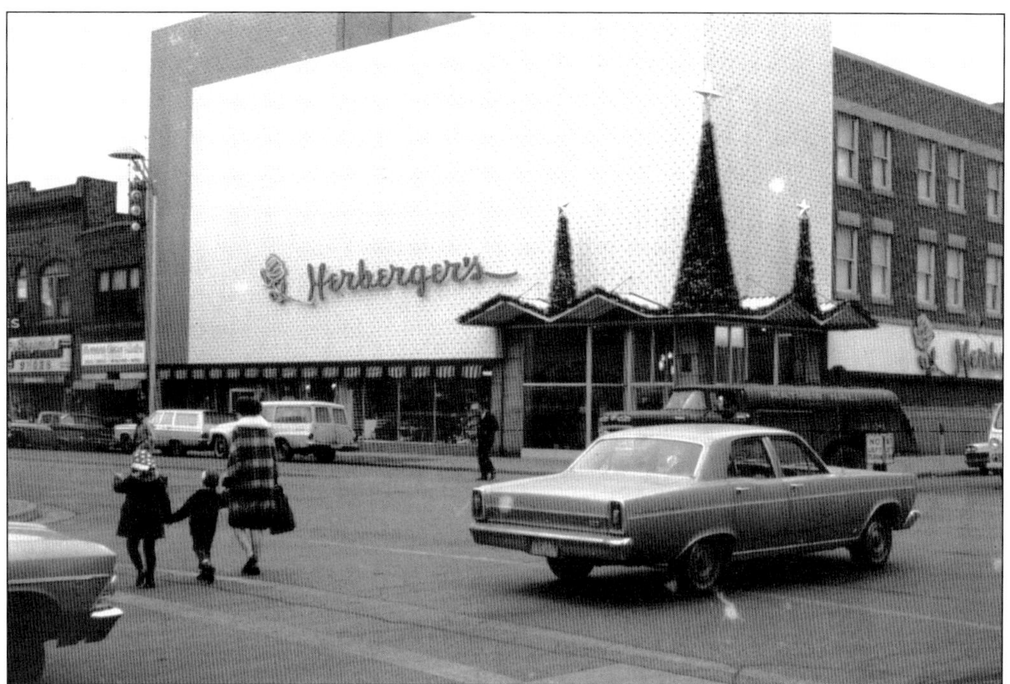

Herberger's at Sixth Avenue and St. Germain Street, c. 1965. Bob Herberger opened the first Herberger's store in St. Cloud in 1927. In 1943, they opened their first store outside of St. Cloud in Watertown, South Dakota, and by 1977, Herberger's had 16 stores in six states, as far west as Great Falls, Montana. St. Cloud remained the headquarters of the Herberger's department store chain until 2000, and in 2018, it went out of business.

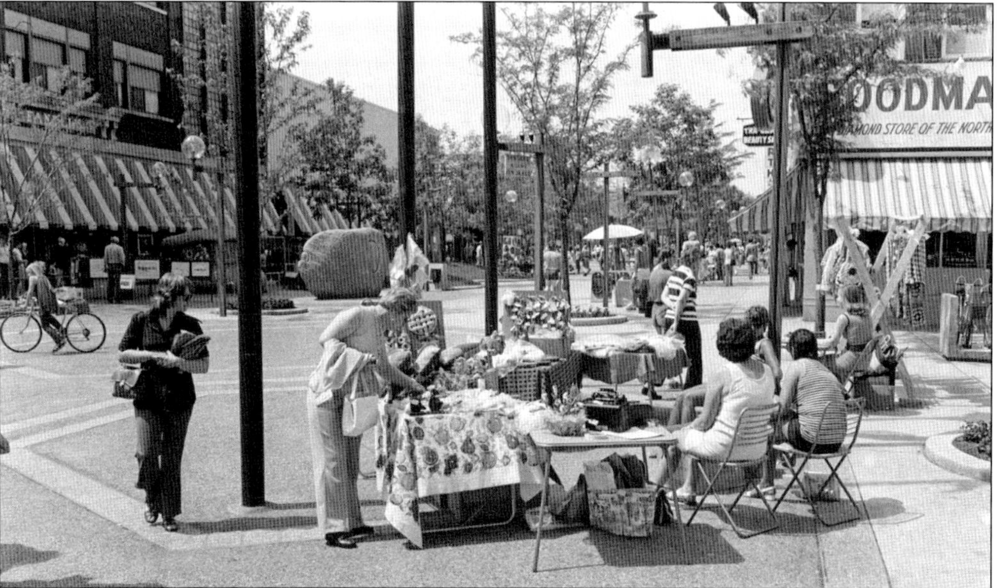

Art Show on Mall Germain, 1975. In 1973, West St. Germain Street from Fourth Avenue to Eighth Avenue was converted into a pedestrian mall as part of a downtown renewal project. Ring Road was installed encircling the Mall Germain to provide passage for vehicles around downtown, while the avenues ended in cul-de-sacs. West St. Germain Street was reopened to vehicular traffic in 1997.

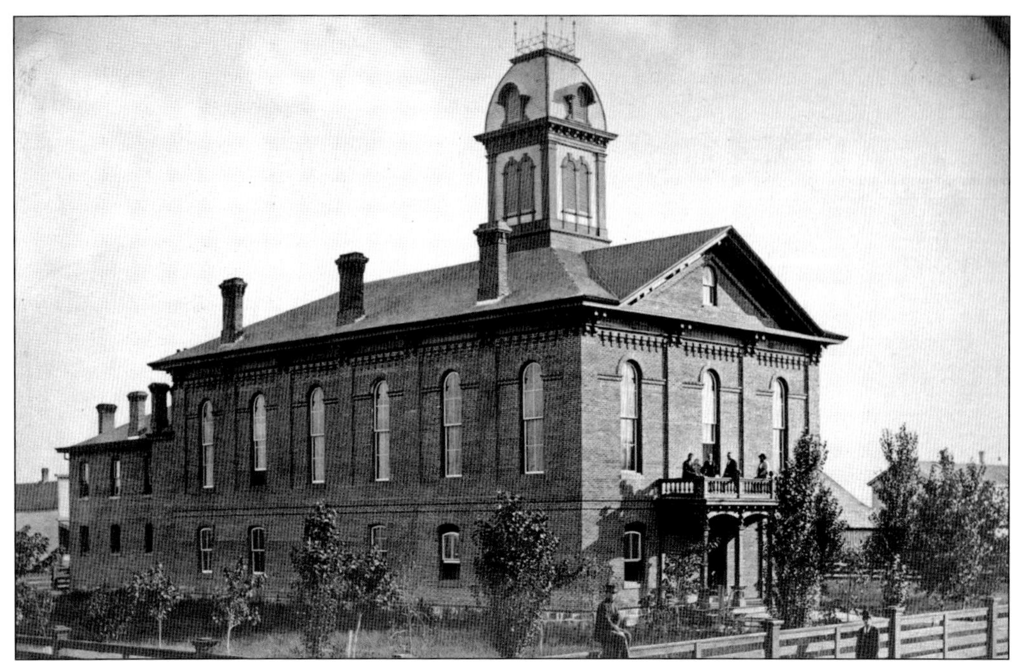

Stearns County Courthouse, c. 1877 (above), and New Courthouse under Construction, c. 1922 (below). Before the first courthouse was constructed, county records and business were held in rented rooms and halls around St. Cloud. In 1861, J.L. Wilson provided land for the construction of a Stearns County courthouse. Completed in 1863, the first courthouse stood at the center of downtown St. Cloud. By the turn of the century, the volume of the county's business had outgrown this building. It was not until 1920 that this courthouse was demolished, and a new courthouse was built on the same site. Completed in 1922, the Stearns County Courthouse was constructed using granite provided by Rockville Granite Company of Cold Spring. It is adorned with a dome at its center and massive granite columns at the front entrance.

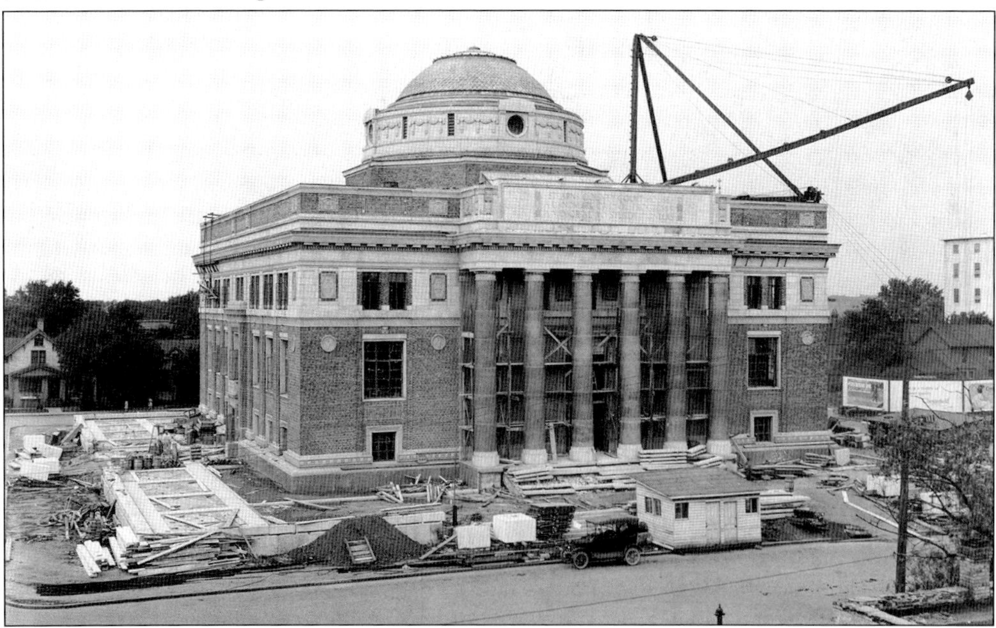

Six

Crossroads of Progress

St. Cloud's location "in the heart of Minnesota" reflects its strategic position at the crossroads of river, rail, road, and bus networks. From early oxcarts and riverboats to modern highways and transit buses, transportation has shaped the city's growth, economy, and identity.

Before railroads, the Mississippi River served as a major freight and passenger route, while the Red River Trails brought oxcart traffic through the area. St. Cloud was a key stop on the Métis Red River cart routes, moving furs and goods between Pembina and St. Paul.

A turning point came in 1866, when the first rail line reached East St. Cloud from St. Paul. Over the following decades, the Great Northern and Northern Pacific Railroads expanded through the city, connecting it to broader freight and passenger networks. The historic St. Cloud station, built in 1909, continues to serve Amtrak's Empire Builder route.

At the turn of the 20th century, electric streetcars arrived, with the Granite City Railway operating for more than 40 years before automobiles and changing transit patterns led to its discontinuation in 1936. During this period, the Pan Motor Company symbolized the city's embrace of the automobile, even though its plans ultimately faltered.

As streetcars ended, St. Cloud shifted to bus transit. In the late 1960s, the Minnesota Legislature authorized the St. Cloud Metropolitan Transit Commission (SCMTC), which began service in 1969 and expanded over time to include fixed routes, paratransit, intercity connections, and a central transit hub. The Northstar Link now connects the city to commuter rail service in Big Lake.

Road and highway infrastructure also became central to connectivity. Interstate 94, US Highway 10, and Minnesota Highways 15 and 23 anchor the city's links to the region. Bridges such as the Veterans Bridge (1971), University Bridge (1985), and Granite City Crossing (2009) span the Mississippi, supporting both vehicles and pedestrians.

Transportation shaped neighborhoods and communities as well. Thirty-four historic sites are tied to the "Transportation and Shipping" context, including homes built by railway workers, engineers, and transit-related entrepreneurs.

St. Cloud's transportation history is one of continual adaptation. From riverboats and oxcarts to streetcars, railroads, buses, and highways, the city has continually evolved to meet changing technologies and economic demands, leaving a lasting mark on its landscape and community.

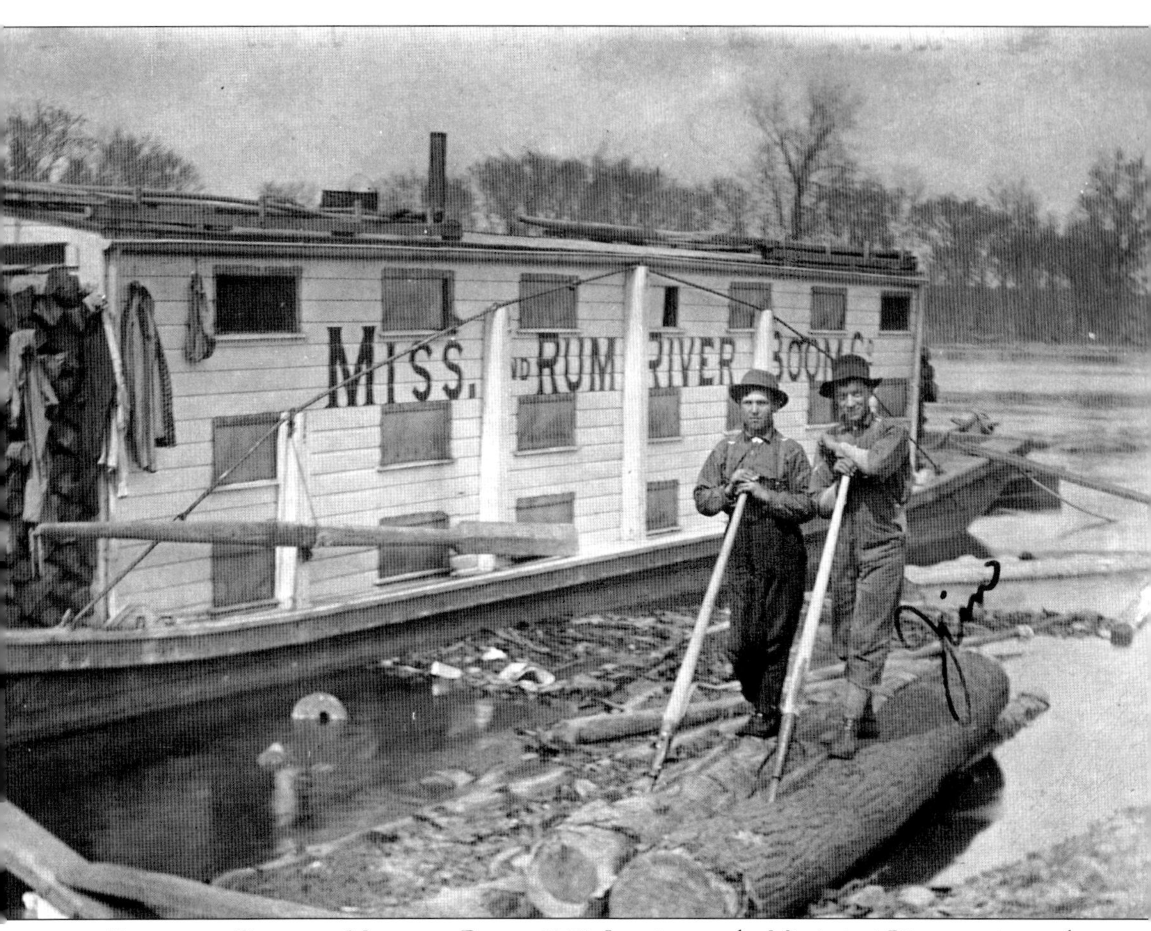

Bunkhouse Boat, the Mississippi River, 1908. Logging on the Mississippi River was integral to the town's early economic development, serving as a primary transportation route for timber from the late 19th to the early 20th century. Log drives and boom operations were common methods for moving lumber downstream. During the logging season, lumberjacks lived in rustic bunkhouses, often housing more than 70 men. Sleeping arrangements were sparse, with two men per bunk on coarse hay-stuffed mattresses.

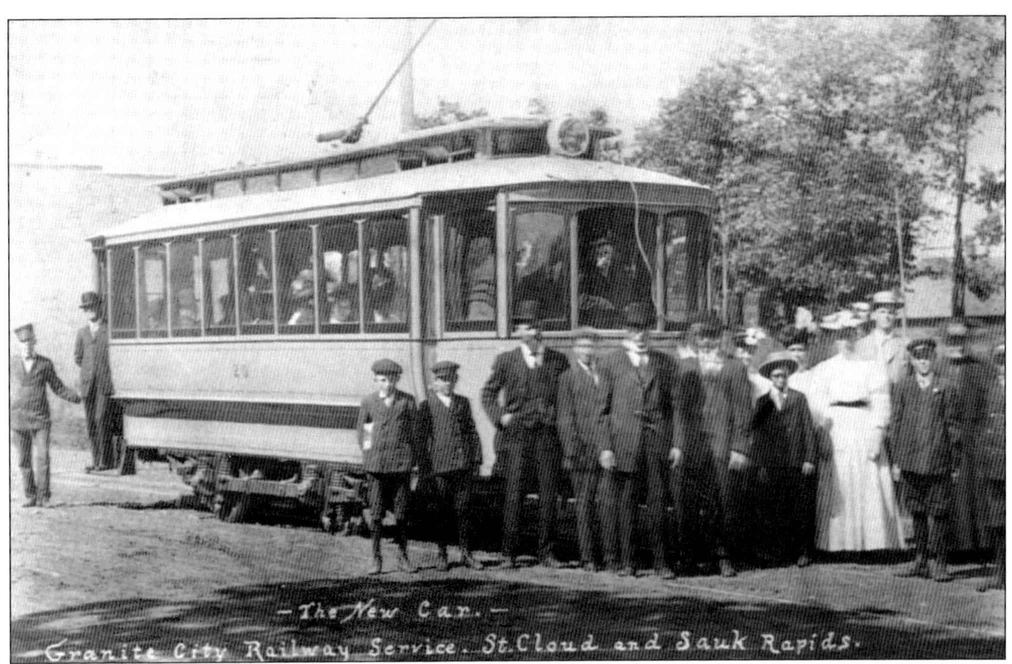

St. Cloud Streetcars, 1910. St. Cloud's first electric streetcar line opened on June 24, 1892, bringing with it a new metropolitan experience for the city. Originally horse-drawn, the line soon converted to electricity under the Granite City Railway Company, which expanded service into Sauk Rapids and Waite Park. At its peak in 1914, the system featured nine miles of track, a large brick carbarn, and 17 streetcars equipped with lights, stoves, and cushioned seats. The service quickly became essential, carrying residents and commuting railroad workers reliably every 20 minutes.

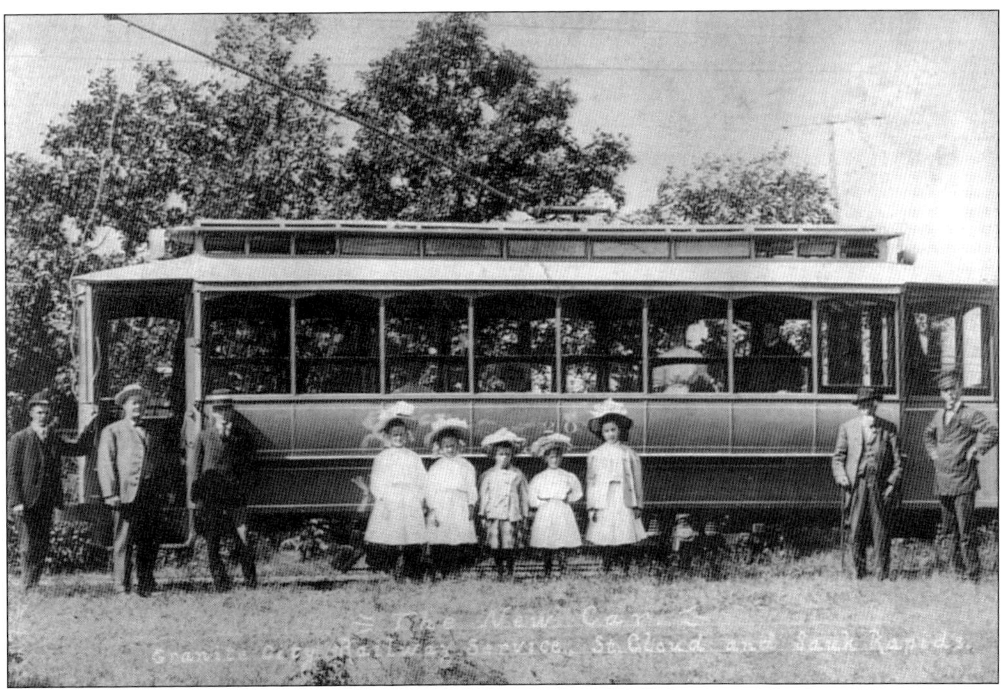

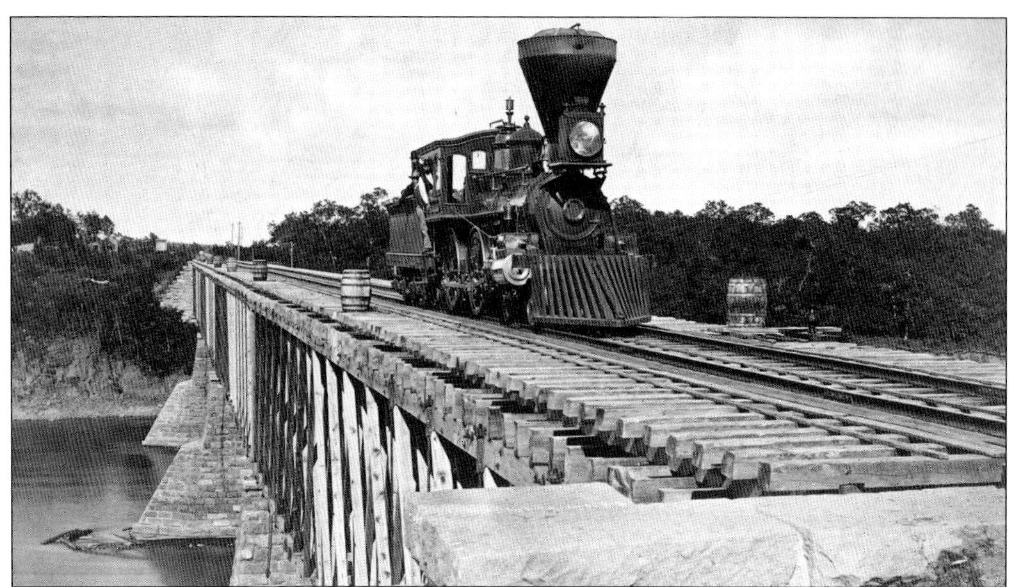

Train Crosses Railroad Bridge, 1877. In 1872, the St. Paul & Pacific Railroad announced plans to construct a bridge across the Mississippi River, marking its first expansion into St. Cloud's west side. The bridge was completed in June 1873, and soon, passenger service extended westward from St. Cloud to Melrose, with stops along the way. By 1889, as many as 16 passenger trains arrived in St. Cloud each day.

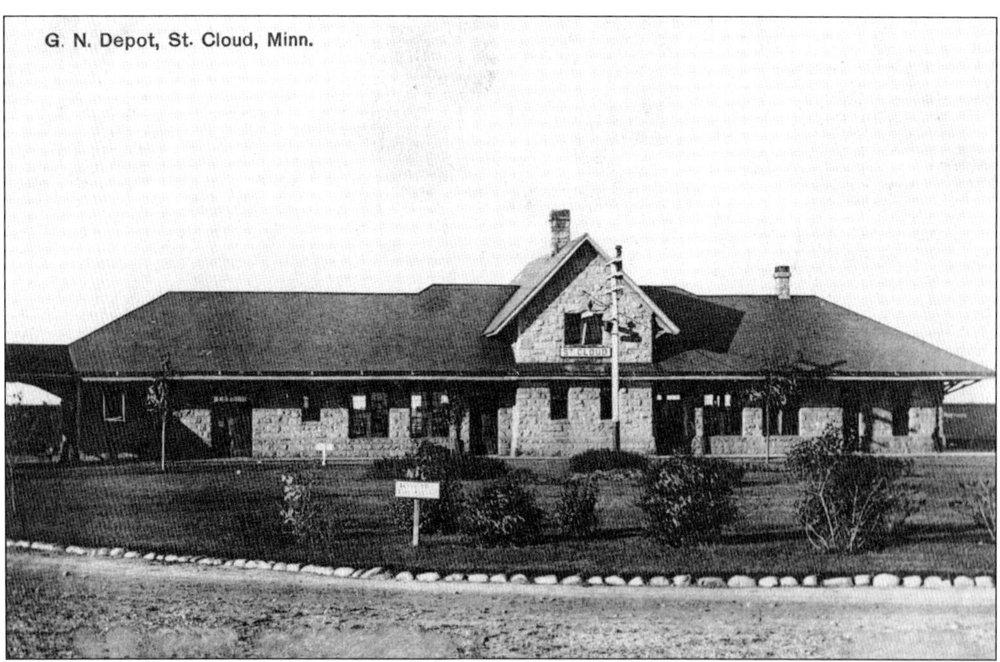

Great Northern Depot, c. 1910. The Great Northern Railway built the city's first depot in 1883 on the east side. In 1887, the company expanded by purchasing 300 acres for major facilities, including a paint shop, repair shop, and woodworking shop. On the west side, the Northern Pacific Railway constructed its own depot in 1889, later replacing it with a new building in 1909 and a roundhouse in 1923. By 1970, the two major lines merged to form the Burlington Northern.

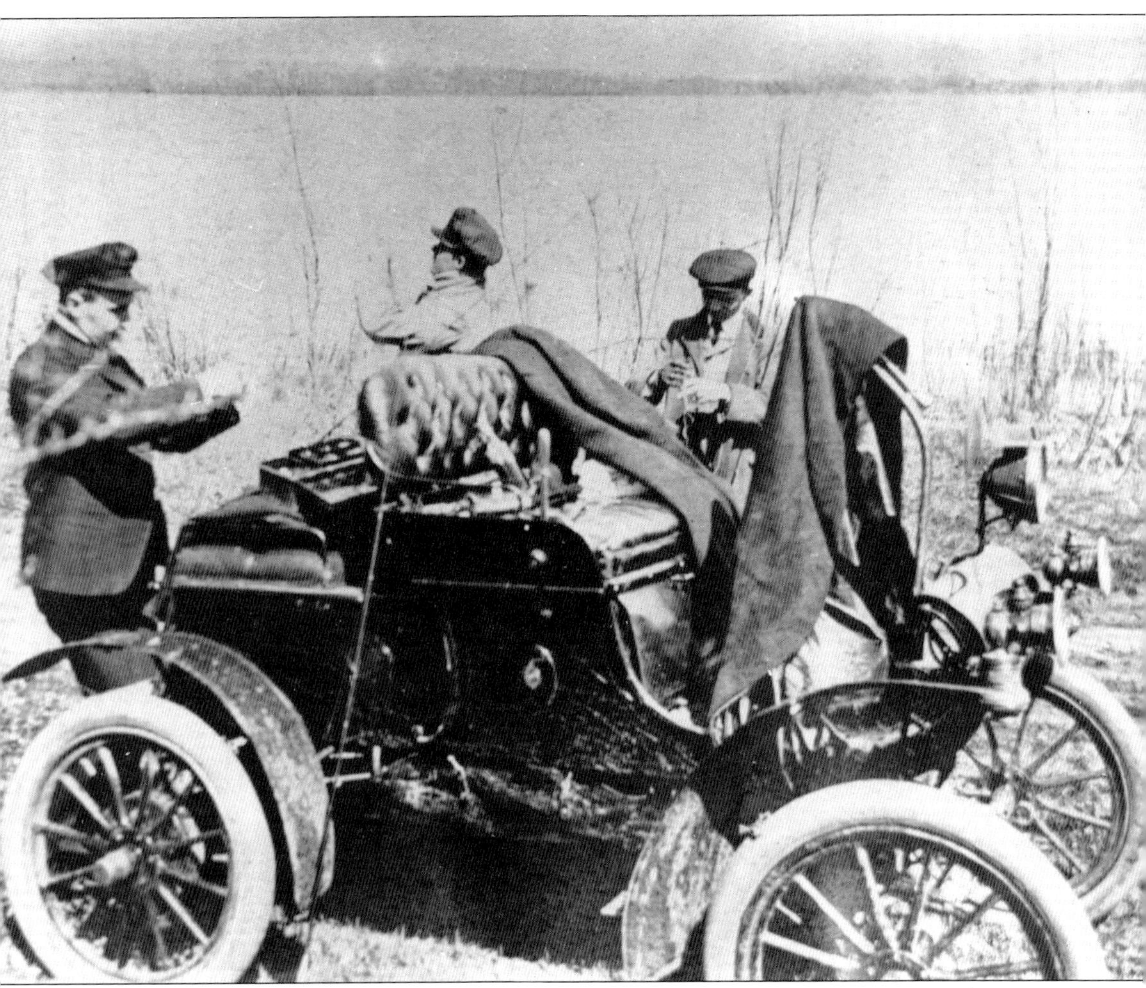

FIRST AUTOMOBILE IN ST. CLOUD, 1899. In 1899, St. Cloud witnessed a transportation milestone when the first automobile arrived in the city. Steve Tenvoorde and his friend P.R. Thielman, known locally as "the Daredevils," drove a Milwaukee Steamer 70 miles from Minneapolis over a rugged oxen trail to bring the car home. Their daring journey introduced residents to a new era of travel and marked the beginning of St. Cloud's connection to the automobile industry.

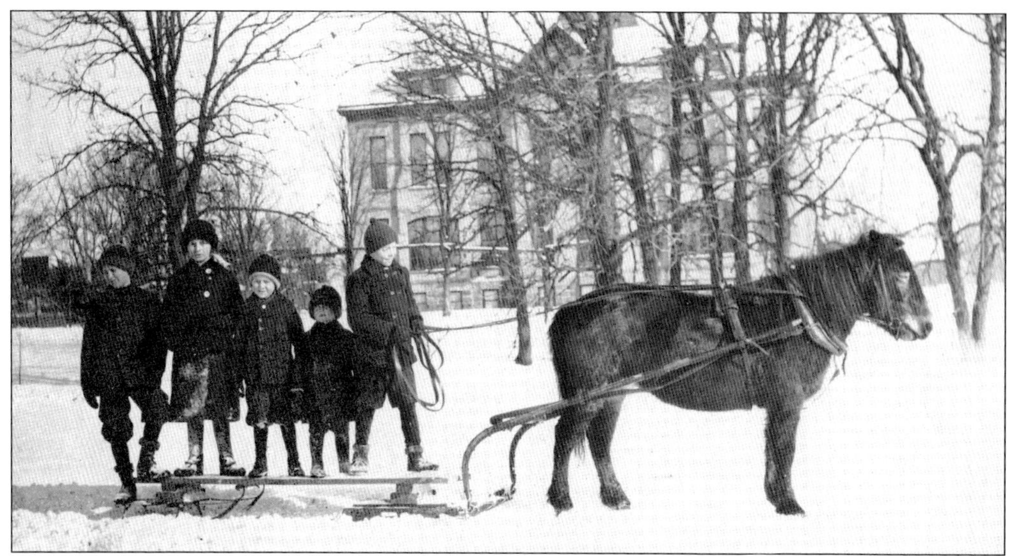

Donkey Pulls a Sled-Sleigh with Children, Washington School, c. 1915. In the early 20th century, parents and children in snowy areas had to think creatively for practical ways to travel when roads were unpaved or uncleared. More rural inhabitants of St. Cloud often sent farm animals and sleds to carry their children to school.

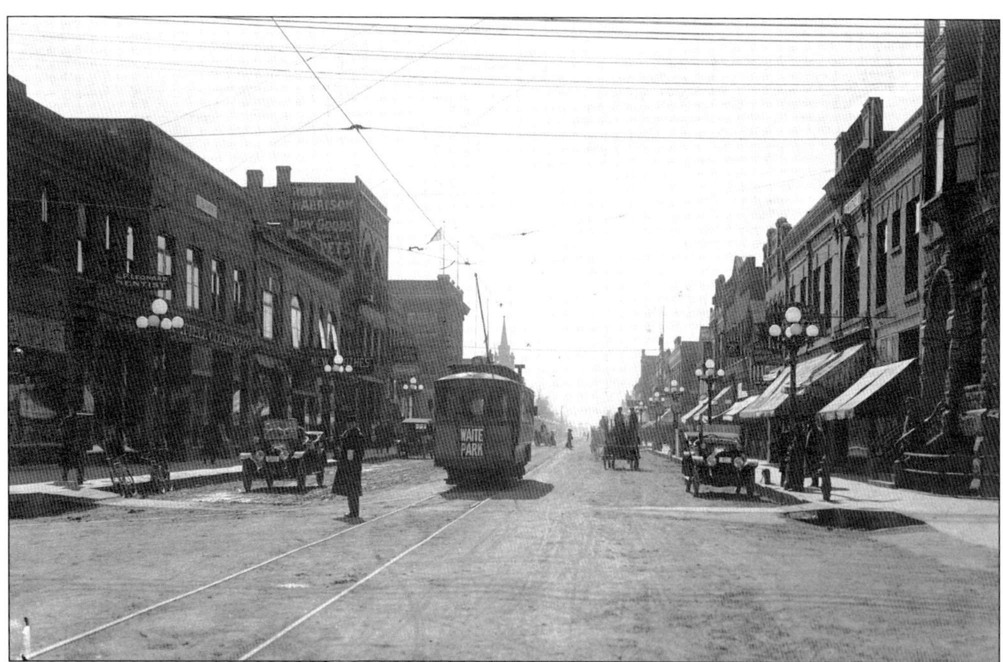

St. Germain Street Transportation, c. 1916. Despite its success, the rise of the automobile in the 1930s led to the decline of the streetcar. Service officially ended on April 29, 1936, when 15,000 people gathered to bid farewell during the final run to Waite Park and back. Soon after, the tracks were removed, and buses replaced the streetcars that had faithfully served St. Cloud for more than four decades.

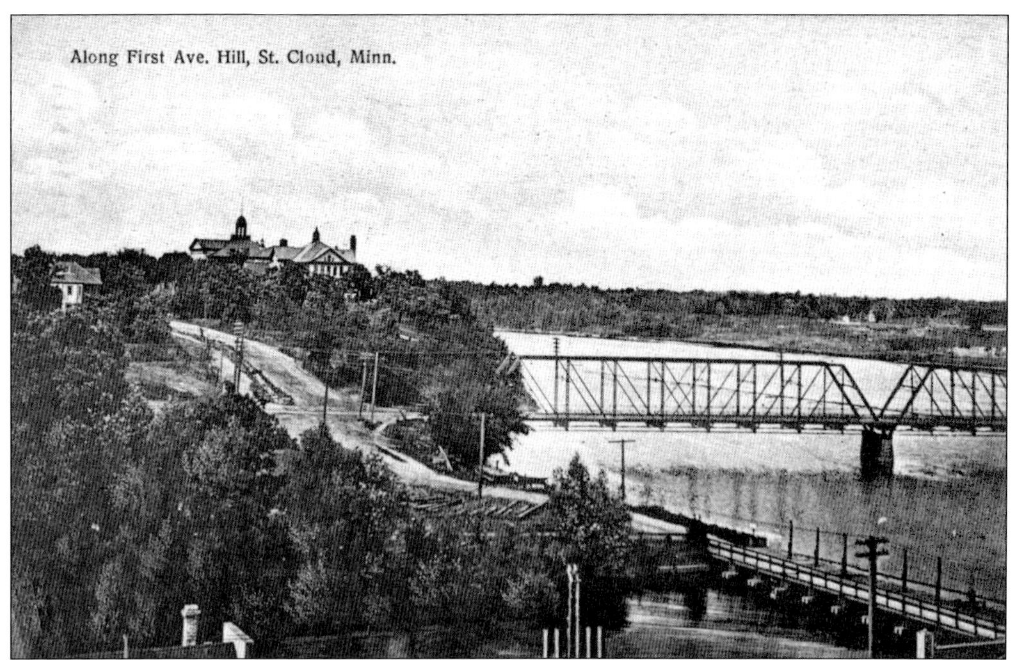

JEFFERSON HIGHWAY AND FIRST AVENUE, C. 1912. Built in 1910 as part of the National Auto Trail system, the Jefferson Highway extended from New Orleans to Winnipeg. In St. Cloud, the highway followed Division Street through Rice before continuing south. On the east side, Lincoln Avenue held the Jefferson Highway, which then crossed the St. Germain Street bridge. From there, the route passed St. Cloud Teachers College, crossed the Mississippi River again, and continued past the St. Cloud Reformatory.

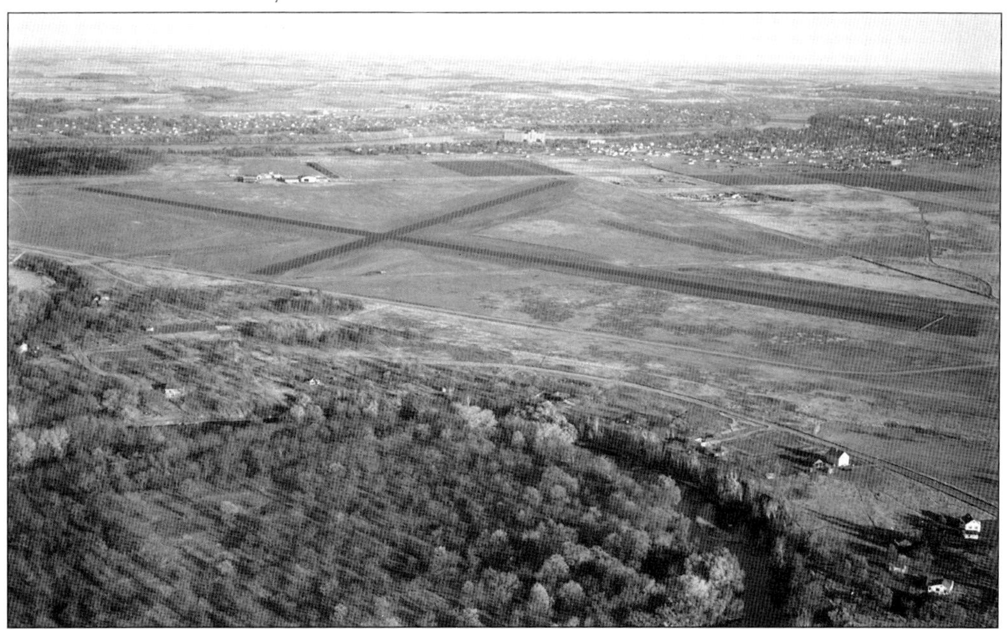

WHITNEY MEMORIAL AIRPORT, 1947. In 1935, land donated by Alice Whitney, widow of Albert Whitney, a land developer, civic leader, and businessman, became Whitney Memorial Airport. It was St. Cloud's first airport.

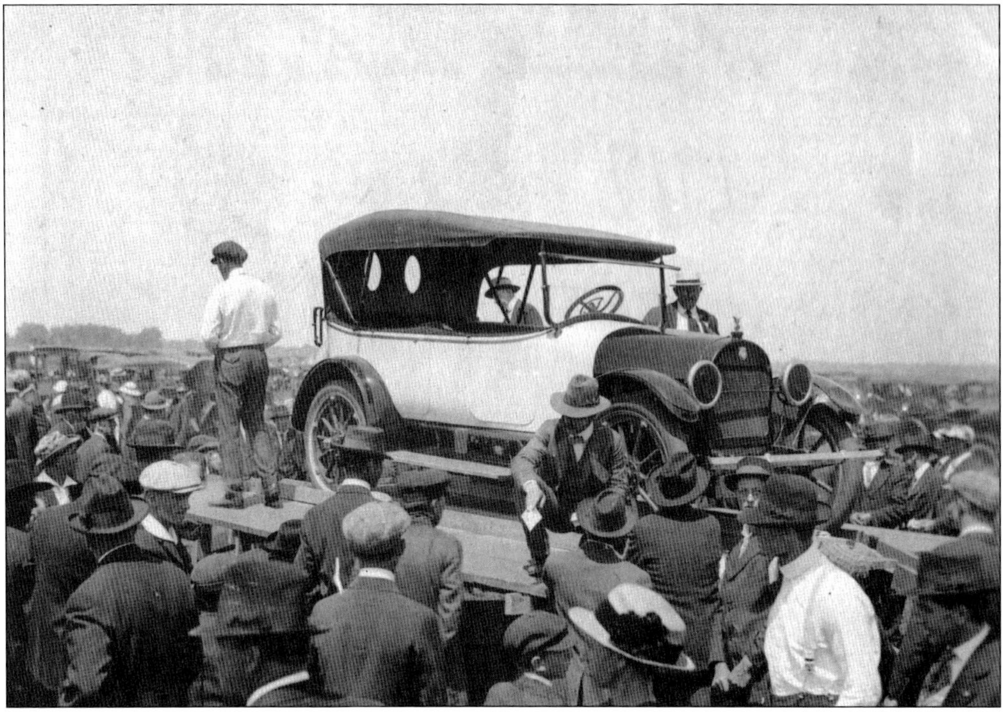

First Unveiling of the Pan Car, Pan Motor Company Picnic, 1917. Sam Pandolfo envisioned a traveler-friendly car with fold-down seats, tool and fuel compartments, high clearance, and space for food. In 1916, he began selling stock, gaining 9,000 investors by 1917. That March, St. Cloud was chosen as the Pan Motor Company's site for its access to rail lines, iron ore, and hydroelectric power. On July 4, 1917, Pandolfo unveiled the Pan automobile at Minnesota's largest-ever picnic. The massive crowd consumed 15,434 pounds of beef and 8,000 loaves of bread—and it still was not enough to feed everyone.

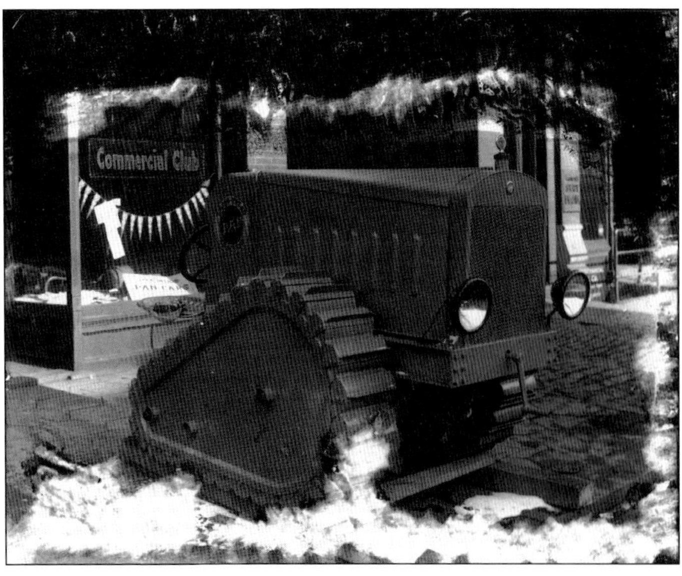

Pan Tank-Tread Tractor, c. 1918. The Pan Tank-Tread Tractor, developed by the Pan Motor Company around 1919, was an ambitious attempt to modernize farming equipment. Powered by a Buda engine, the machine featured a distinctive full-track design and could be operated either from a traditional tractor seat or directly from a trailing implement. Financial troubles soon derailed the project, and only a single prototype was ever produced.

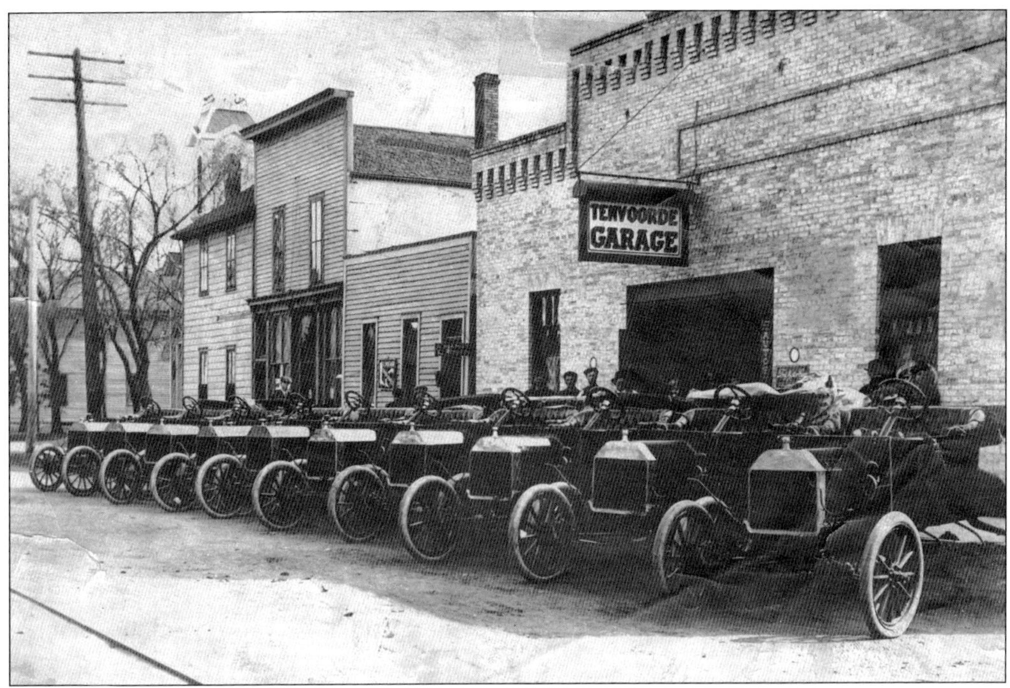

TENVOORDE GARAGE, C. 1905 (ABOVE), AND TENVOORDE SHOWROOM, C. 1918 (BELOW). In 1903, Steve Tenvoorde signed an agreement that made his business the second Ford dealership in the nation, a legacy that today stands as the oldest Ford dealership in the world. Fascinated by machinery, he contracted with several early car manufacturers, including Oakland, Saxon, Buick, and Oldsmobile, before shifting exclusively to Ford vehicles within just over a decade. The dealership operated from a brick building in downtown St. Cloud, featuring a five-car showroom that allowed passersby to view the latest models even in the depths of Minnesota winters. Beyond sales, the shop became a trusted resource for mechanical repairs and bodywork, establishing a reputation for reliability and service.

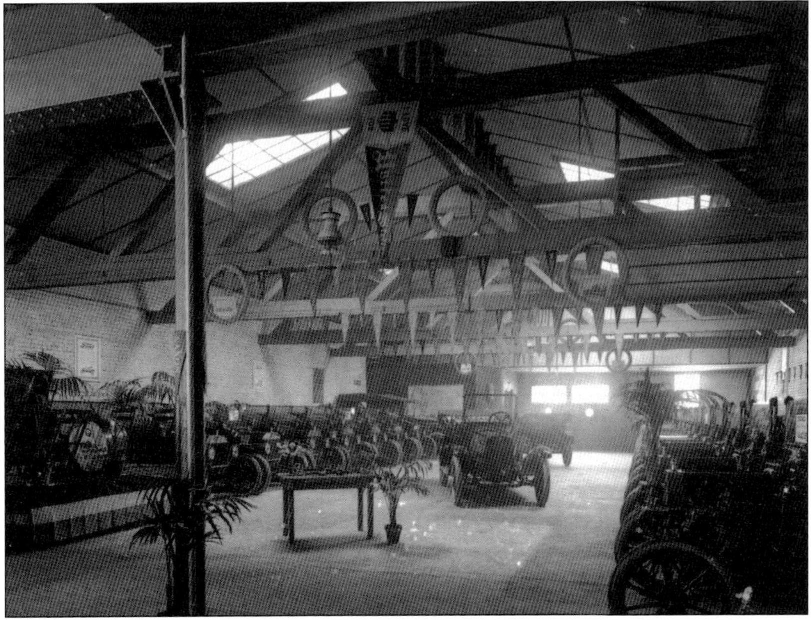

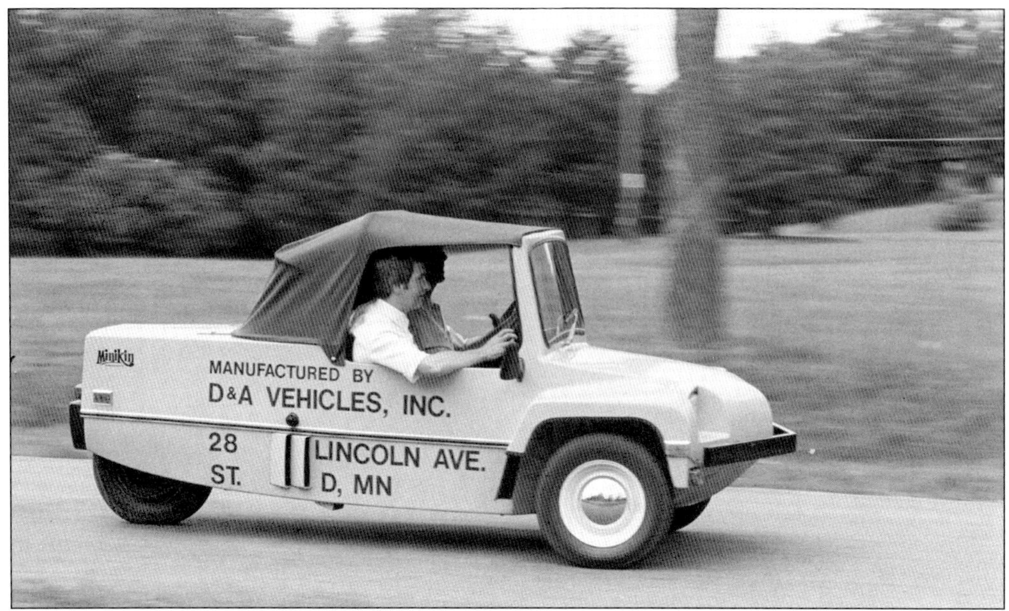

MINIKIN INVENTORS DRIVE A MINIKIN, 1983 (ABOVE), AND TWO MINIKINS ON THE ROAD, 1985 (BELOW). In the early 1980s, Don Schirmers and Allen Tank launched D&A Vehicles with hopes of reshaping commuter transportation. After acquiring the rights to the H-M Vehicles Freeway, a tiny three-wheeled car known for its 100 miles-per-gallon rating, they redesigned it into a two-seat convertible called the Minikin. Built in St. Cloud, the Minikin featured a lightweight frame, a central steering wheel, and a 16-horsepower engine that promised up to 80 miles per gallon. Marketed as a fun, affordable second car, it was also pitched for RV owners, island rentals, and even pizza delivery. Despite its ambition and efficiency, only about 16 Minikins were ever sold. Though short-lived, the project reflected central Minnesota's role in experimenting with alternative, fuel-efficient transportation during a time of rising gas prices. (Both photographs by Mike Knaak; courtesy of the *St. Cloud Times*.)

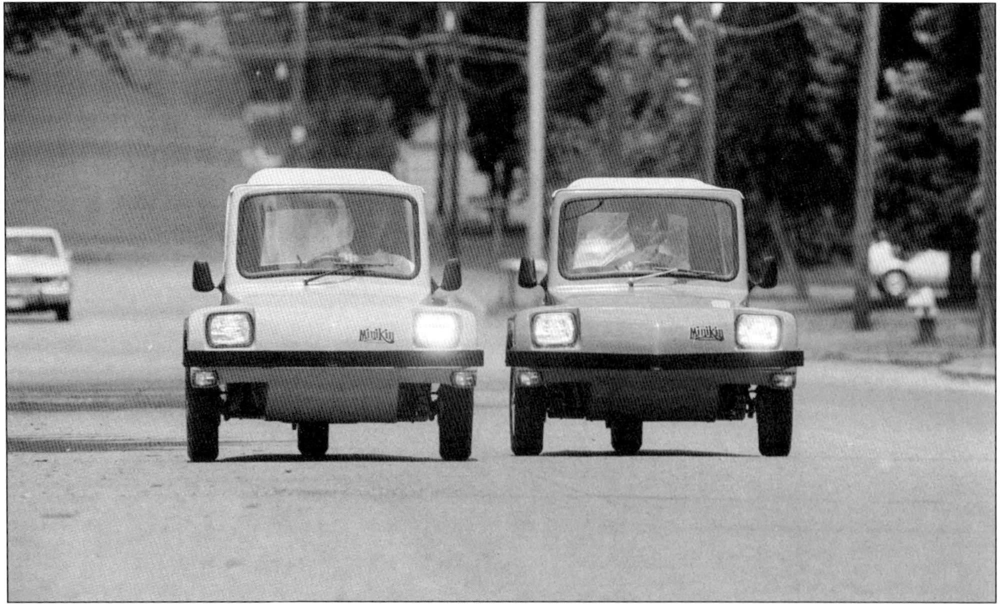

Seven

Pillars of Care

From its earliest days, St. Cloud's story has not just been about settlement and growth but about how communities cared for one another in illness, hardship, and crisis. Social services and institutions, hospitals, orphanages, libraries, police and fire departments, and welfare organizations have long shaped the rhythms of public life in the city. A variety of local organizations, faith groups, government agencies, and citizens responded to the changing demands of care, public health, and social welfare over time to improve life for its residents.

Institutions formed the backbone of these efforts. The Benedictine Sisters established the St. Cloud Children's Home and a hospital, which grew into a long-standing center of child welfare and medical care. In the 1920s, the federal government chose St. Cloud as the site of a veterans' hospital, a facility that expanded through the mid-century and became a major provider of medical and mental health care for former service members.

But care in St. Cloud was never confined to large institutions. The city's police, fire, and library services also represent threads of civic welfare. Public safety and education services also strengthened mid-century, with the police, fire department, and public library expanding to meet the needs of a growing city.

As the city grew, so did the complexity of its welfare networks. By the late 20th century, coordination became increasingly important, and in 1992, local agencies, nonprofits, and government bodies formed the St. Cloud Area Human Services Council. The goal was to reduce duplication, expand cooperation, and respond more effectively to housing, health care, and social needs. Today, the city continues to grapple with issues of affordable housing, mental health, veterans' needs, child welfare, refugee resettlement, and more, pushing local systems to adapt and innovate.

Through these institutions and the individuals who built and ran them, St. Cloud built its social service architecture and responded to epidemics, war, and social change. Those systems, in turn, shaped the community itself.

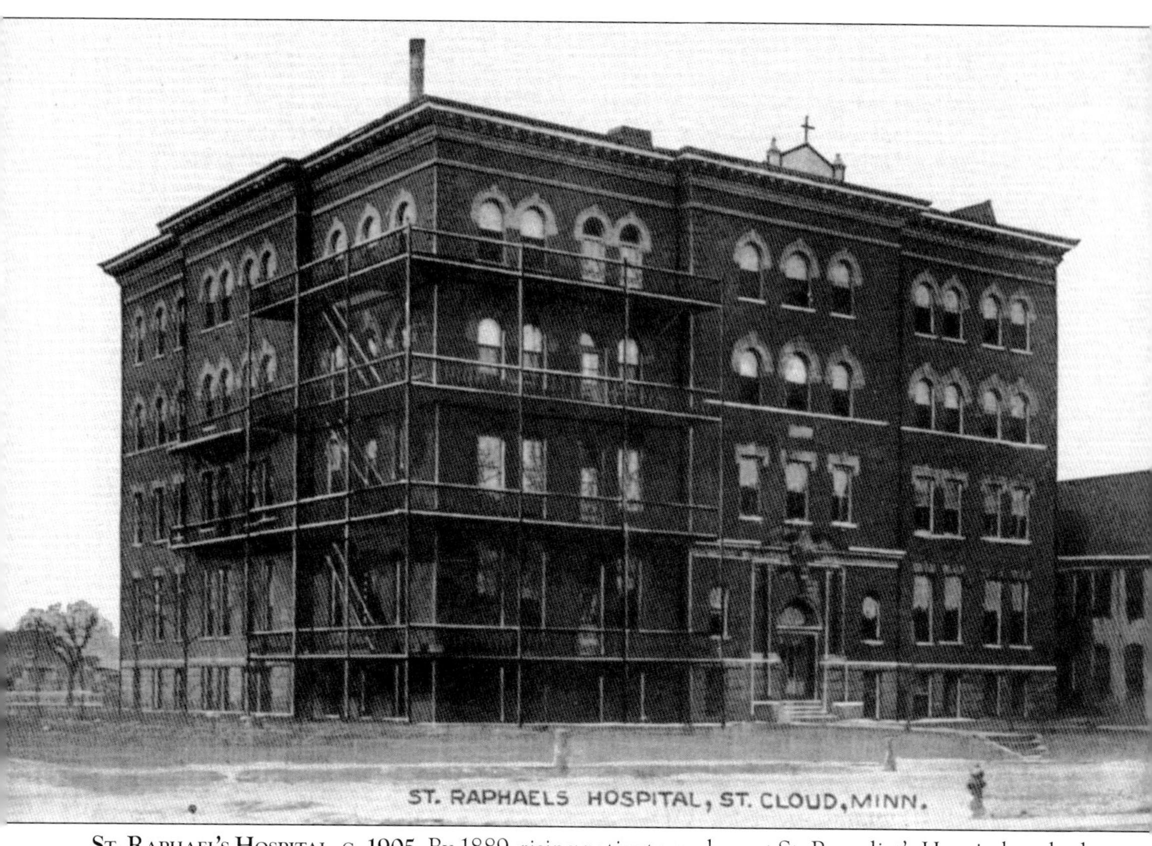

St. Raphael's Hospital, c. 1905. By 1889, rising patient numbers at St. Benedict's Hospital pushed the sisters to seek a larger space. Local donors offered land across the Mississippi, and in 1890, they built St. Raphael's Hospital, a modern three-story facility. Promised bridges and streetcar access never came, leaving the site isolated. After a decade of struggle, the sisters returned to Ninth Avenue, building a new St. Raphael's Hospital beside their original St. Benedict's Hospital.

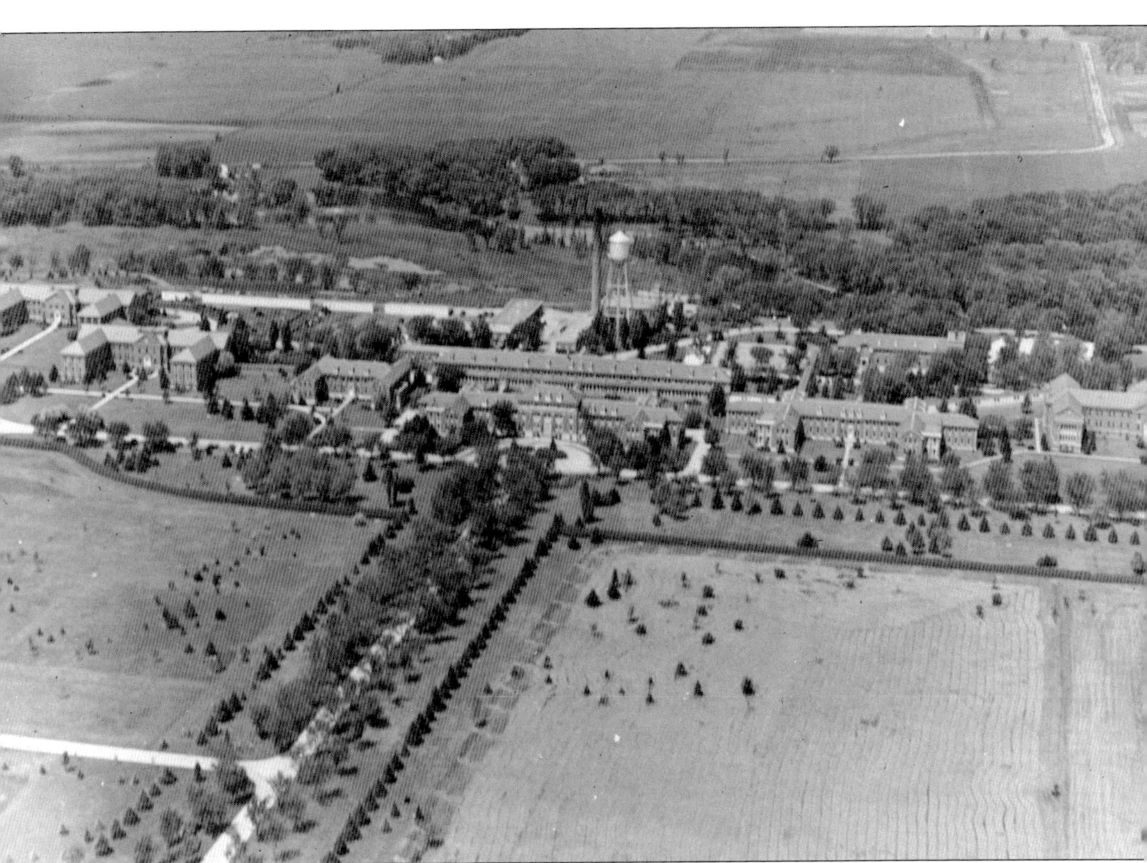

Aerial View of Veterans Administration (VA) Hospital, 1946. Originally called the Soldier Hospital, the "Veterans Hospital" (known now as the St. Cloud VA Health Care System) opened with 275 beds, primarily for psychiatric care. Dr. Hans Hansen, the first hospital manager, secured donors to landscape the grounds and introduced farm work as therapy, utilizing land now occupied by Apollo High School and industrial facilities. By 1936, the hospital had expanded to 47 buildings, serving 760 patients with a growing staff. Patients contributed to the evolving landscape, creating rock gardens, arbors, and pathways that shaped the hospital's surroundings.

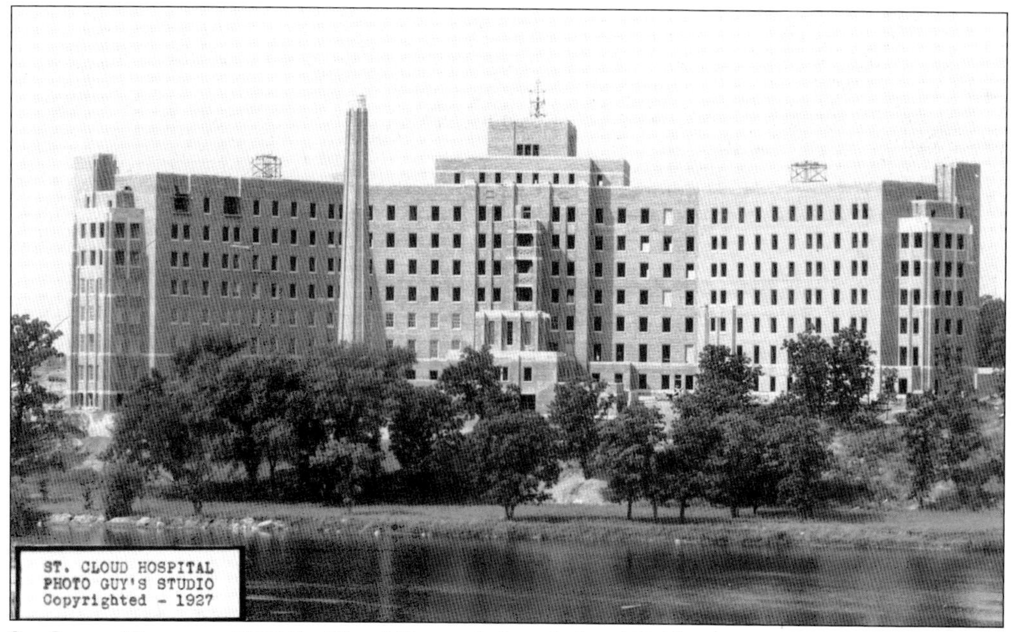

St. Cloud Hospital, 1927. St. Cloud Hospital, founded in 1886 by the Sisters of the Order of St. Benedict, began as St. Benedict's Hospital to serve the growing community in St. Cloud, Minnesota. It gained prominence after providing critical aid during the 1886 Sauk Rapids Cyclone. The hospital evolved through expansions and was renamed St. Cloud Hospital in 1928 at its current location. In 1962, it became a Catholic, not-for-profit institution and later merged with the St. Cloud Clinic in 1995 to form CentraCare Health.

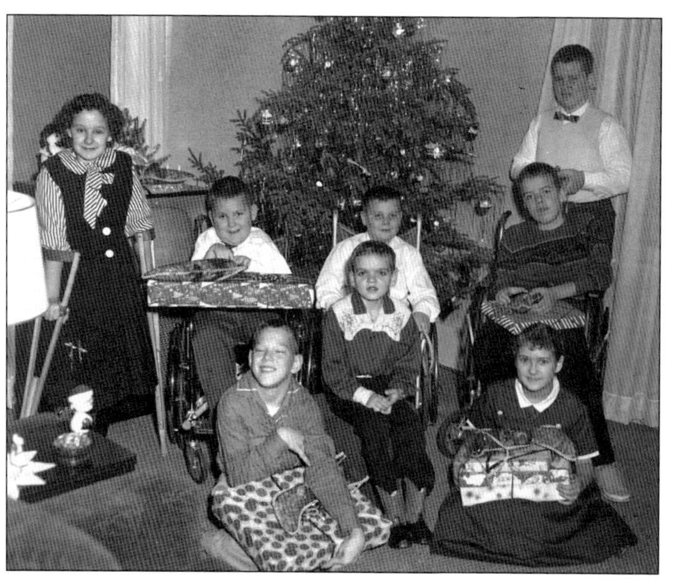

Christmas Party for Homebound Children, 1959. The "homebound" teaching program brought educators to students unable to leave their homes. Initially funded by the WPA, it was set to end in 1942 when the agency disbanded. Martha Van Brussel, city director of elementary education, recalled appealing to Eleanor Roosevelt to save the program. A month later, a letter from the White House granted a one-year extension, during which Minnesota passed legislation to ensure its ongoing funding.

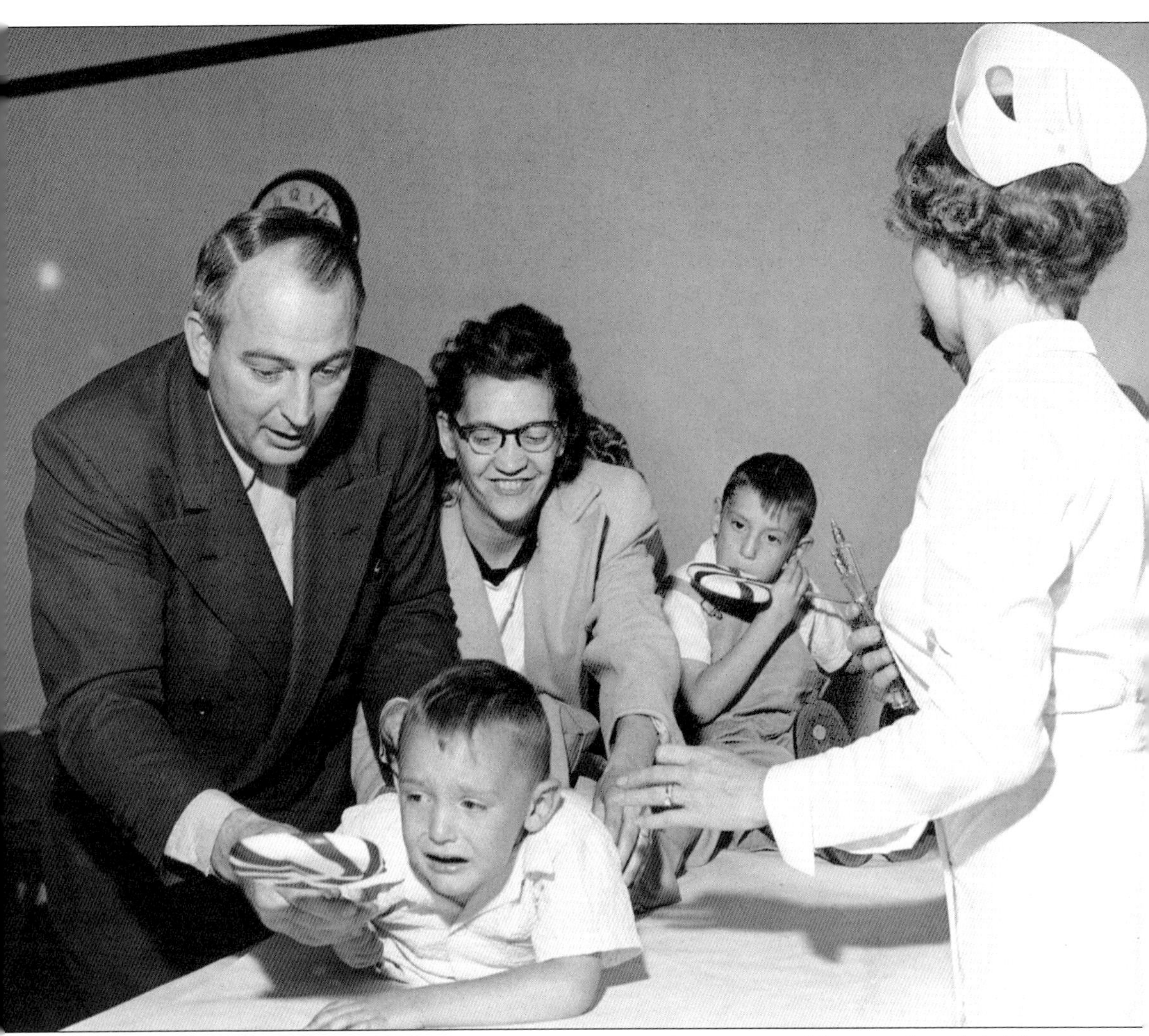

Doctor Inoculates Child with Polio Vaccine, 1953. Polio was one of the most feared childhood diseases of the 20th century, causing paralysis, death, and lasting disabilities. In 1953, after the polio vaccine was deemed safe, Stearns and Benton Counties participated in the nation's third-largest gamma globulin mass inoculation. Known as Operation Lollipop, the free and voluntary clinics were held across the region, with parents rushing to protect their children. Local businesses donated over 30,000 lollipops, which were distributed to participants.

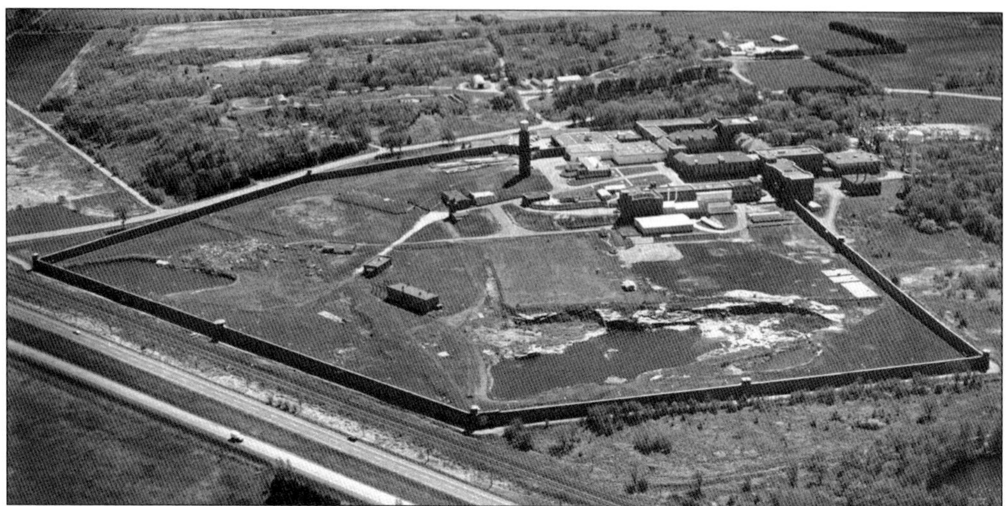

St. Cloud Reformatory, 1979. Founded in 1887, the St. Cloud Reformatory was created to give young, first-time offenders a chance at rehabilitation. Inmates contributed to their communities through granite work, farming, logging, and vocational training in trades like printing, clothing, and shoe manufacturing. For decades, the institution emphasized productive labor and skills that could prepare men for life beyond prison. Now known as the Minnesota Correctional Facility, it remains a long-standing part of the community's history.

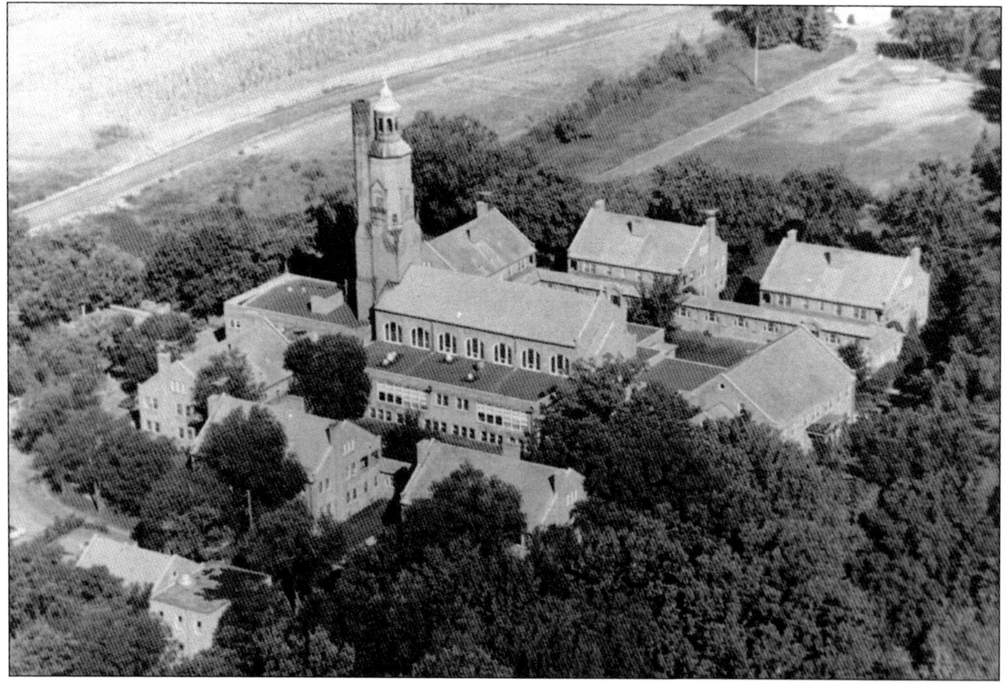

St. Cloud Children's Home, c. 1965. Orphan care in central Minnesota began in 1875 with the Benedictine Sisters sheltering seven children in Pierz. In 1924, the St. Cloud Orphanage opened with six cottages, housing up to 150 children. Over time, evolving child welfare philosophies transformed it into a treatment center. Renamed the St. Cloud Children's Home in 1950, it shifted focus to supporting children with emotional and behavioral challenges, moving beyond traditional orphan care.

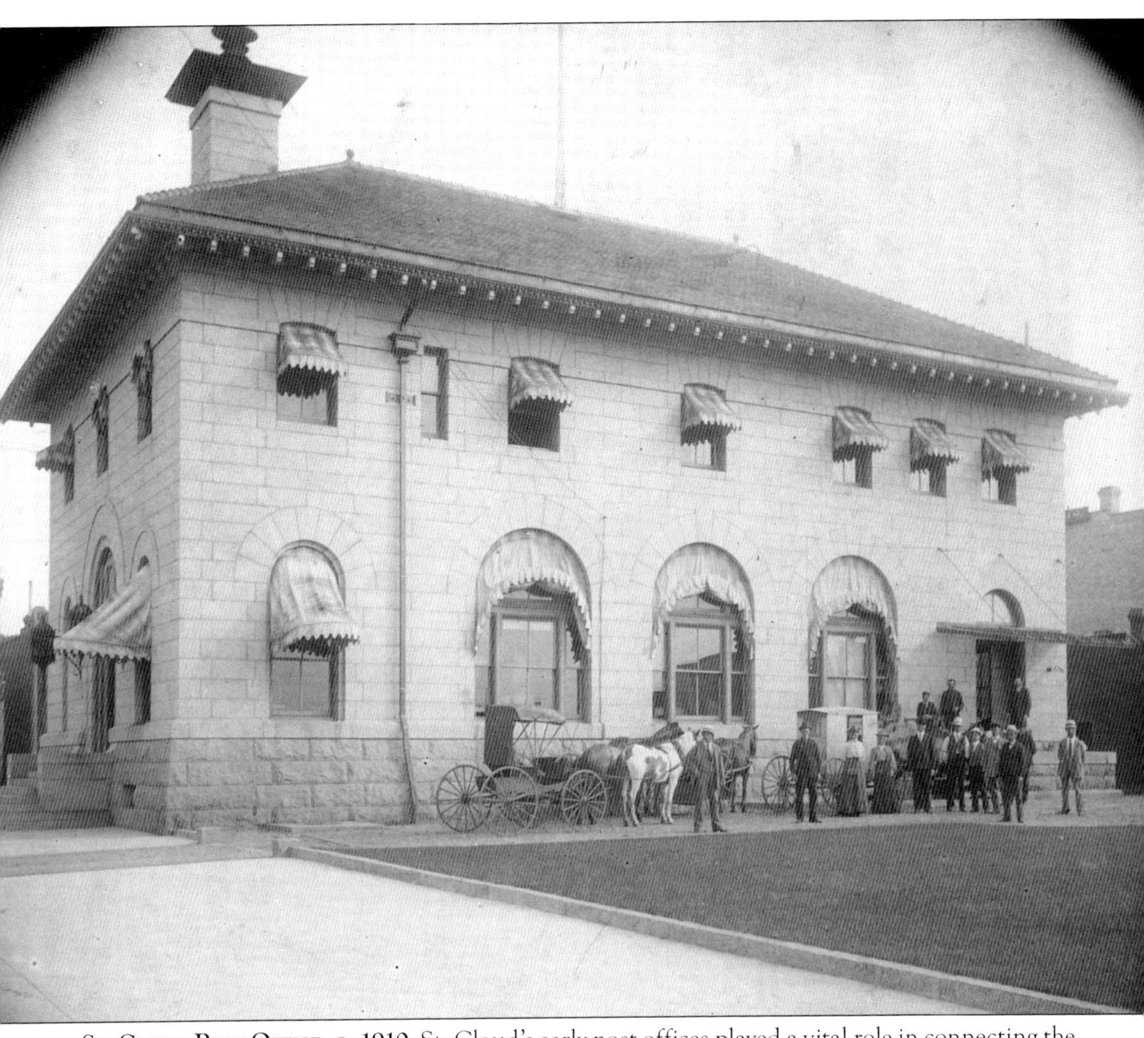

ST. CLOUD POST OFFICE, C. 1910. St. Cloud's early post offices played a vital role in connecting the community. From Frank Sisson's small log store in the 1850s to Joseph Edelbrock's Acadia post office, residents relied on local postmasters to distribute mail and keep people connected. The 1938 St. Cloud Post Office, now in the National Register of Historic Places, served as the city's central hub for 30 years, helping residents with daily correspondence and even military enlistments during World War II.

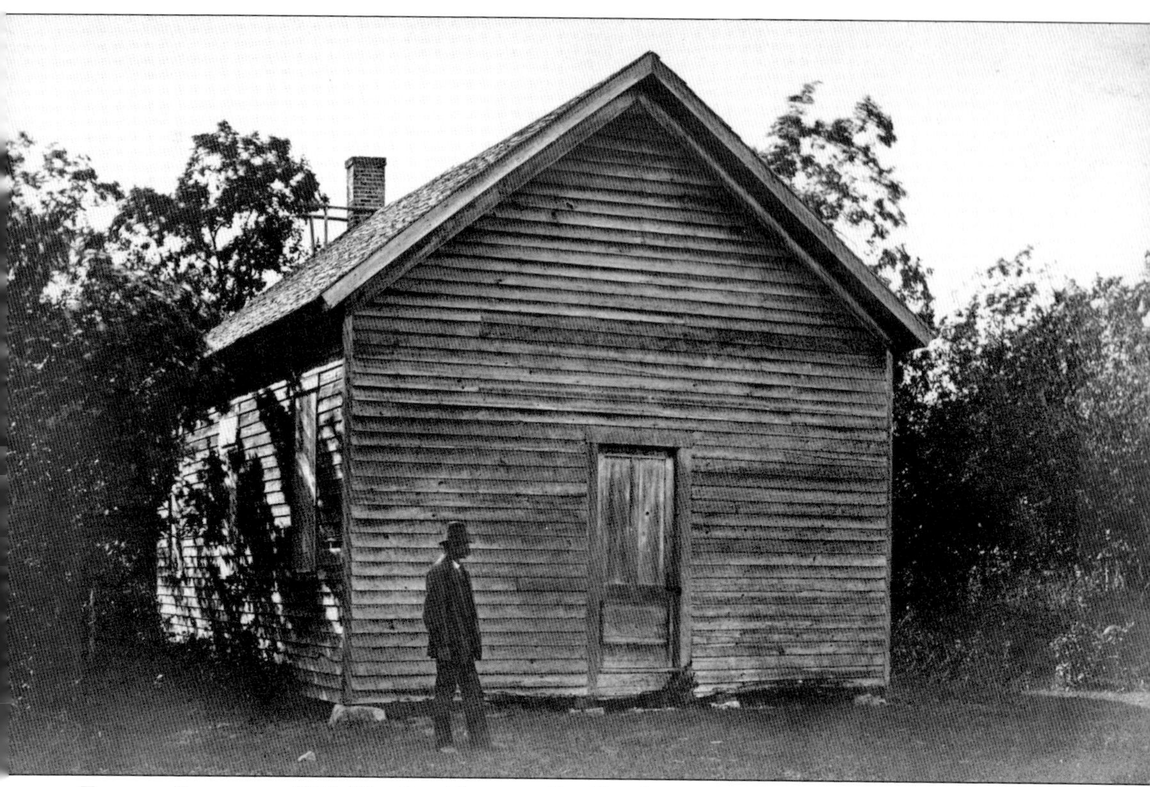

Everett School, c. 1877. The first library in St. Cloud was not a public library. It began in 1858 with 130 books donated by Boston native Edward Everett, after learning a local school was named in his honor. The books were intended for use in the school's library.

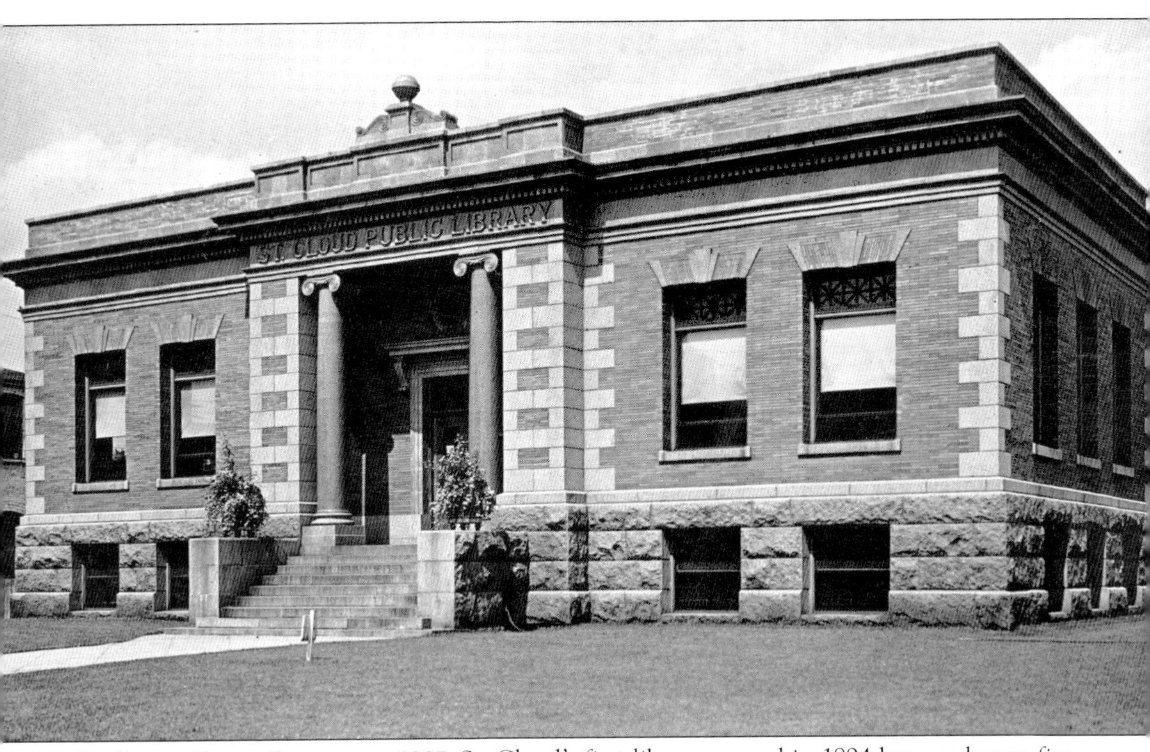

ST. CLOUD PUBLIC LIBRARY, C. 1907. St. Cloud's first library opened in 1894 but was lost to fire in 1901. The Reading Room Society secured $25,000 from Andrew Carnegie and local funds to build a new library, which opened in 1902. A WPA-funded wing was added in 1939. By the 1970s, the structure no longer met the city's needs, and in 1979, the library moved to West St. Germain Street, with the old Carnegie building later demolished. For much of the 20th century, the library symbolized St. Cloud's dedication to education and community.

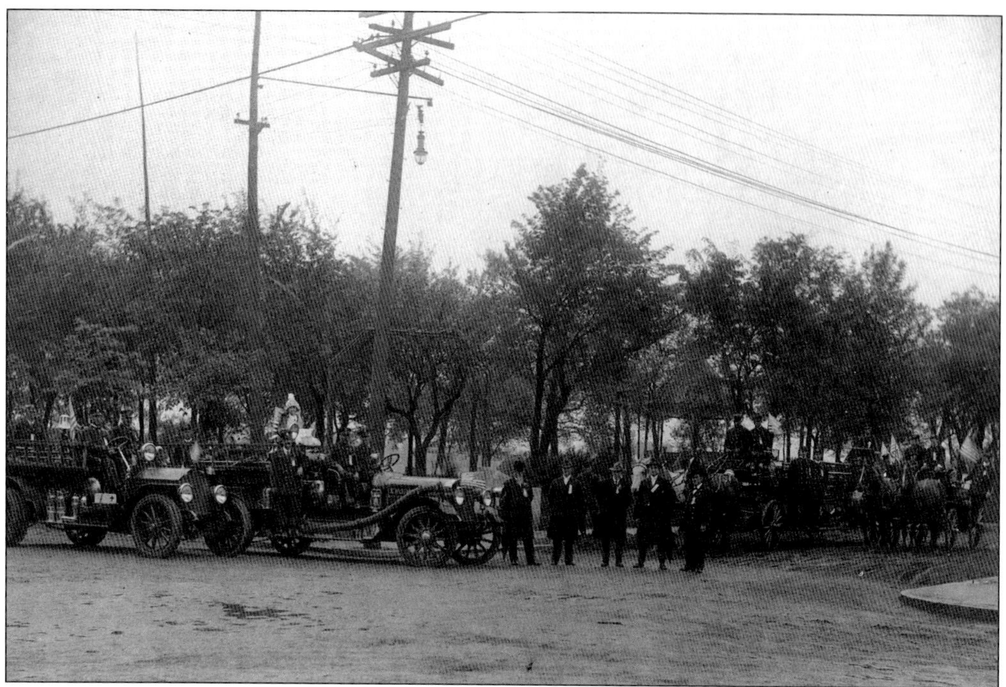

FIRE HALL, 1918. In 1861, St. Cloud recorded its first fire, causing $1,000 in damage but no deaths. Two years later, Mayor Evans allocated funds to upgrade the "bucket brigade's" equipment. Returning Civil War soldiers soon joined the volunteers, forming the St. Cloud Pioneer Fire Company No. 1 in 1864. Over time, despite several major fires, the department advanced rapidly and by 1917 was among the best equipped in Minnesota.

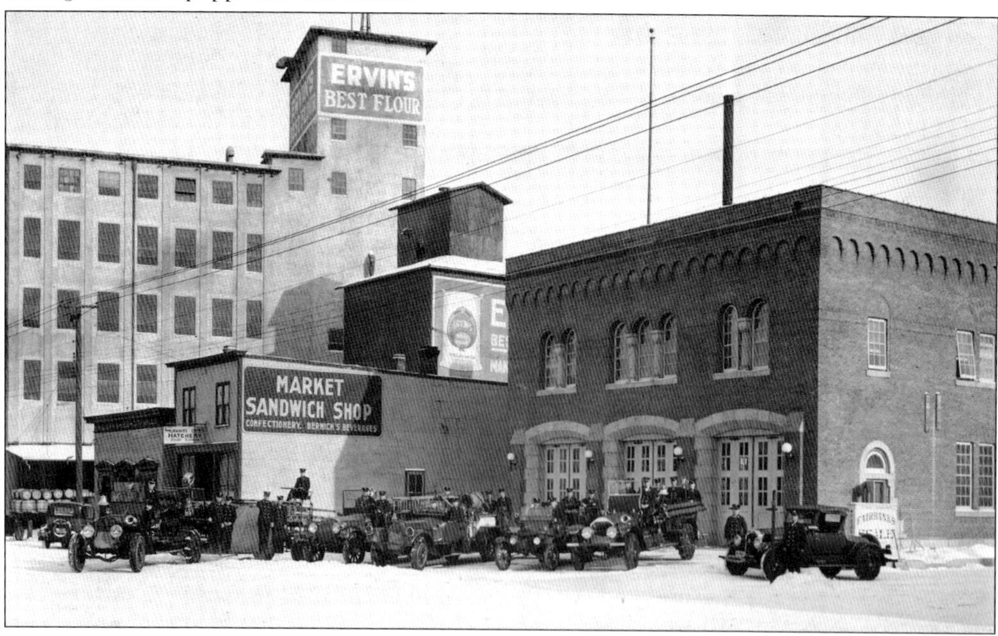

FIRE DEPARTMENT, 1930. In 1929, the fire department moved into a brand new $100,000 station. The year 1930 saw the donation of an old ambulance from the police department; although few firefighters knew first aid, they agreed to operate it for citizens who could not afford a private ambulance service.

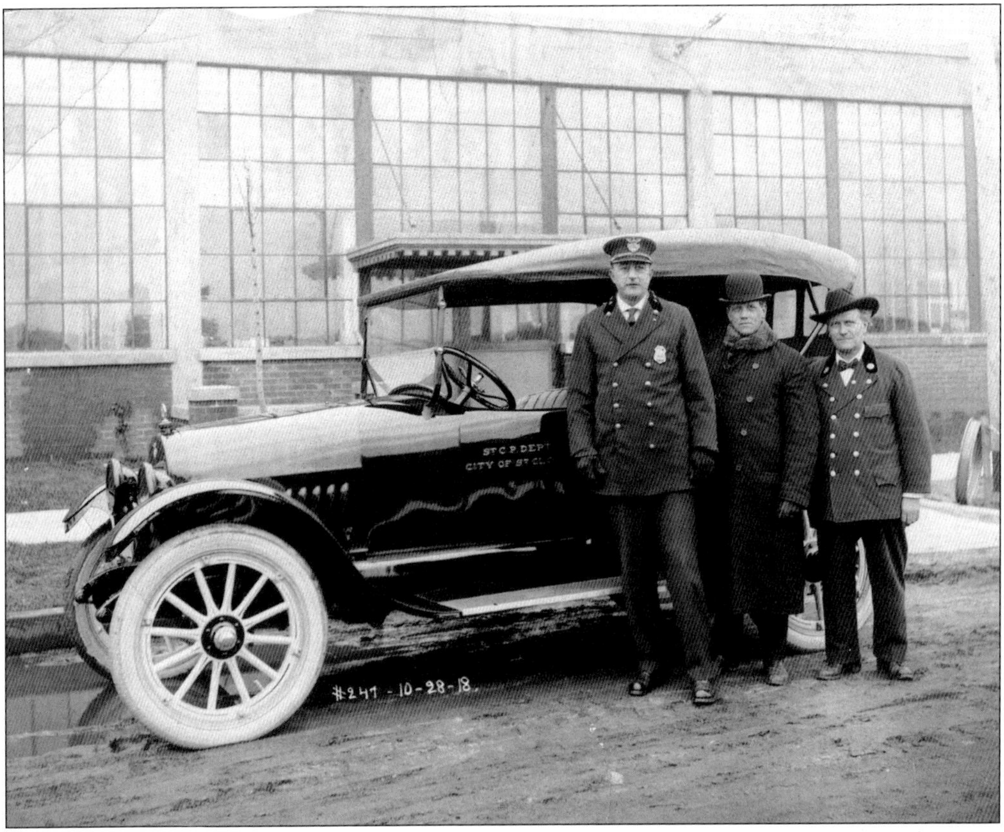

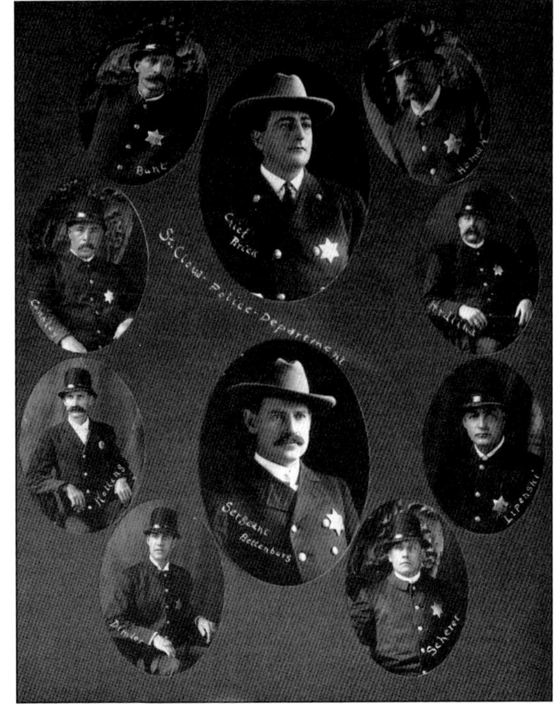

Chief Ed Brick with Pan Motor Police Car, 1918 (above), and St. Cloud Police Department, 1910 (right). The St. Cloud Police Department traces its roots to the first log cabin in St. Cloud, to the early courthouse and jail constructed in Columbia Square during the 1860s, before moving into its first dedicated building in 1917. A major milestone came in 1913 when Chief Ed Brick (above, far left) drove the department's first squad car, a Pan automobile equipped with a side-mounted bell to signal emergencies. At the time, the force included a chief, a sergeant, and eight officers, who had previously patrolled on foot, bicycle, or horseback. The department later shared the 1917 building with the city hall and the fire department until relocating to the Law Enforcement Center in 1987, marking nearly 70 years of service in its original headquarters.

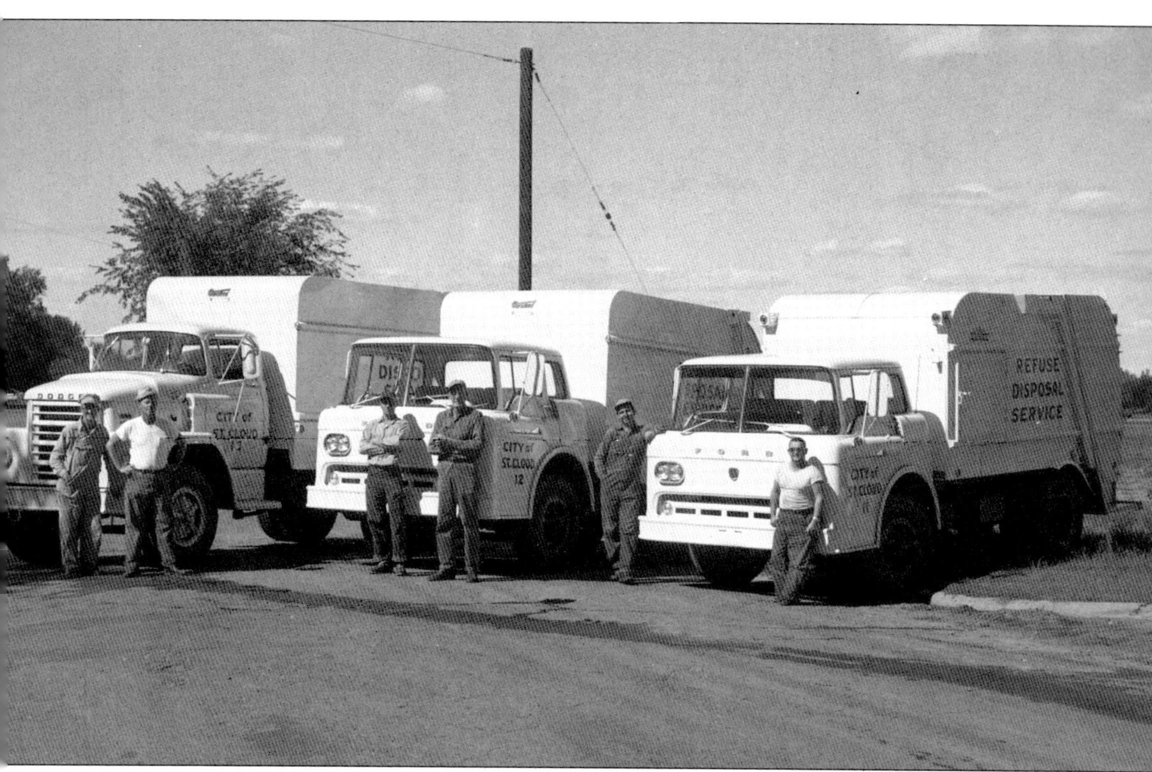

Employees with New Garbage Trucks, 1960. On the front lines of public health, St. Cloud's sanitation crews have always worked hard to collect and safely dispose of the city's waste, protecting the environment and the community. Since 1991's volume-based system cut landfill deposits in half, their dangerous, essential work has kept the city cleaner, healthier, and safer.

Eight

All-America City

In 1974, St. Cloud won the All-America City award from the National Municipal League. Although the award itself was for community projects, the moniker "All-America City" evokes a separate characteristic that has always been part of the nature of St. Cloud, and that is its classic American culture.

Music, dancing, and theaters were central to the cultural landscape of St. Cloud since its earliest days, providing recreation and entertainment for people across central Minnesota. The Davidson Opera House and Sherman Theatre (later the Paramount) were popular venues for stage plays, musicals, and movies. For years, the St. Cloud Municipal Band performed every Thursday night in Barden Park. The Granite City Coliseum and the Crystal Ballroom were hot spots for dancing with traveling orchestras providing live music. Other popular hangouts included the Press Bar, Dan Marsh, and the Wagon Wheel supper club.

For years, amateur and minor-league baseball were a cultural touchstone in St. Cloud and greater central Minnesota. The Northern League reorganized after World War II in 1945, and the St. Cloud Rox played in the league's first season in 1946. The Rox won the title that year, with a fan turnout of 55,179 over 53 home games. They played their first season in the Municipal Stadium in 1948 to an increased turnout of 66,389 over 60 home games. The St. Cloud Rox were an affiliate team of the then New York Giants until 1960, then became an affiliate of the Minnesota Twins in 1965. Around that time, minor-league baseball attendance began to decline significantly. Despite the skill of the St. Cloud Rox, having won five of the seven final league championships, attendance reached an all-time low in 1971 of 17,071 over 35 home games. The Northern League disbanded later that year.

St. Cloud became the prototypical scene for Minnesota winters when snow fell during the winter months. Children went sledding, made snowmen, and ice-skated on Lake George, while older kids went skiing and rode snowmobiles. St. Germain Street was strewn with Christmas decorations, and Christmas shoppers cluttered the city sidewalks.

Though it received the title due to community projects like the Mall Germain and the St. Cloud Industrial Park, the culture of St. Cloud also made it an All-America City.

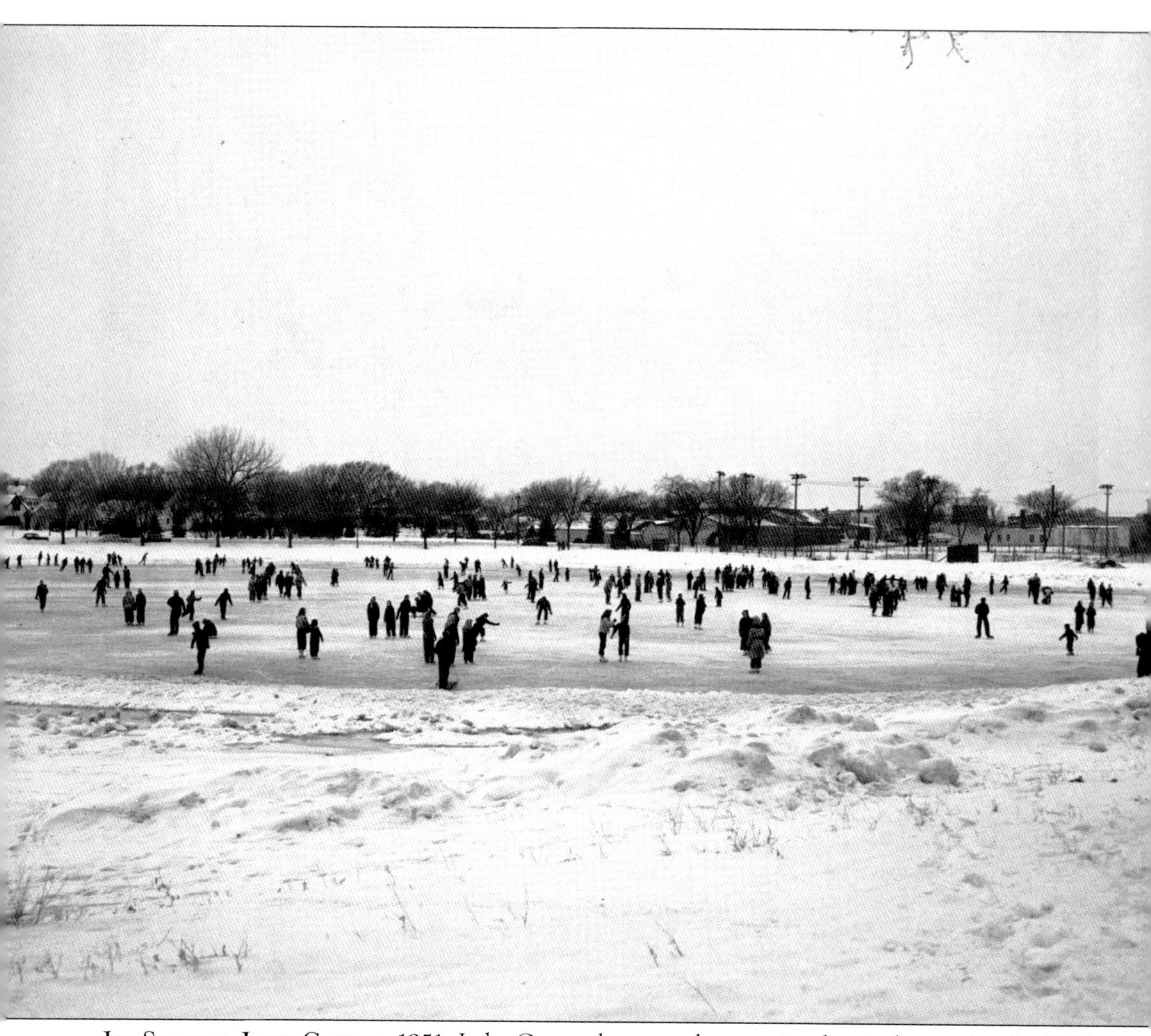

ICE SKATING, LAKE GEORGE, 1951. Lake George has not always existed as it does today. In 1867, John Coates built a skating rink in the park, claiming it was the largest in the state. However, low water levels in the following years led citizens to push the city council to develop a boulevard around the lake. After several delays, the project was completed in the early 1900s. In 1928, after a land donation to the city, workers dredged Lake George, transforming it from a 23-acre swamp into a 7-acre lake, with depths reaching 35 feet in some areas. By the 1930s, a large toboggan slide had been built, making Lake George a popular destination for skating, sledding, and winter carnivals, as pictured here.

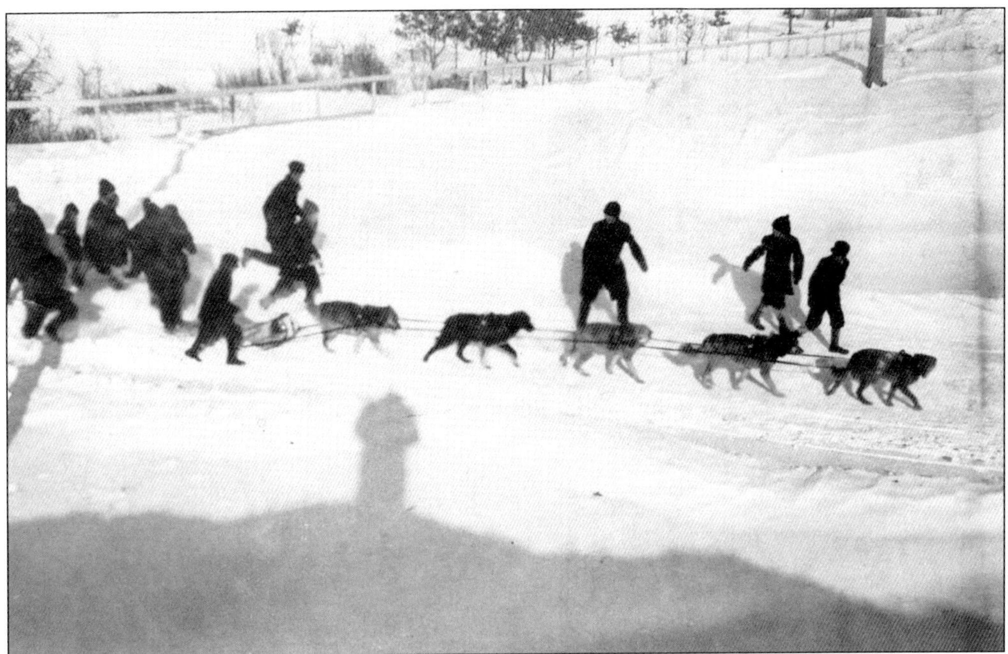

Dogsled Races, 1917. In 1917, the Winnipeg to St. Paul dog sled race captivated St. Cloud's community. Despite freezing temperatures of below 30 degrees Fahrenheit, around 3,000 spectators eagerly awaited Fred Hartman's arrival on February 2. Though seven hours behind, Hartman's imminent arrival thrilled the crowd as he battled past towns like Rothsay and Sauk Centre. The St. Cloud residents enjoyed the exciting spectacle of the mushers and their sled dogs battling harsh winter conditions. Hartman finished last but was celebrated for his courage and perseverance.

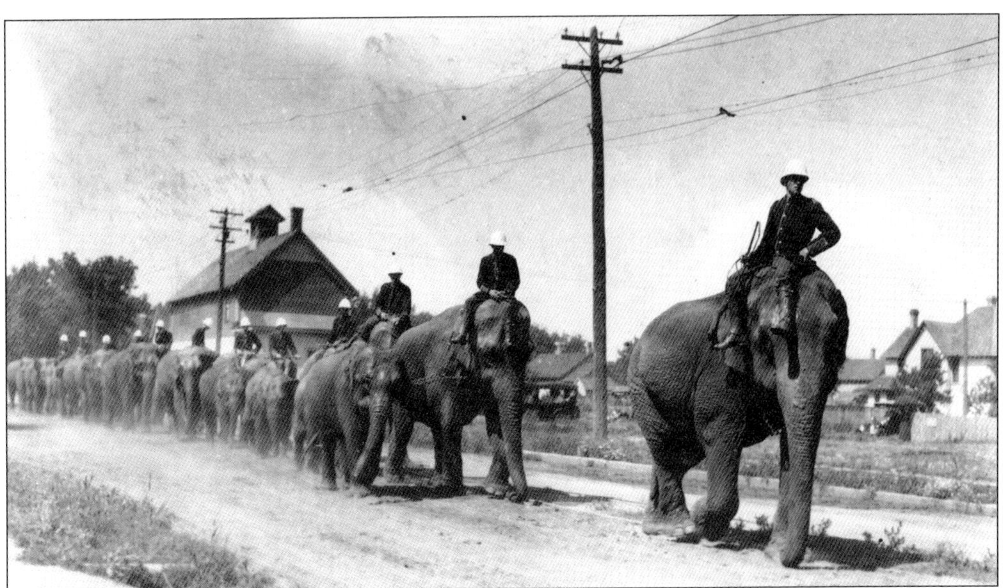

Circus Day, 1915. Traveling circuses were a common and welcome sight in St. Cloud. A variety of groups passed through, with the first on July 25, 1867. July 9, 1915, saw Barnum and Bailey presenting "the greatest show on earth." Tickets were 50¢, with children under the age of 12 at half price.

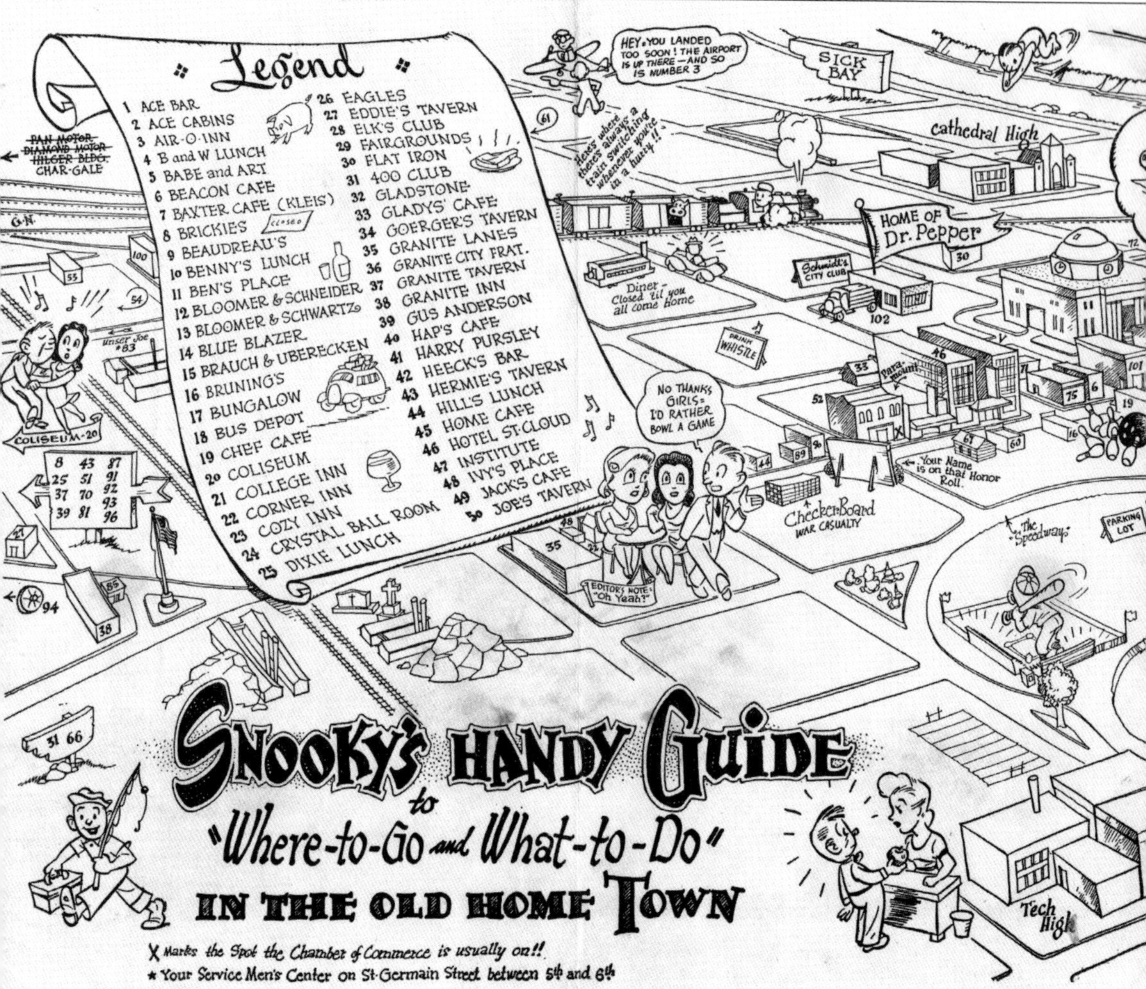

SNOOKY'S HANDY GUIDE, C. 1944. Francis "Snooky" Bernick, president of Bernick's from 1934 to the 1950s, created "Snooky's Handy Guide," an illustrated map for World War II servicemen arriving in St. Cloud. The guide highlighted popular local hangouts like bars, ballrooms, bowling

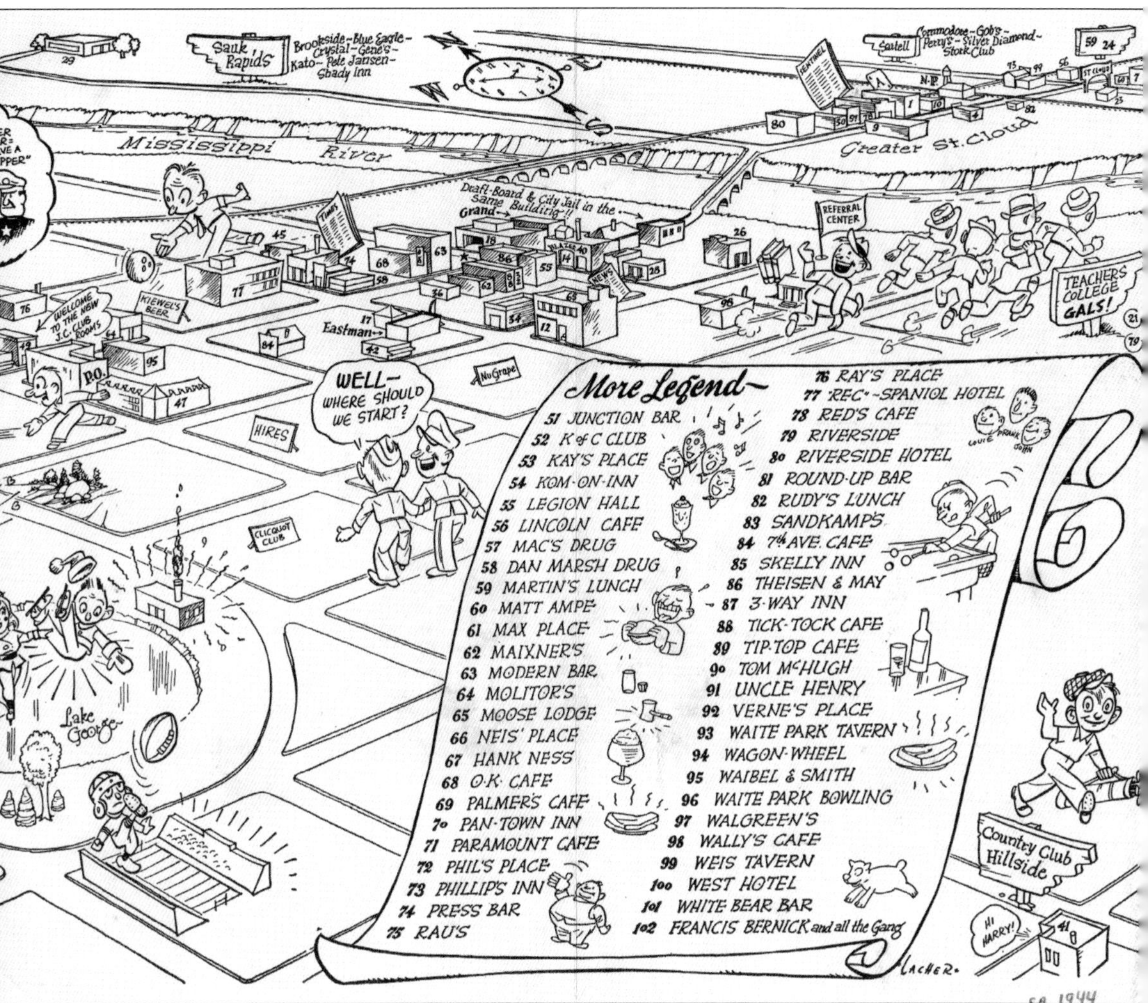

alleys, cafés, theaters, and landmarks, including Cathedral High School and Lake George. Bernick's location was marked as "Home of Dr. Pepper" and a hub for "Francis Bernick and all the Gang."

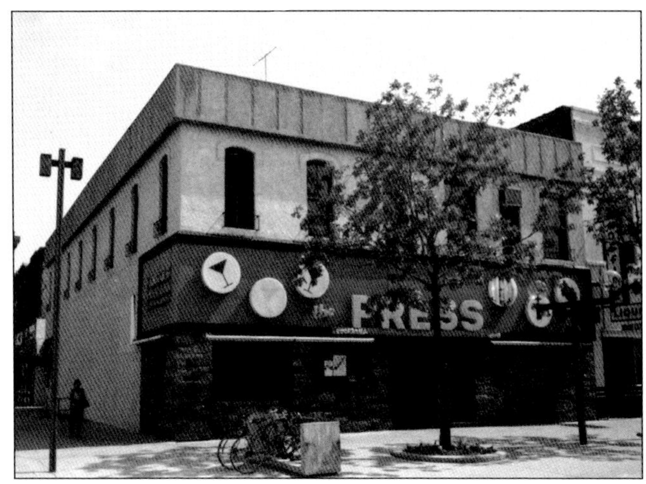

Press Bar, 1979. The Press Bar originally opened on Sixth Avenue, next to the *St. Cloud Times* building, giving the establishment its name. In 1947, the Press Bar took up residence on the corner of Fifth Avenue and St. Germain Street inside a structure built by Joseph Edelbrock in 1881. Since its opening in the 1940s, the Press Bar had been a popular hangout for St. Cloud State University students and St. Cloud residents alike. It was destroyed by fire in 2020.

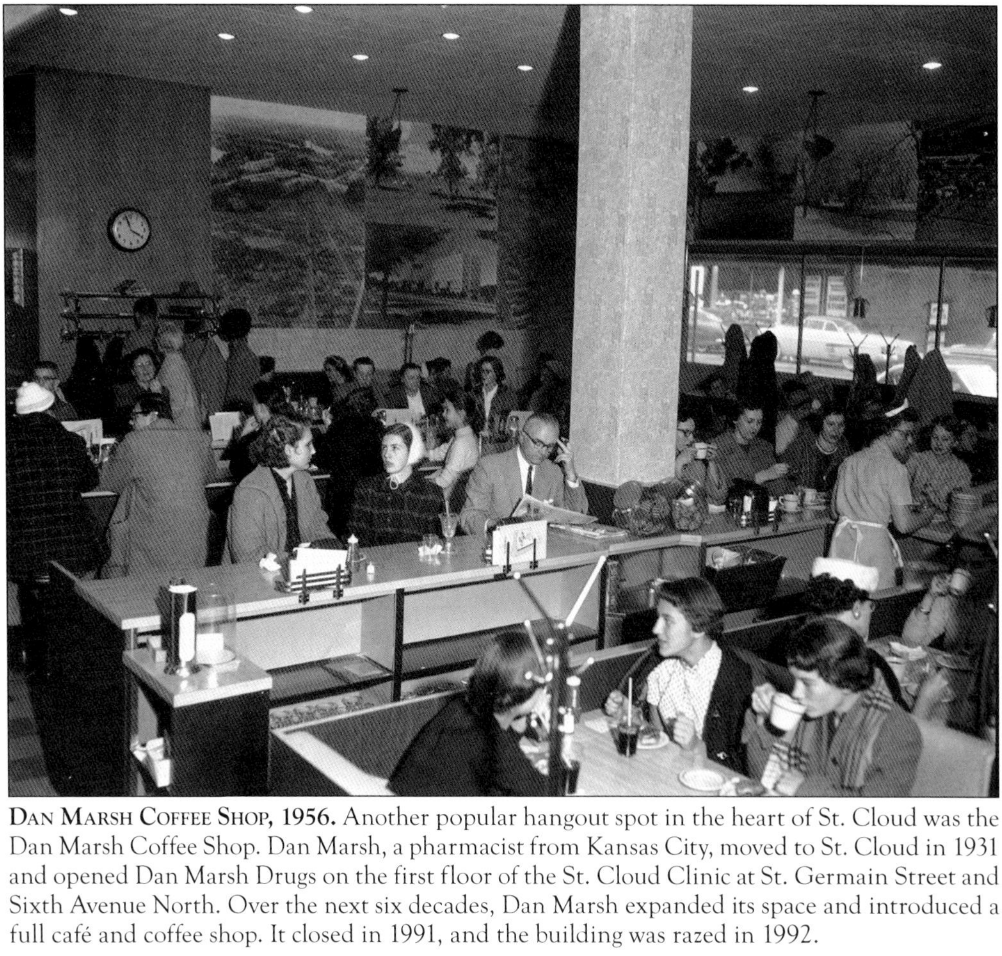

Dan Marsh Coffee Shop, 1956. Another popular hangout spot in the heart of St. Cloud was the Dan Marsh Coffee Shop. Dan Marsh, a pharmacist from Kansas City, moved to St. Cloud in 1931 and opened Dan Marsh Drugs on the first floor of the St. Cloud Clinic at St. Germain Street and Sixth Avenue North. Over the next six decades, Dan Marsh expanded its space and introduced a full café and coffee shop. It closed in 1991, and the building was razed in 1992.

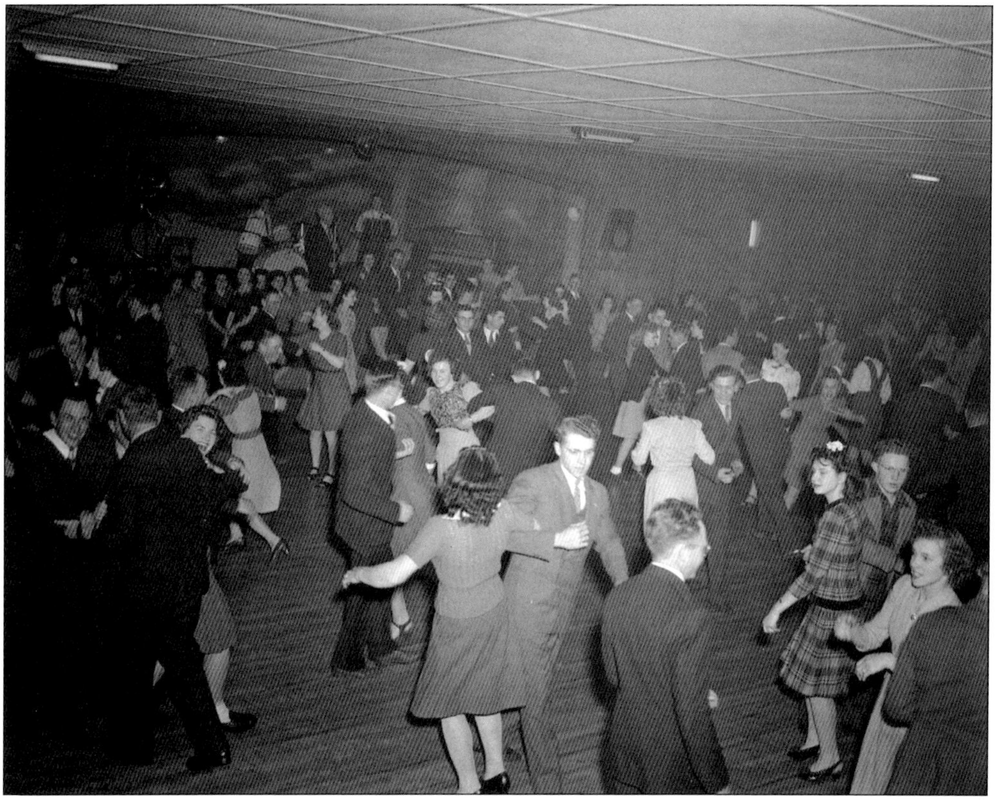

DANCING, GRANITE CITY COLISEUM, 1945. Dancing at local halls and ballrooms was a popular pastime in the St. Cloud area for decades. Ballrooms like the Granite City Coliseum featured regional bands and provided a venue for events hosted by local organizations, like the Beaux and Belles square dancing club. Granite City Coliseum provided a space for entertainment and recreation for 40 years until it burned down in 1972.

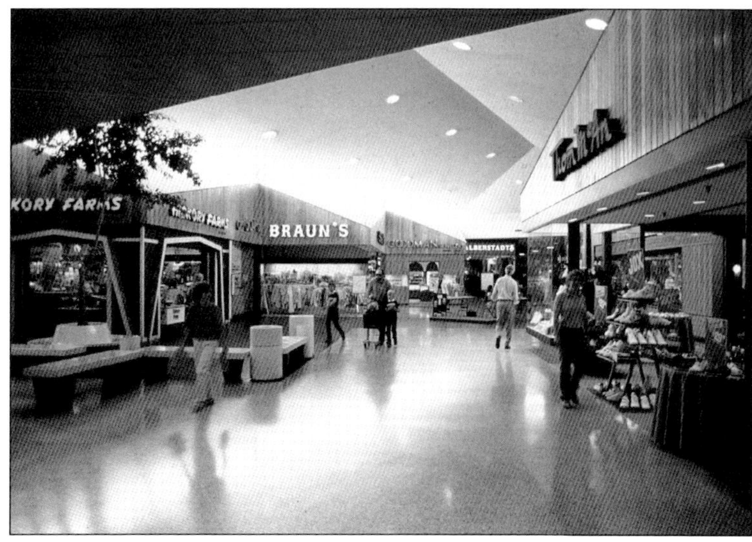

CROSSROADS CENTER, 1985. Crossroads Center was built on 400,000 square feet of swampland on the outskirts of St. Cloud in 1965. It opened in April 1966 and expanded to such an extent over the next four decades that it crossed into the Waite Park city limits and spanned nearly a million square feet.

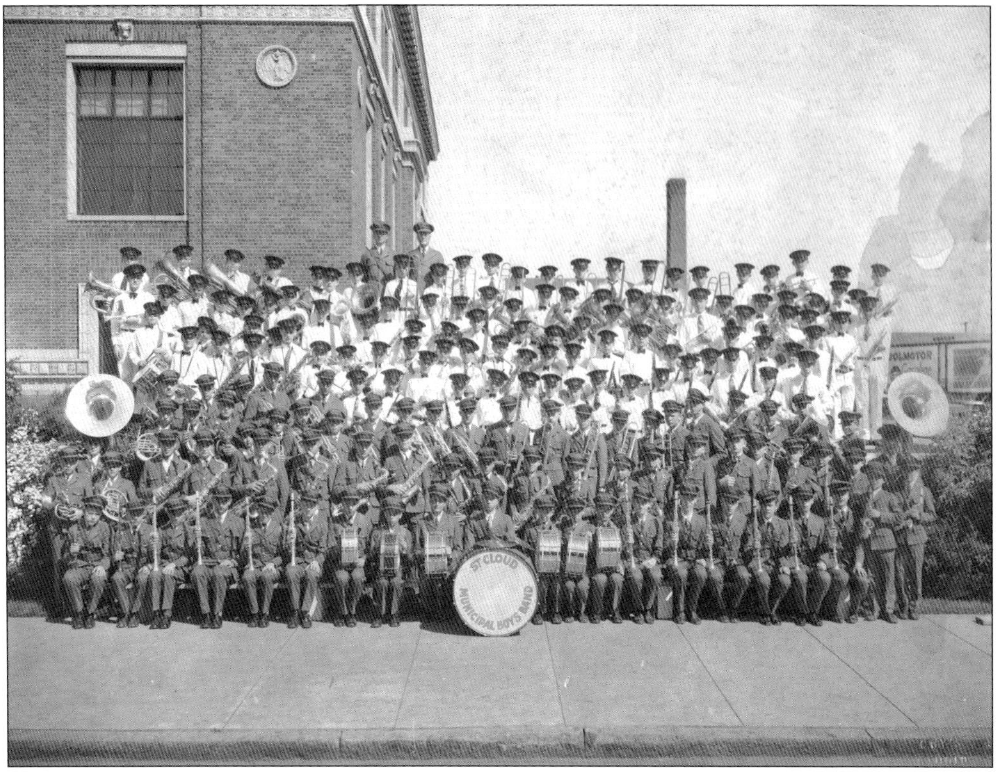

St. Cloud Municipal Boys Band, c. 1930. A St. Cloud city band existed in some form since 1887, beginning with the St. Cloud Union Band. But in 1923, a group of St. Cloud businessmen asked the "Minnesota Music Man," G. Oliver Riggs (top row, on the right), to form the St. Cloud Municipal Boys Band. Those who performed in the boys' band under the direction of Riggs began a municipal band for adults in the 1930s, forming the St. Cloud Municipal Band. The band began receiving official sponsorship from the City of St. Cloud in 1947.

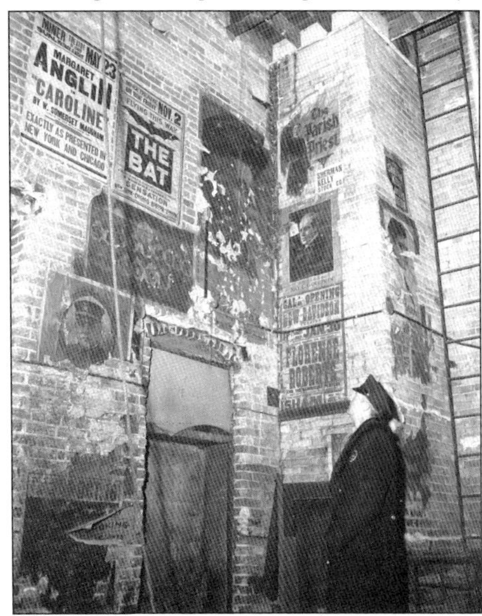

Posters on the Walls of the Old Davidson Opera House, 1958. The Davidson Opera House was built on Fifth Avenue in 1897. It featured live traveling shows as they passed through St. Cloud from Chicago to Fargo. At the time, it was said to be the northwest's finest theater, with performances attended by St. Cloud socialites like the Whitneys and the Mitchells. When it was purchased during World War I, it was renamed the Miner Theater, and movies soon replaced live performances.

Larry Saatzer Works on Statue of Liberty Snow Sculpture, 1983. Lawrence "Larry" Saatzer transformed his front yard into a gallery of snow sculptures for nearly 20 years. He constructed figures such as George Washington, the Statue of Liberty, and the Apollo moon landing. Though he won several awards, he remained humble, saying he sculpted simply for the joy of others. As he liked to put it, "Snow is free, why not do something with it?" (Courtesy of St. Cloud State University Archives.)

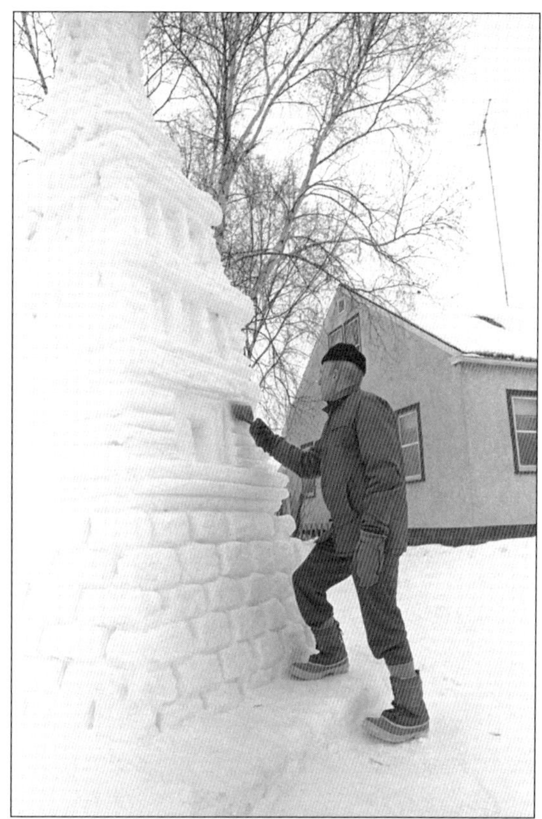

Caponi-Granite Trio. The Granite Trio, created by Minnesota artist Anthony Caponi in 1973, is a three-piece granite sculpture in downtown St. Cloud. Quarrying began at Moonlight Grey Quarry, with Caponi carving the 32-ton pieces on-site. The largest, Castle, features ovals and supports; Sentinel is tall and narrow, and the smallest, Jewel Stone, is a richly detailed glacial boulder donated by a local farmer. The sculpture symbolizes the crown jewel of the Mall Germain area.

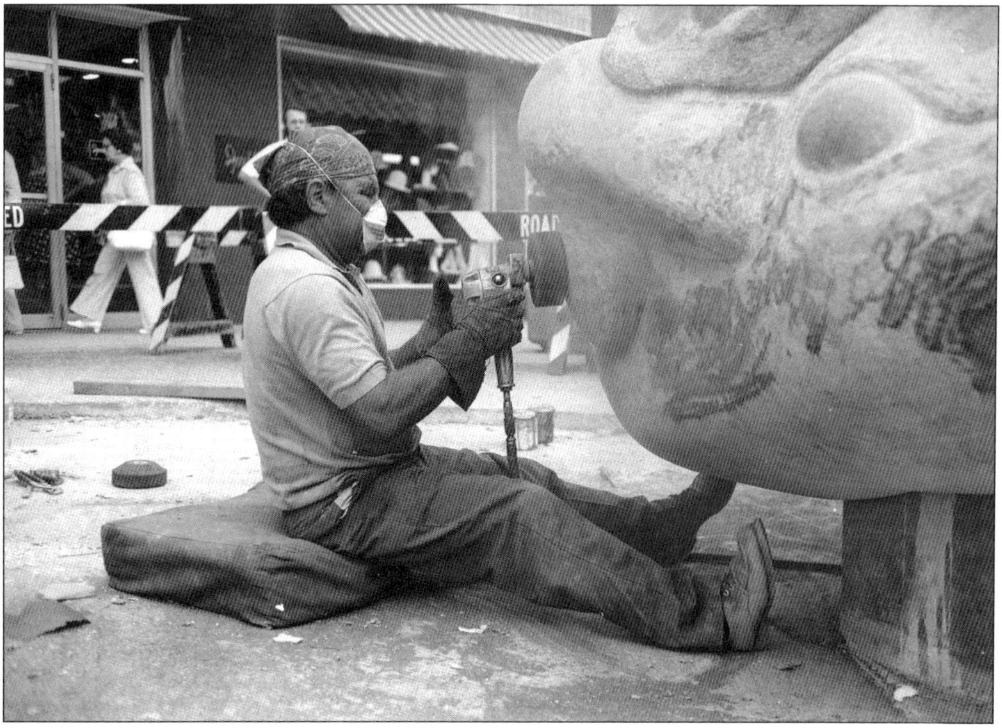

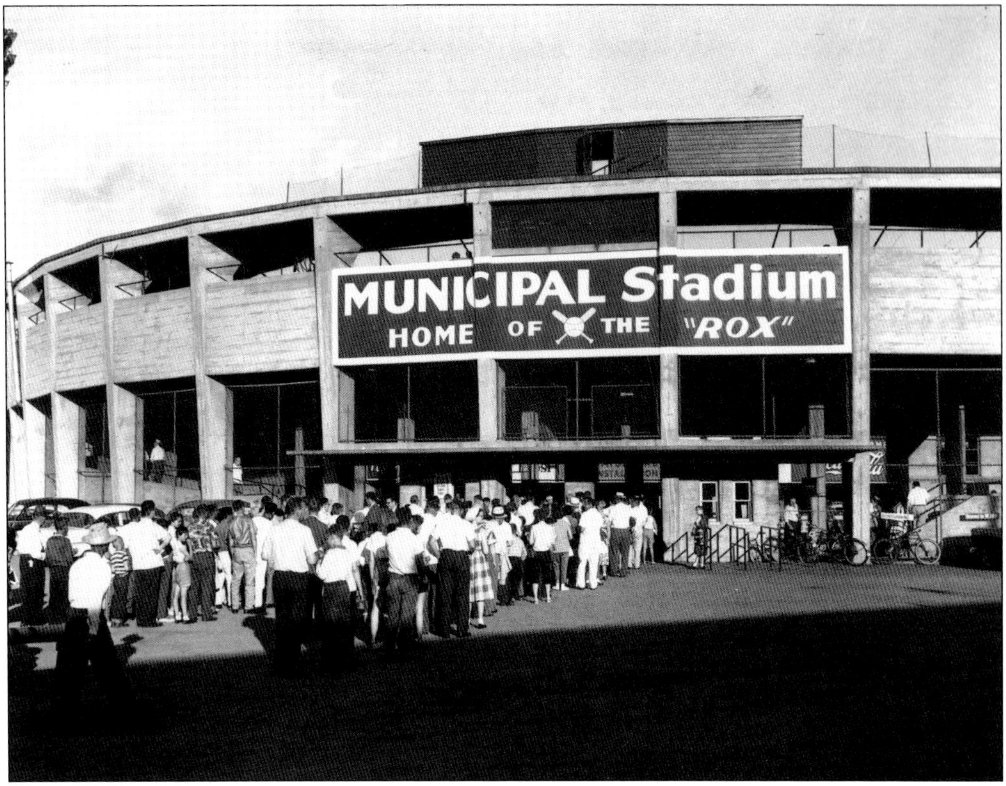

St. Cloud Rox Municipal Stadium, c. 1955. After the Northern League was reorganized in 1945, the St. Cloud Rox played their 1946 season in an open field enclosed by a snow fence. In 1947, construction began on the Municipal Stadium located at Division Street and Twenty-Fifth Avenue South. When it was dedicated in 1948, about 2,500 people attended, including then-mayor of Minneapolis and future vice president Hubert Humphrey. The final Rox game at the Municipal Stadium was in September 1970. Sixty-one St. Cloud Rox alumni made it to the major leagues, including Charlie Fox, Gaylord Perry, and Ozzie Virgil.

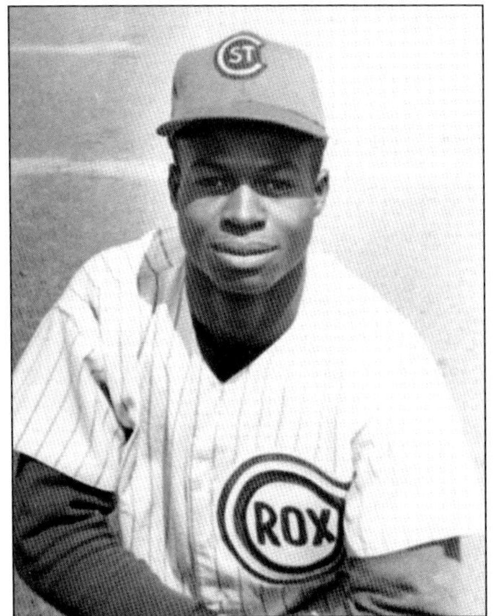

Lou Brock, 1961. Lou Brock's journey to the Baseball Hall of Fame began in St. Cloud. In the summer of 1961, Brock played for the St. Cloud Rox, a season that saw the Rox at the Northern League championship. Brock also played in the Northern League All-Star Game and won Rookie of the Year. He went on to play for the St. Louis Cardinals, with whom he won the 1964 World Series. He was inducted into the Hall of Fame in 1985.

Nine

St. Cloud at War

Every major US conflict since the Civil War has impacted St. Cloud. Early settlers like James M. McKelvy, Stephen Miller, and Christopher Andrews served in the Union army during the Civil War, Miller rising to the rank of colonel and Andrews to major general. And although the violence of the Dakota War of 1862 in southwest Minnesota never reached St. Cloud, its citizens prepared for it in case it came to their doors. Broker Block, a three-story brick building erected in 1861, and Fort Holes, constructed in 1862, were built as points of defense in the event of an attack. Such an attack never came, but both were used as a refuge for white settlers fleeing the war. In 1898, James E. McKelvy raised a company of volunteers from St. Cloud to fight in the Spanish-American War. The company fought in the Battle of Manila, which resulted in Spain's surrender of the city.

Tensions were high on the home front in St. Cloud during World War I. In 1917, Austrian immigrant George Huber was arrested in St. Cloud and sentenced to 10 days in a detention camp for expressing support for Germany. In compliance with newly passed laws, noncitizens of Stearns County were forced to surrender their firearms, and *Der Nordstern*, a German-language newspaper based in St. Cloud, was subjected to an investigation of its files and records. When the St. Cloud National Guard unit returned from action at the Mexican border in March 1917, it was almost immediately mobilized for the war in Europe.

In November 1942, Reelife Motion Pictures producer Robert Allen filmed *St. Cloud at War*, a documentary that featured daily life in St. Cloud, with particular focus on the ways in which St. Cloud was responding to World War II on the home front. It is unknown if a copy of the film still exists, but it undoubtedly captured St. Cloud's solidarity and quintessential response to the demands of World War II. Kids collected rubber, scrap, and waste paper, and victory gardens sprang up in yards across the city. St. Cloud men were drafted or enlisted into the armed forces, and women signed up for the Women's Army Corps (WAC) and Women Accepted for Volunteer Emergency Service (WAVES), the Army and Navy's noncombatant military units for women. Local schools and organizations organized Victory Book campaigns, patriotic community singings, and sold war bonds and stamps. St. Cloud was also instrumental in training central Minnesota women for war production.

From the Civil War to the Vietnam War and beyond, the citizens of St. Cloud have served and sacrificed for their country, on the home front and the front lines.

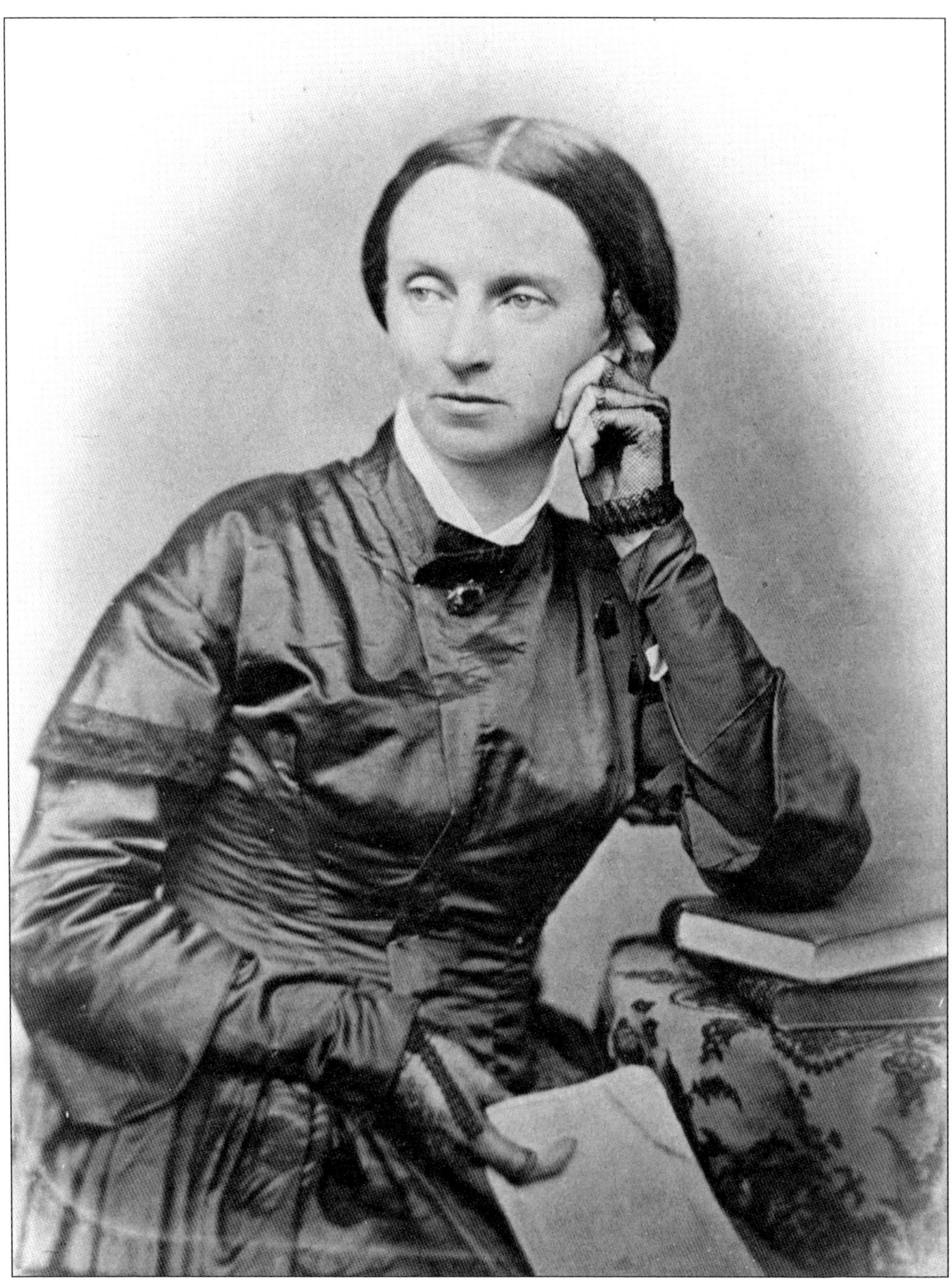

Jane Grey Swisshelm, c. 1850. Jane Grey Swisshelm was a journalist, abolitionist, and women's rights activist. She migrated to Stearns County from Pennsylvania in 1857. In 1858, she began publishing the *St. Cloud Visiter*, but soon after, her press was destroyed by a group of men who supported slavery. Undeterred, she established a second newspaper called the *St. Cloud Democrat*, where she continued to speak out against slavery and criticize St. Cloud's proslavery residents, especially Sylvanus B. Lowry. Swisshelm sold the *Democrat* to her nephew William Bell Mitchell and returned to Pennsylvania in 1863. (Courtesy of Minnesota Historical Society.)

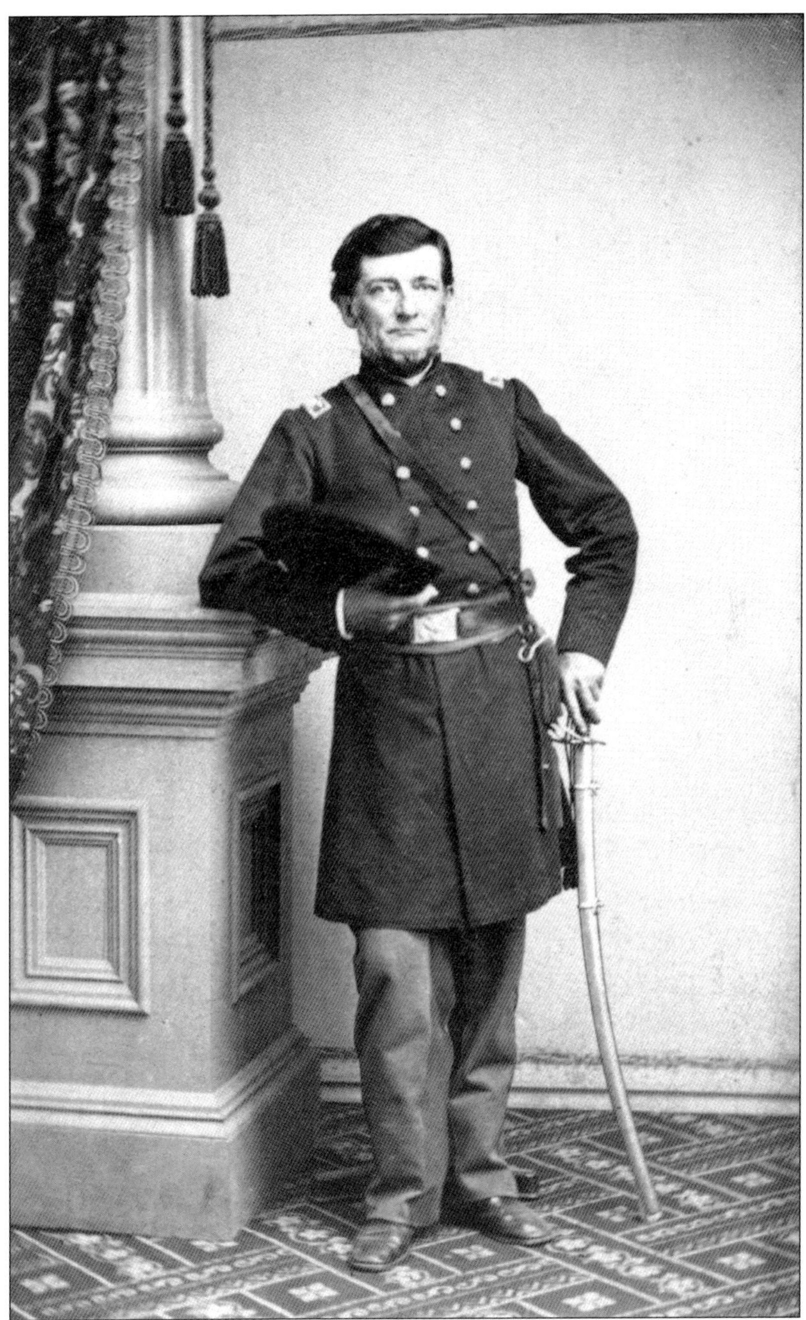

Stephen Miller, c. 1862. Stephen Miller migrated from Pennsylvania to St. Cloud in 1858 and established a mercantile business with Jane Grey Swisshelm's brother-in-law. He enlisted in the 1st Minnesota Infantry Regiment in 1861 and was appointed to the rank of lieutenant colonel. In 1862, he was promoted to colonel and appointed as the commander of Camp Lincoln in Mankato, where 300 Dakota were imprisoned at the conclusion of the Dakota War of 1862. Miller protected those prisoners from vigilantes who wished to murder them but ultimately oversaw the mass execution of 38 Dakota ordered by President Lincoln. Miller was later elected governor of Minnesota and served from 1864 to 1866. (Courtesy of Minnesota Historical Society.)

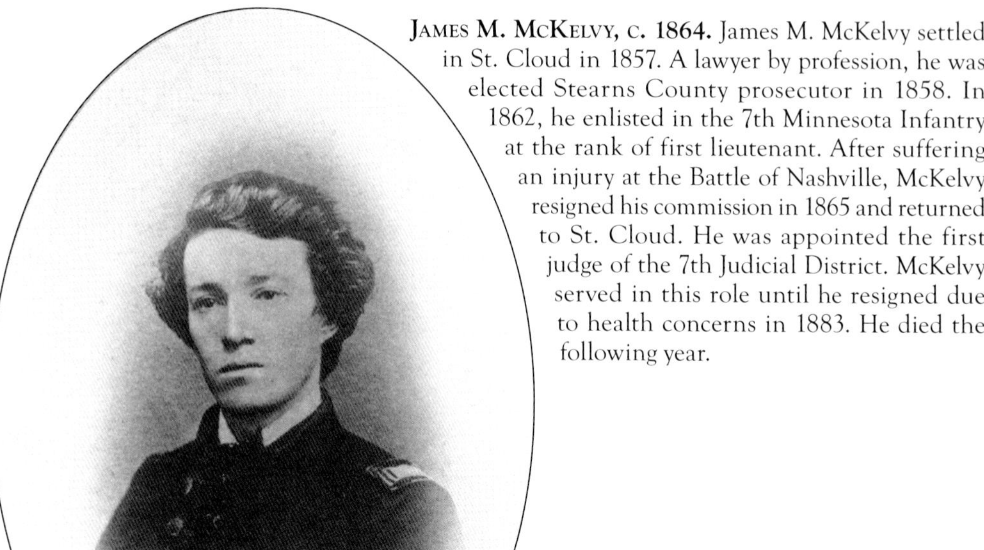

James M. McKelvy, c. 1864. James M. McKelvy settled in St. Cloud in 1857. A lawyer by profession, he was elected Stearns County prosecutor in 1858. In 1862, he enlisted in the 7th Minnesota Infantry at the rank of first lieutenant. After suffering an injury at the Battle of Nashville, McKelvy resigned his commission in 1865 and returned to St. Cloud. He was appointed the first judge of the 7th Judicial District. McKelvy served in this role until he resigned due to health concerns in 1883. He died the following year.

James E. McKelvy, 1898. James E. McKelvy was the son of James M. McKelvy. When the Spanish-American War began in 1898, McKelvy raised a company of St. Cloud volunteers, which elected him captain. Attached as Company M to the 13th Minnesota Infantry Regiment, the company served in the Philippines and fought in the Battle of Manila, which resulted in the Spanish surrender of the city. Company M remained in the Philippines until 1899, engaging with Filipino insurgents in Manila at the beginning of the Philippine-American War.

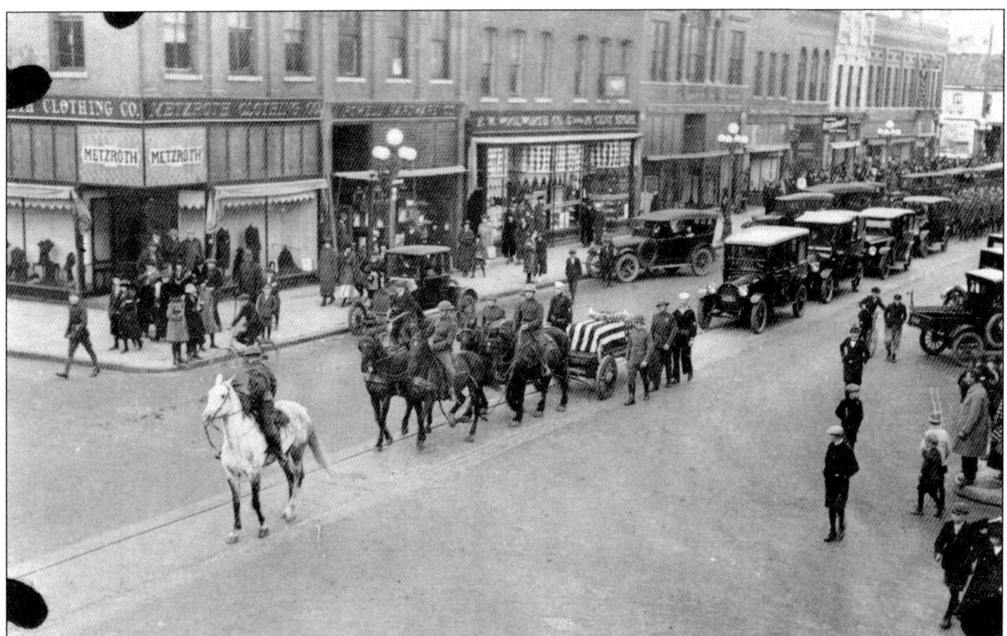

Funeral Procession for Wallace Chute on St. Germain Street, 1920. Wallace Chute was a St. Cloud native and locally known as a star athlete. He graduated from high school in 1915, and in 1917, he enlisted in the US Army. Having the opportunity to remain at Camp Cody, New Mexico, to train incoming troops, he instead chose to go to France to fight. In October 1918, he was wounded at Verdun and succumbed to his injuries in December. His remains were returned to St. Cloud in 1920, where he was honored with a funeral procession along St. Germain Street.

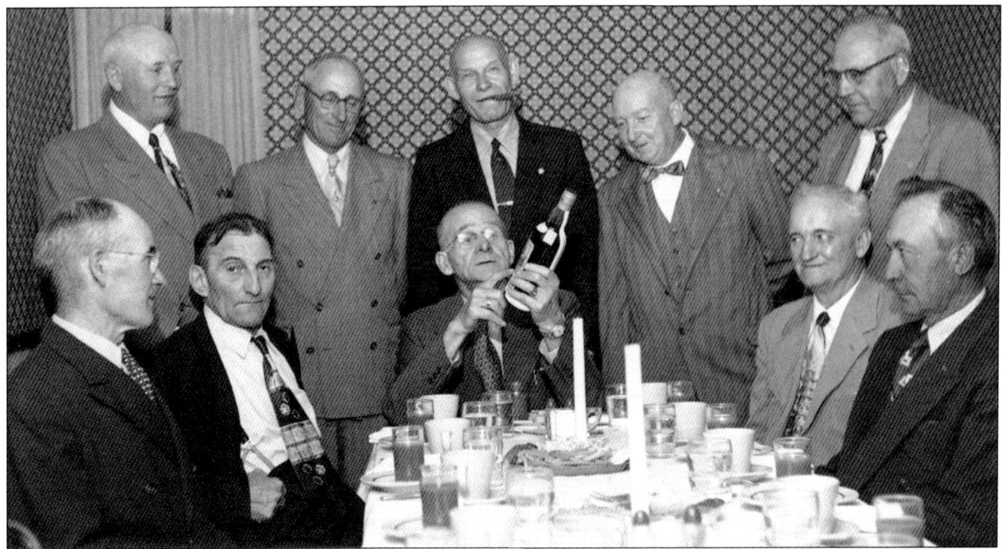

Last Man's Club, 1949. The Last Man's Club of St. Cloud was made up of survivors of the "Lost Battalion" of World War I. On October 2, 1918, units of the 308th Infantry Regiment were cut off and surrounded during an assault into the Argonne Forest. For the next six days, the soldiers were without food and water while suffering German assaults and artillery fire. After six days, Allied forces rescued the stranded soldiers. The Last Man's Club gathered annually and kept a bottle of wine down through the years for the last man left of their fraternity.

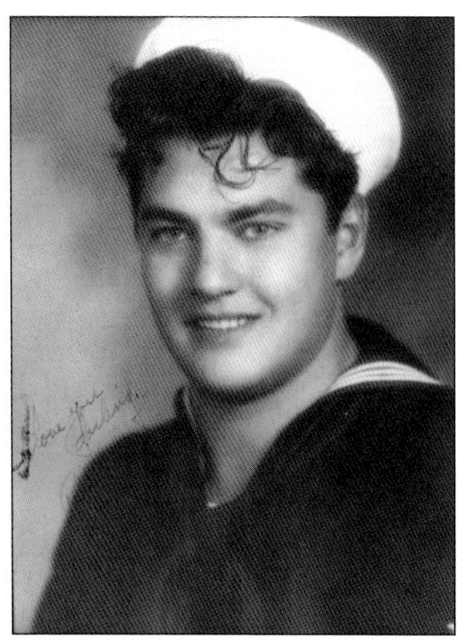

Ralph Krafnick, c. 1942. Like Wallace Chute, Ralph Krafnick was a St. Cloud native who excelled in sports. Krafnick enlisted in the Navy in 1937. In December 1941, Krafnick was stationed at Pearl Harbor on the USS *New Orleans*. On the morning of December 7, Krafnick was practicing baseball on the deck of the *New Orleans* when the Japanese began their assault on the naval base. Krafnick survived the attack and went on to serve 32 months in the Pacific theater. Years after the war, Krafnick founded the Minnesota Chapter of the Pearl Harbor Survivors Association.

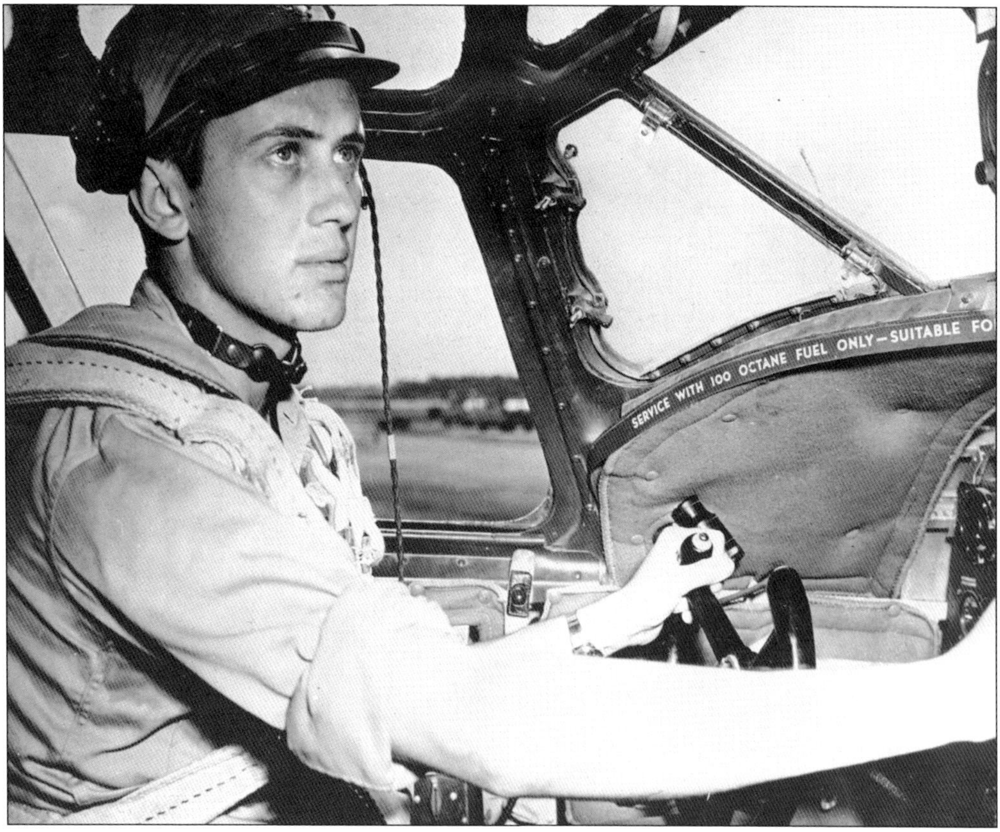

George McDowall, c. 1944. George McDowall was a B-24 Liberator bomber pilot in the Pacific theater of World War II. He flew over 40 bombing missions, including a particularly intense raid on Brunei Bay that resulted in extreme damage to his aircraft. After his father's death in 1952, George and his mother, Grace, took over the family business, the McDowall Company of St. Cloud. The company was instrumental in the renovation of downtown St. Cloud in the 1980s. McDowall Company is still in business today.

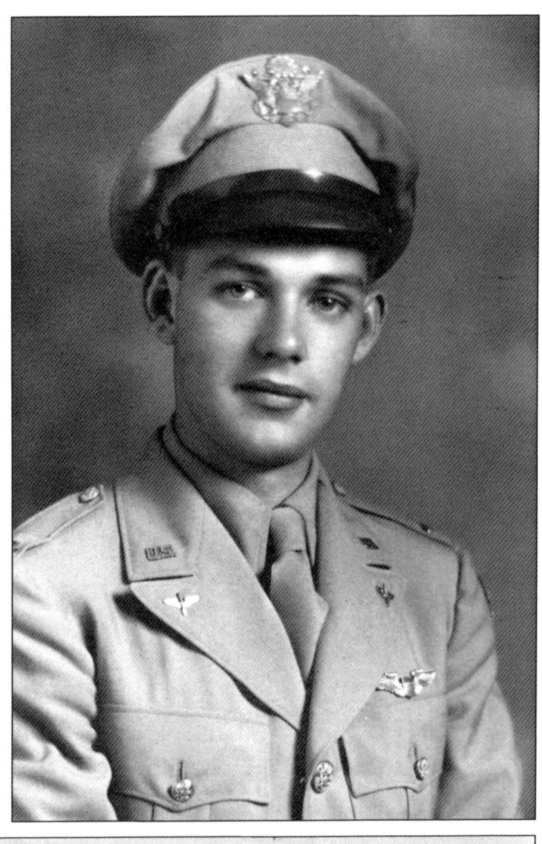

George Fish, c. 1944. Brothers George and Howard Fish grew up in St. Cloud, their father working for the City of St. Cloud and the Great Northern Railway. Both men enlisted in the Army Air Corps in 1942. George became a pilot and crew commander of a B-24. On February 22, 1944, George's aircraft became separated from the rest of his flight group over Germany. When he and his crew did not return to the air base in England, they were listed as missing in action. In October 1945, George was declared killed in action. He has never been found or recovered.

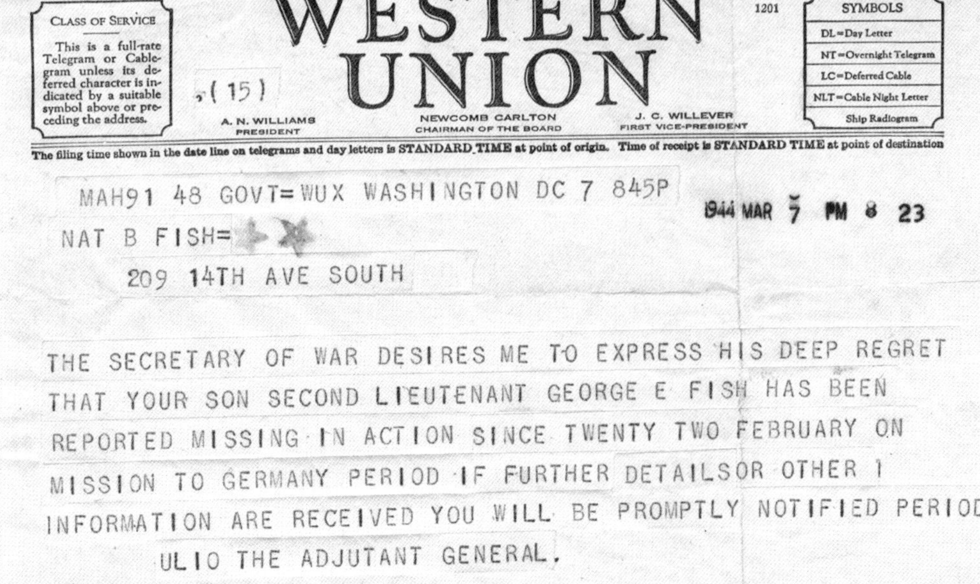

WESTERN UNION

1201

CLASS OF SERVICE
This is a full-rate Telegram or Cablegram unless its deferred character is indicated by a suitable symbol above or preceding the address.

SYMBOLS
DL=Day Letter
NT=Overnight Telegram
LC=Deferred Cable
NLT=Cable Night Letter
Ship Radiogram

,(15)

A. N. WILLIAMS, PRESIDENT — NEWCOMB CARLTON, CHAIRMAN OF THE BOARD — J. C. WILLEVER, FIRST VICE-PRESIDENT

The filing time shown in the date line on telegrams and day letters is STANDARD TIME at point of origin. Time of receipt is STANDARD TIME at point of destination

MAH91 48 GOVT=WUX WASHINGTON DC 7 845P

1944 MAR 7 PM 8 23

NAT B FISH=

209 14TH AVE SOUTH

THE SECRETARY OF WAR DESIRES ME TO EXPRESS HIS DEEP REGRET THAT YOUR SON SECOND LIEUTENANT GEORGE E FISH HAS BEEN REPORTED MISSING IN ACTION SINCE TWENTY TWO FEBRUARY ON MISSION TO GERMANY PERIOD IF FURTHER DETAILSOR OTHER INFORMATION ARE RECEIVED YOU WILL BE PROMPTLY NOTIFIED PERIOD

ULIO THE ADJUTANT GENERAL.

THE COMPANY WILL APPRECIATE SUGGESTIONS FROM ITS PATRONS CONCERNING ITS SERVICE

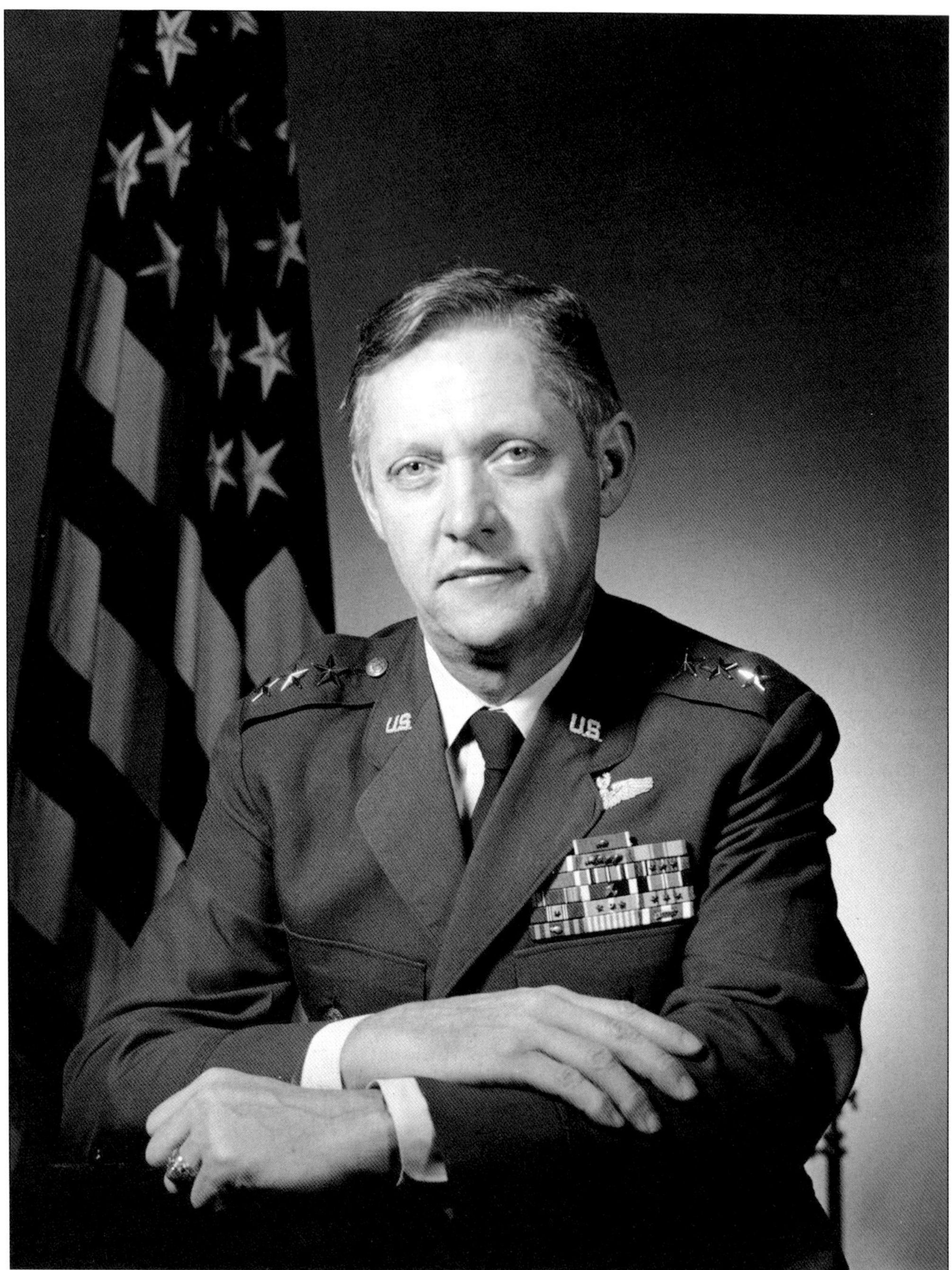

Lt. General Howard Fish, c. 1974. George's younger brother Howard was assigned as a navigator on a B-17. A year after George went missing, on February 7, 1945, Howard's aircraft was shot down over Vienna, Austria. He bailed from the plane and landed in a field, suffering minor injuries. He was taken captive by the German army and held as a POW for the remainder of the war. After the war, Howard remained in the Air Force and ultimately reached the rank of lieutenant general in 1974. He also served as the assistant vice chief of staff of the US Air Force. Howard retired from the Air Force in 1979 and died in Tyler, Texas, in 2020.

Joan Trebtoske Jenks, c. 1940. While attending St. Cloud Teachers College, St. Cloud native Joan Jenks (neé Trebtoske) joined the school's pilot training program. When the United States entered World War II, she joined the Women Airforce Service Pilots group, a unit of women who flew war planes from factories in the United States' interior to ports on the coast where they would be shipped to the war front. Jenks flew P-51s, P-47s, C-47s, and B-17 bombers. In 1989, she received the Pioneer in Aviation award at the Florida International Air Show.

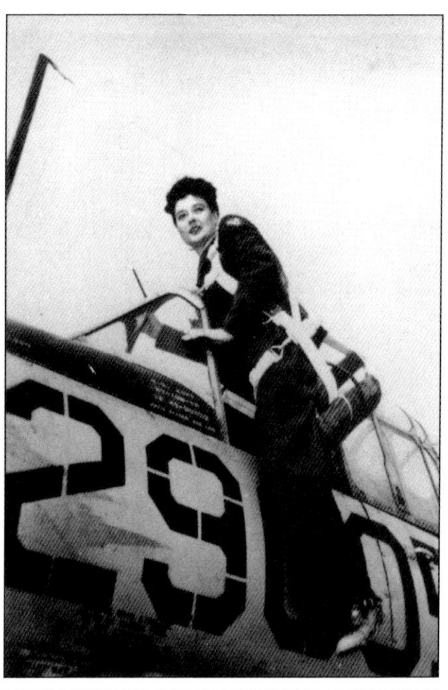

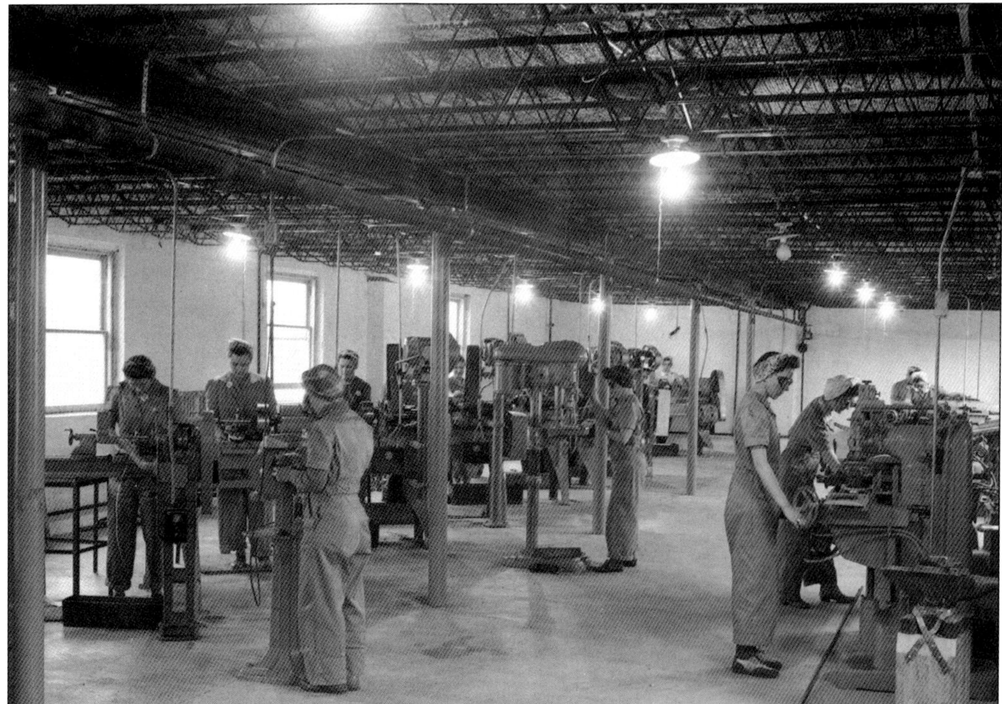

National Youth Administration School Sheet Metal Shop, 1942. St. Cloud played a key role in training central Minnesota women for war production. The National Youth Administration (NYA) opened a school for training women ages 16–25 in operating machines and working with sheet metal. The vocational school at Technical High School trained women in a variety of trades, including welding, machine and auto repair, radio operating, and more. Women trained in St. Cloud gained employment all over the country, including Boeing Aircraft in Seattle.

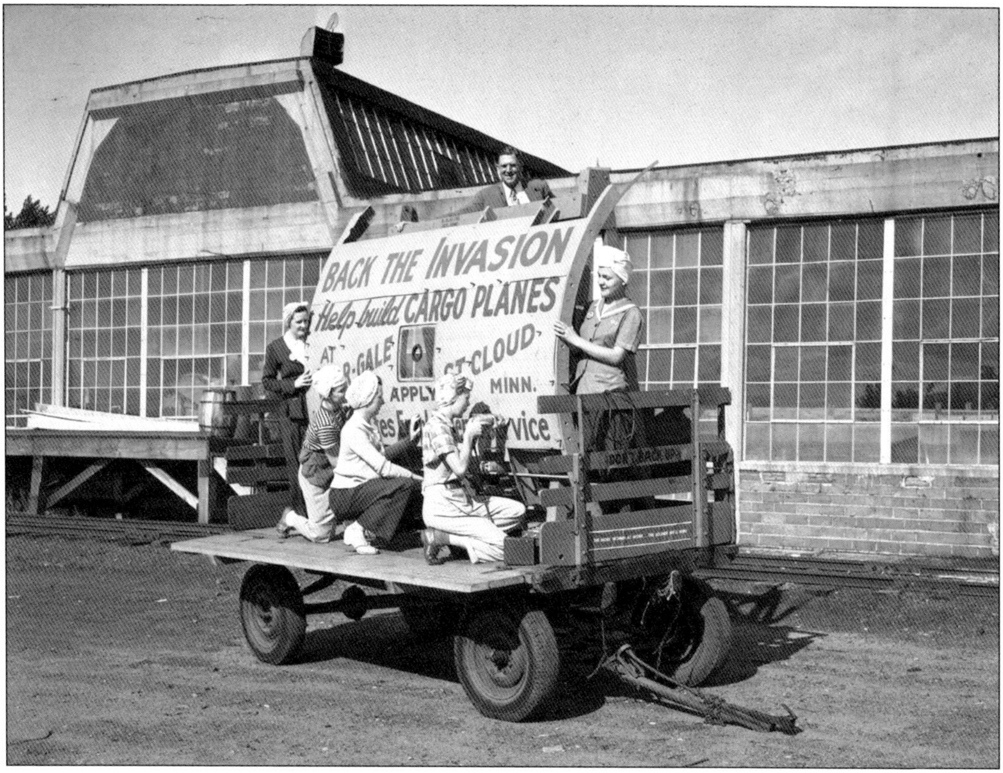

Char-Gale, 1944. In 1943, women's position in the labor force was at its peak in the United States, totaling almost 40 percent of all workers. St. Cloud followed the same trend. In 1941, Twin Cities company and defense contractor Char-Gale purchased the former Pan Motor Company manufacturing plant. During the war, the Char-Gale Assembly Plant manufactured wings and fuselages for military cargo planes. At the beginning of 1942, only men were employed at the plant, but by 1943, Char-Gale depended on women laborers to continue fulfilling its defense contracts. The pictured fuselage mounted to a trailer was driven around the St. Cloud area and used as an advertisement for open positions at Char-Gale. The sticker on the front of the trailer reads, "The more women at work . . . the sooner we'll win!"

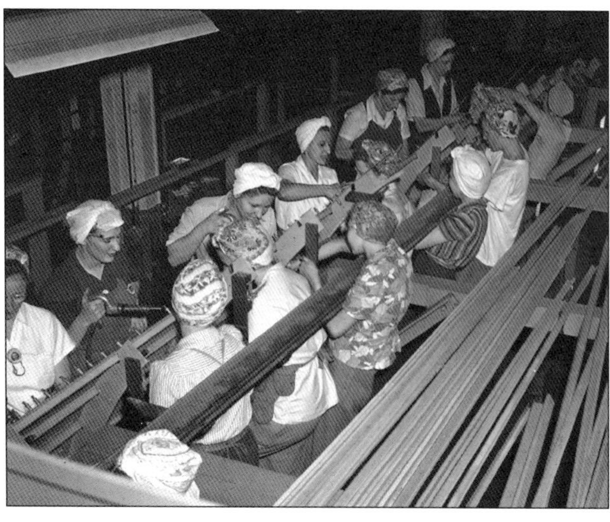

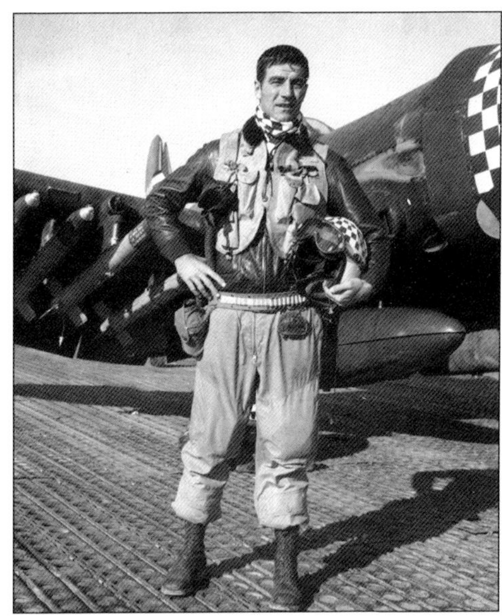

Capt. George Byers, c. 1950. Capt. George Byers was one of four brothers who served in World War II. He received his commission as a second lieutenant in the Marine Corps after receiving advanced flight training in May 1944. He served for the remainder of the war, and in 1951, he was recalled from the Marine Reserves to serve in Korea. There, he flew 102 combat missions with the Checkerboard Squadron and received the Gold Star for his conduct in battle. After the war, he was the youngest man to become the mayor of St. Cloud.

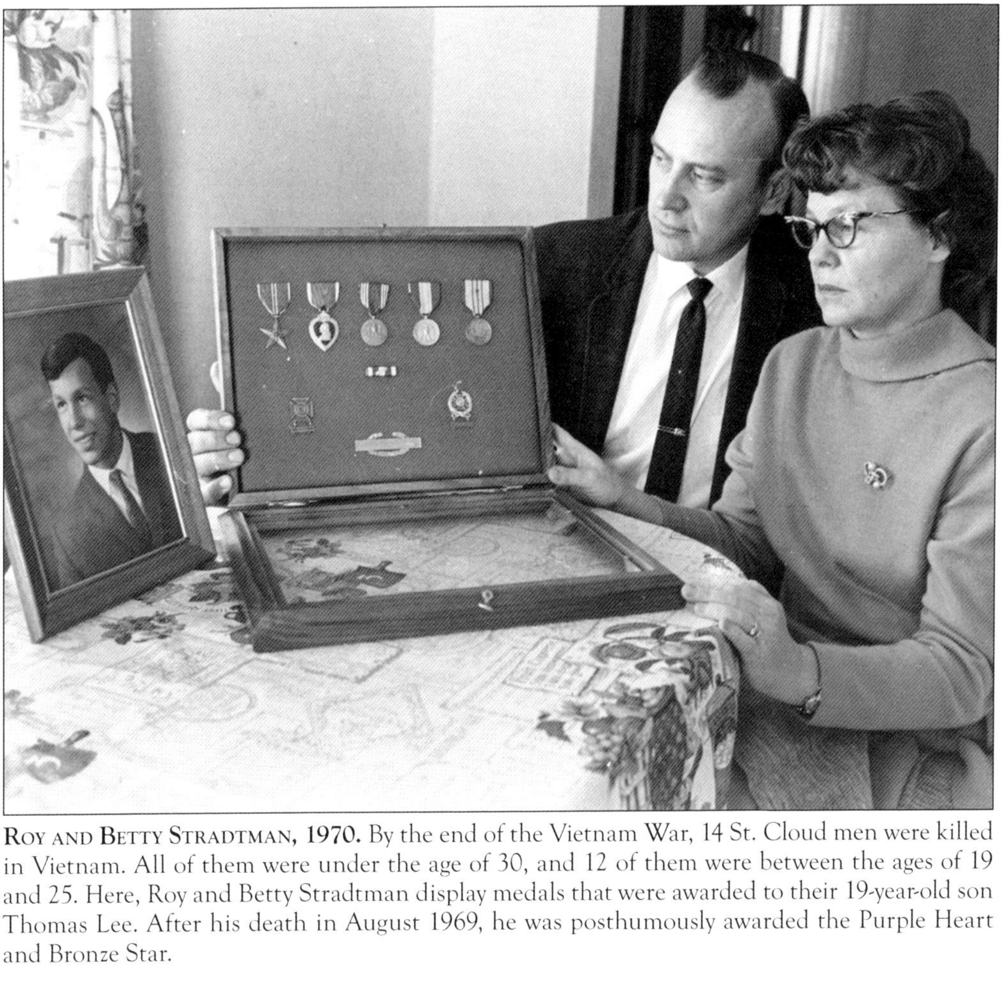

Roy and Betty Stradtman, 1970. By the end of the Vietnam War, 14 St. Cloud men were killed in Vietnam. All of them were under the age of 30, and 12 of them were between the ages of 19 and 25. Here, Roy and Betty Stradtman display medals that were awarded to their 19-year-old son Thomas Lee. After his death in August 1969, he was posthumously awarded the Purple Heart and Bronze Star.

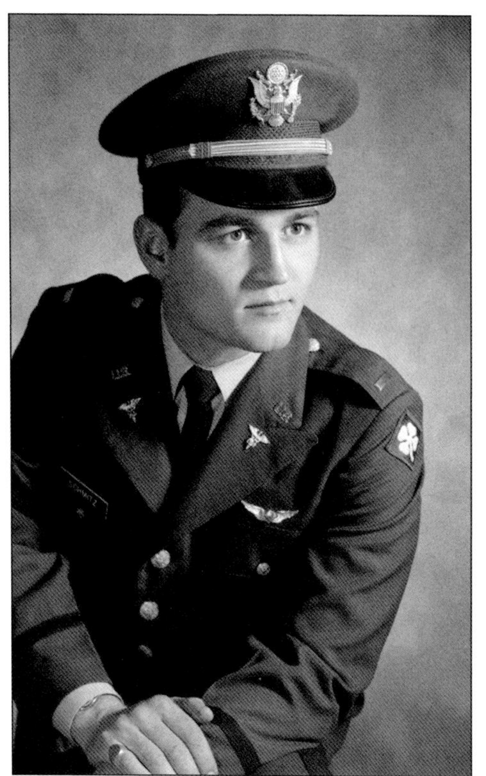

Lt. Phillip Schmitz, 1970. Twelve days into his education at Stanford University Law School, 24-year-old Phillip Schmitz was drafted into the US Army. He trained as a medical transport officer and was assigned to helicopter medical evacuation duty. He died May 10, 1970, when his helicopter was shot down during a rescue mission. He had been in Vietnam for only 17 days.

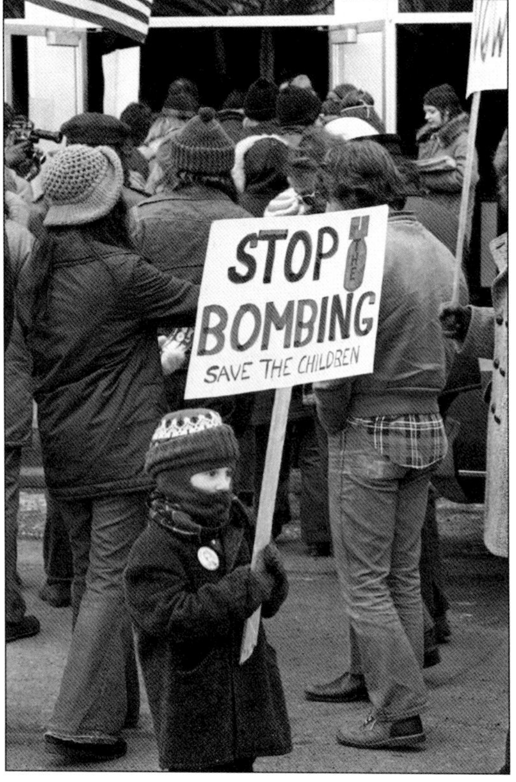

Child at Vietnam War Protest, 1973. In 1973, a national protest against the Vietnam War was organized on the day of Richard Nixon's presidential inauguration, January 20. In St. Cloud, 500 people marched to the St. Cloud Civic Center while carrying protest signs and chanting "One, two, three, four, we don't want Nixon's war!" A rally was held at the civic center, where anti-war speakers advocated for peace and an end to US involvement in South Vietnam. (Courtesy of St. Cloud State University Archives.)

Ten

Once Upon a Time in St. Cloud

The annals of the history of St. Cloud reveal remarkable narratives that draw a distinctive portrait of the rural Minnesota city. These stories share the highs and lows of the community, its claims to fame, and its tragedies.

St. Cloud is the birthplace of movie stars and world-class performers like June Marlowe and Gig Young. Robert Breen, son of Breen Hotel proprietor Henry Breen, became a world-famous Shakespearean actor, performing in the titular role of *Hamlet* at Kronberg Castle in Denmark in 1949 at the request of King Frederick IX and Queen Ingrid of Denmark. St. Cloud has also played host to distinguished guests, including Eleanor Roosevelt, Maya Angelou, and Ray Bradbury. In 1952, Dwight D. Eisenhower visited St. Cloud and spoke to a crowd of 8,000 people in downtown St. Cloud.

The history of St. Cloud also reveals its years as a "den of iniquity" in the 1880s and 1890s. A combination of a loose interpretation of city ordinances and St. Cloud city officials' unwillingness to enforce the laws led to a bevy of "houses of ill fame," supplying venues for prostitution and gambling. On July 31, 1893, Catholic and Protestant faith leaders and a crowd of concerned St. Cloud citizens gathered at a local opera house to voice their indignation at the moral state of the city. Bishop Otto Zardetti believed there to be a financial motivation for city officials to allow these houses to continue their business. It would not be until 1894, when all but one city official was voted out of office, that the city would be rid of such houses.

Tragedy has also shaped the history of St. Cloud. Tornadoes have devastated the area, taking lives while destroying homes and businesses. Fires have claimed dozens of historic buildings over the past 170 years. The Armistice Day Blizzard of 1940 devastated central Minnesota, and every winter since, it looms in the memories of St. Cloud residents who lived through it.

Although a typical American city in many ways, St. Cloud has its own distinct and remarkable history shaped by marvelous highs and devastating lows.

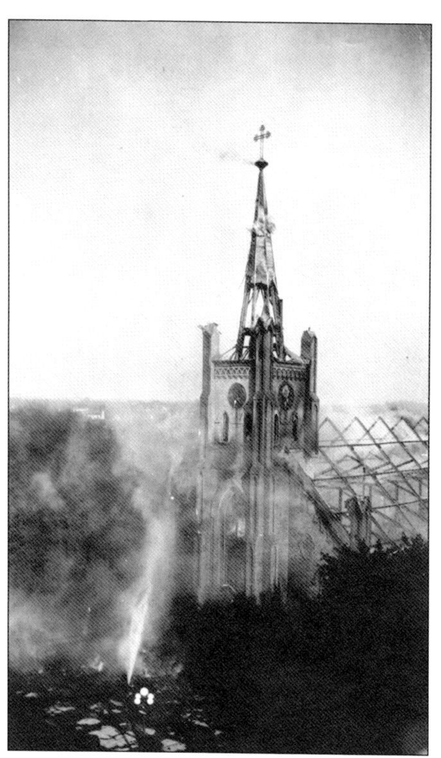

IMMACULATE CONCEPTION CHURCH FIRE, 1920. The second iteration of the Church of St. Mary of the Immaculate Conception (now St. Mary's Cathedral) was constructed in 1864. The Gothic structure stood at St. Germain Street and Ninth Avenue for a little over 55 years. In August 1920, passersby first noticed smoke coming out of the steeple of the church. Soon, the entire church was engulfed in flames, and less than an hour later, the steeple toppled over. The cause of the fire is still unknown.

HOLY ANGELS CATHOLIC CHURCH AFTER FIRE, 1933. Thirteen years after the destruction of the Immaculate Conception Church, the Holy Angels Pro-Cathedral suffered the same fate. During a storm in September 1933, lightning struck the steeple, and the entire church was destroyed by the resulting fire. It was rebuilt on the same site.

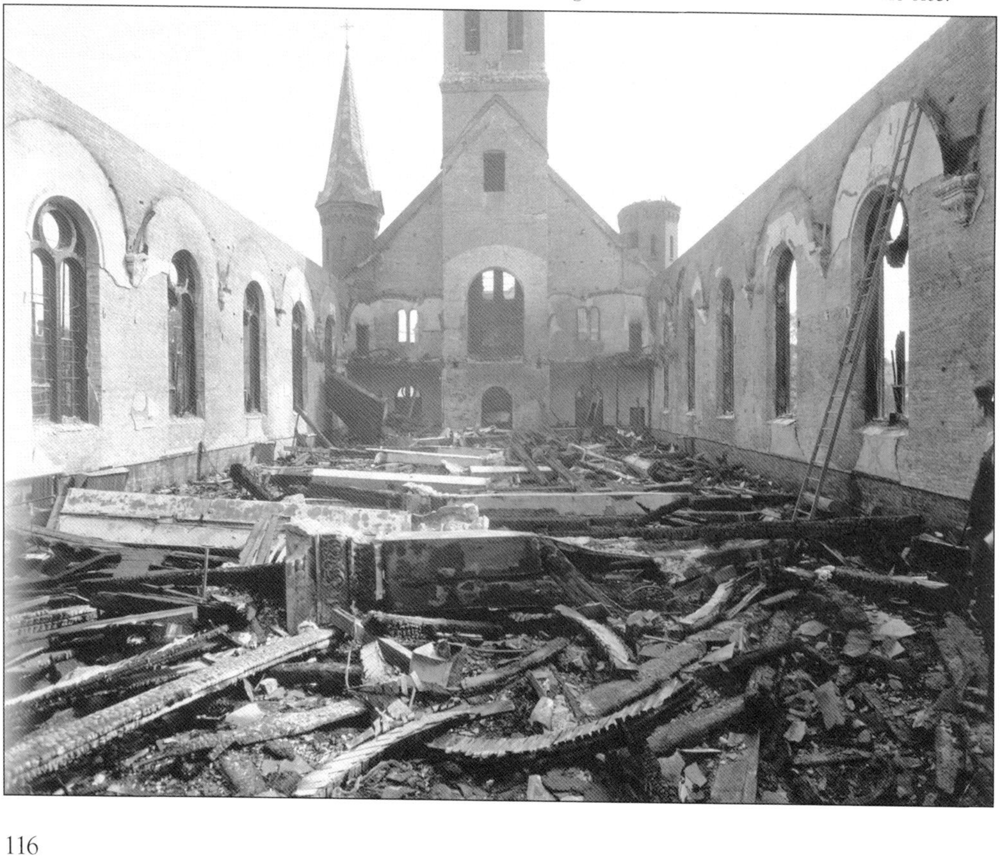

St. John's Episcopal Church Fire, 1969. In August 1969, lightning struck a gable of St. John's Episcopal Church, causing a devastating fire. The fire quickly spread through the 19th-century timbers of the church roof. Although the greater part of the structure was saved from the fire, the water used to put it out caused significant harm to the interior of the building.

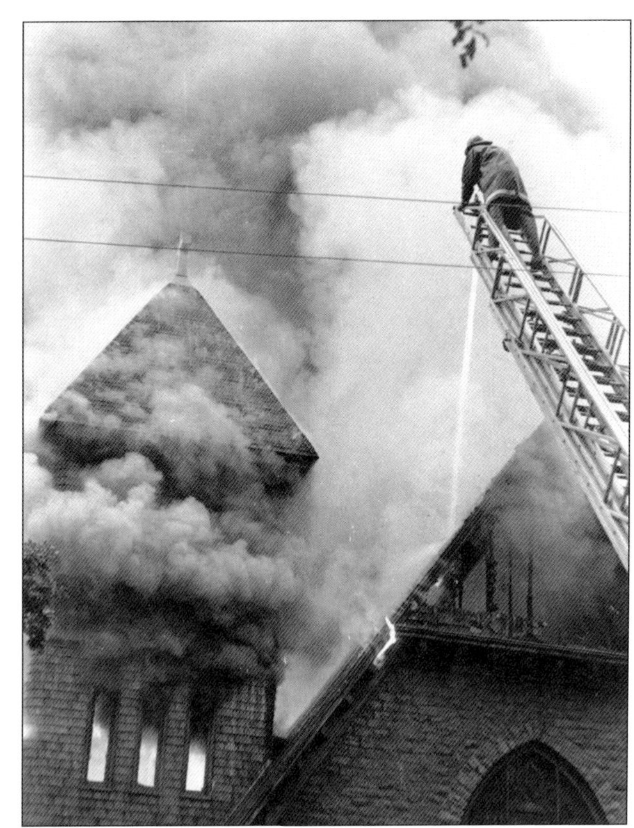

Destroyed Warehouse after Tornado, 1953. In March 1953, a powerful tornado ripped through the heart of St. Cloud. Telephone poles and power lines were torn down, and windows were blown out of downtown businesses. It destroyed a lumber storage warehouse and lifted a portion of the roof of Holy Angels Church. The roof of St. Cloud Launderette on Ninth Avenue North collapsed, killing a 16-year-old boy.

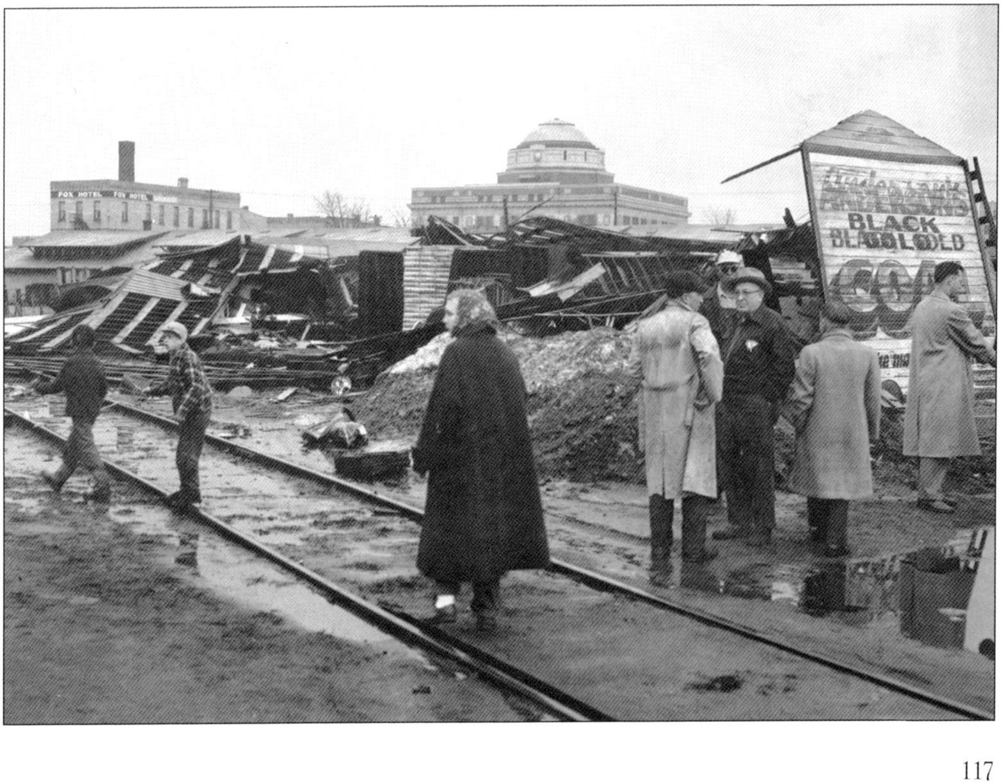

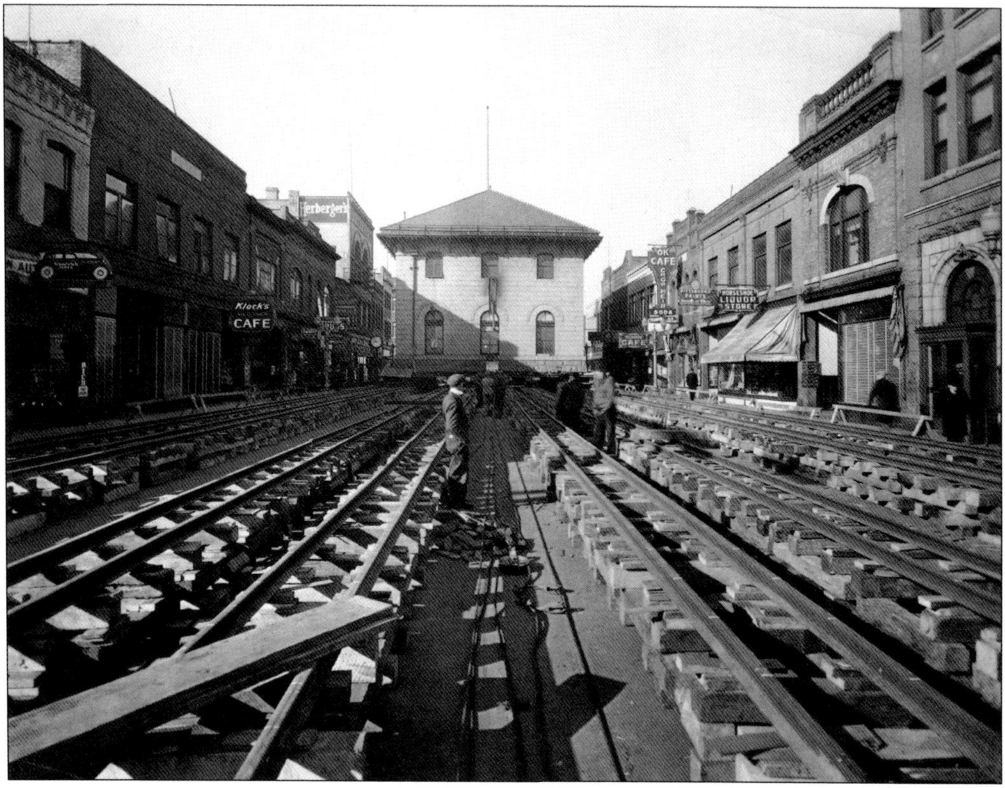

Moving St. Cloud Post Office down St. Germain Street, 1937 (above), and Graphic Tracing Path of Post Office, *St. Cloud Times*, 1937 (below). In the mid-1930s, federal funds were allocated to St. Cloud to replace the outdated post office and federal building located at Eighth Avenue and St. Germain Street. Rather than destroy the historic structure, the City of St. Cloud opted to use the building as its new city hall. However, the building was located at a pristine location in the heart of St. Cloud, which allowed easy access for area residents to use the post office and federal building's services. The solution decided upon was to move the 2,400-ton granite structure to an empty lot five blocks down St. Germain Street and build a new post office at its former location. The move was done in 32 days at a rate of approximately 150 feet per day; the building was lifted onto rails and pulled by horses.

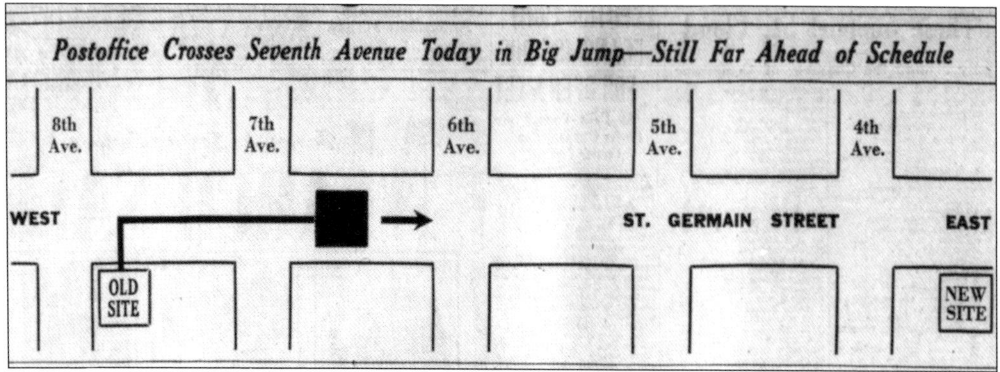

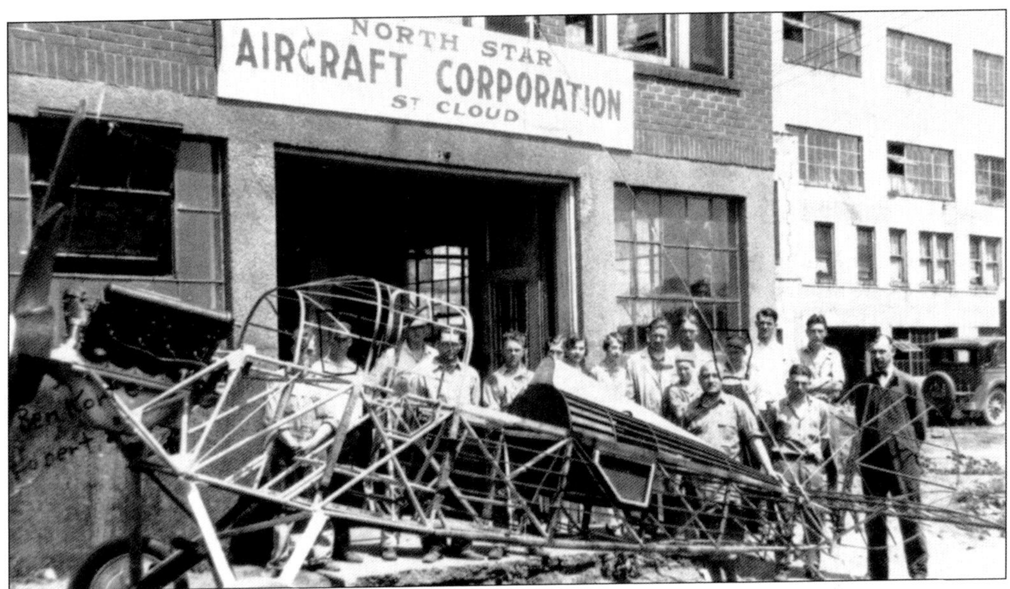

North Star Aircraft, 1928. In March 1928, "Captain" Hoseas Mohlar arrived in St. Cloud searching for an opportunity to produce an aircraft supposedly of his design. He claimed to be a veteran pilot who became an aircraft designer and production superintendent after World War I. In May, he began the North Star Aircraft Corporation with a board and investors of local businessmen. Production began on Mohlar's design, the first of which was to be called the *Spirit of St. Cloud*. However, delay after delay postponed its completion, while Mohlar kept promising results if he just had more funds.

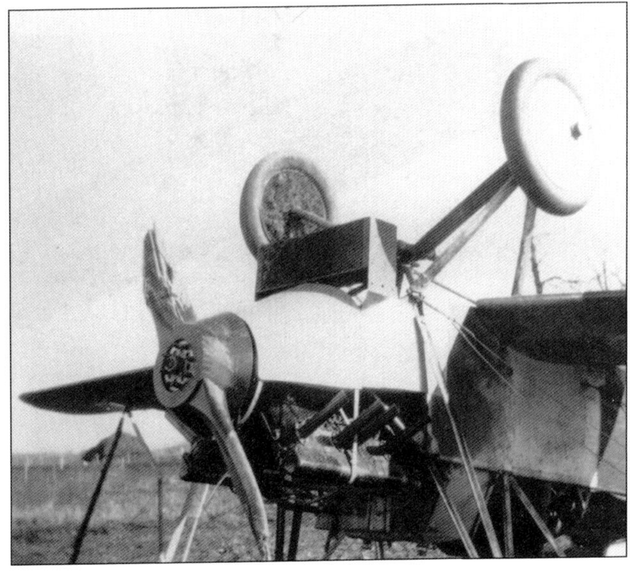

The *Spirit of St. Cloud* after its First Test Flight, 1928. In September 1928, Mohlar abandoned St. Cloud after emptying the company's safe of plans, blueprints, and minute books. The remnant members of North Star Aircraft Corporation completed the *Spirit of St. Cloud*, and on October 15, 1928, it finally had its first trial flight. After reaching an altitude of 40 feet, its nose tipped upward, fell tailfirst, and landed on its back. The seven-month saga of con man "Captain" Hoseas Mohlar and North Star Aircraft Corporation in St. Cloud had unceremoniously come to an end.

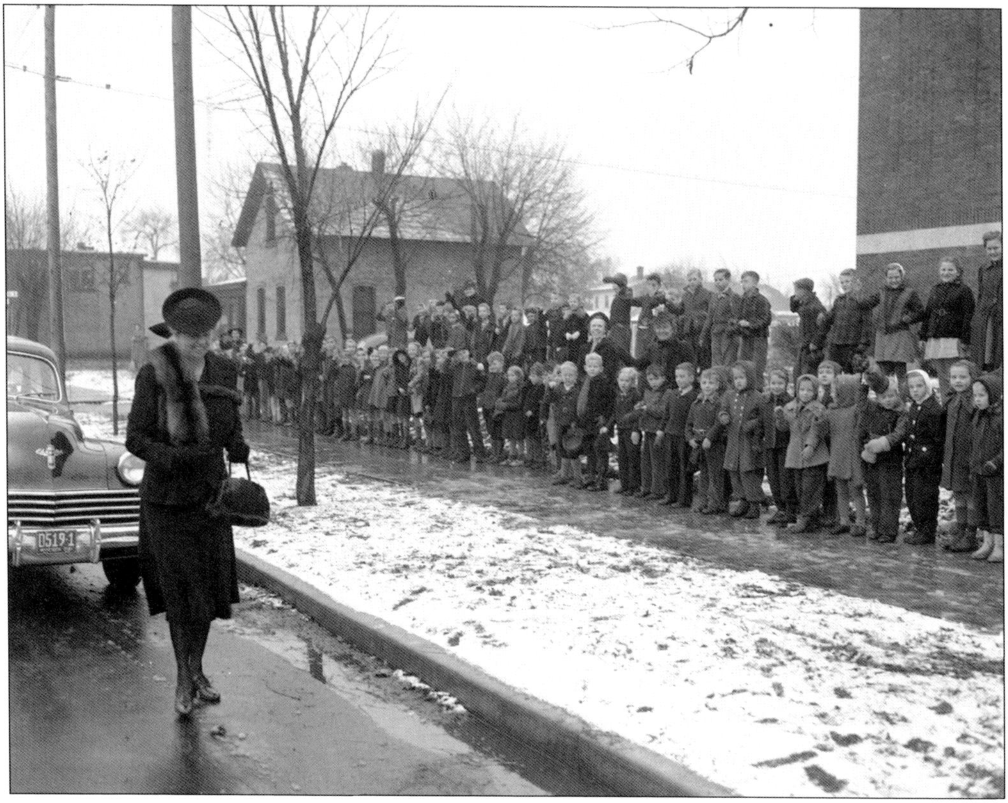

Eleanor Roosevelt Visits St. Cloud, 1941. In October 1941, First Lady Eleanor Roosevelt visited St. Cloud to speak to the Central Minnesota Institute. Although she requested no parades or public welcome, 2,000 central Minnesota citizens greeted her when her train arrived in St. Cloud. Roosevelt was generous with her time, visiting every school in St. Cloud, the Veterans Administration Hospital, and the St. Cloud Orphanage. Alice Wheelock Whitney hosted the first lady during her time in St. Cloud.

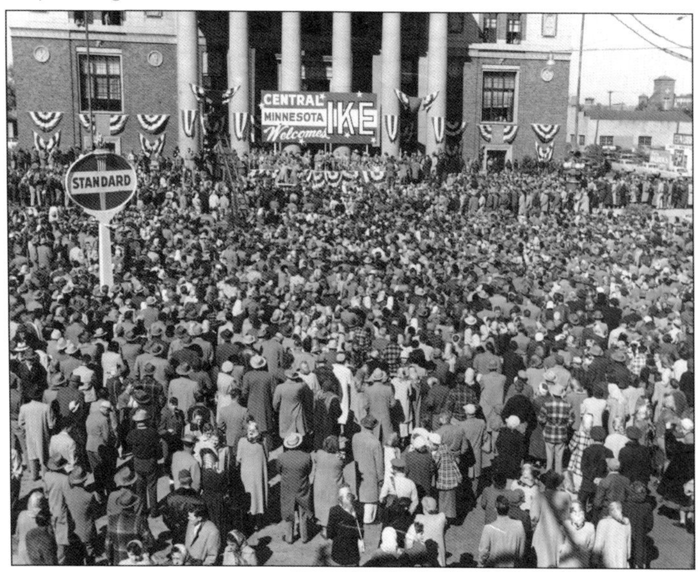

Dwight D. Eisenhower Visits St. Cloud, 1952. During his 1952 presidential campaign, Dwight D. Eisenhower visited St. Cloud. After parading through Sauk Rapids and St. Cloud, Eisenhower spoke to a crowd of 8,000 people in front of the Stearns County Courthouse.

Myron Hall, c. 1940. Myron Hall was the photographer for the *St. Cloud Times* for nearly 40 years, from 1937 to 1976. In a memorial letter published in the *St. Cloud Times* in August 1996, Mike Knaak, former *St. Cloud Times* photograph editor and successor to Hall, said after Hall's death, "For half a century, Myron was the eyes of Central Minnesota. The photographic record he compiled is a priceless part of our community's history." In 1988, Hall donated his entire body of work to the Stearns County Historical Society.

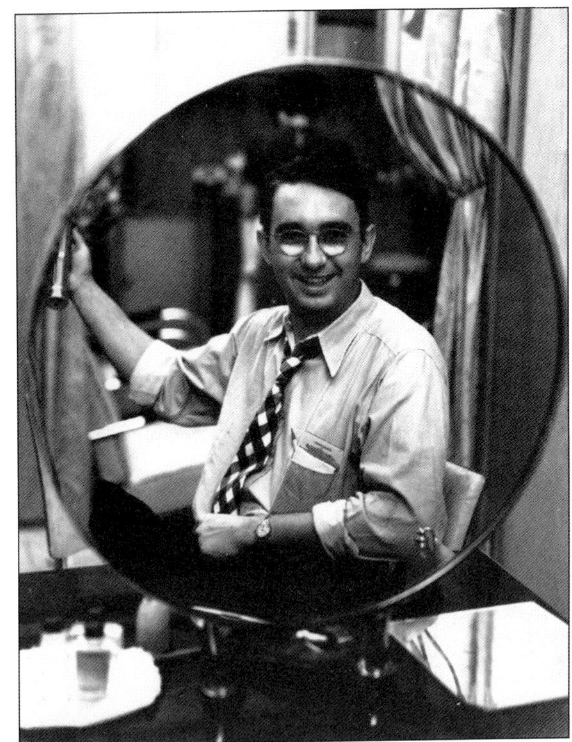

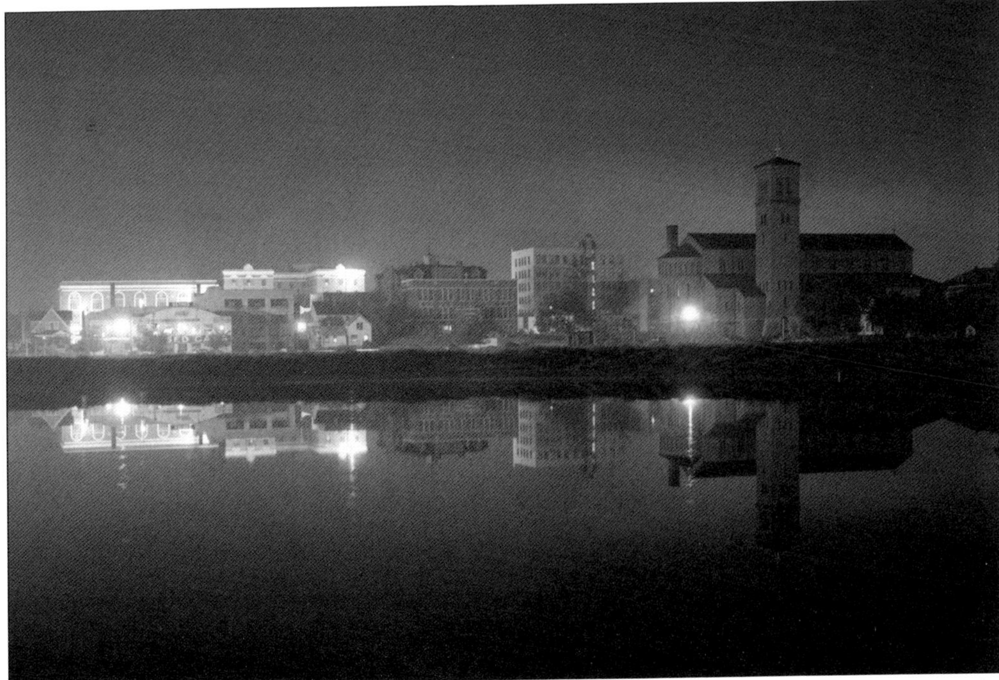

St. Cloud Skyline, 1939. Myron Hall captured this image of St. Cloud's skyline from across Lake George, published in the *St. Cloud Times* on September 7, 1939. From here, the viewer can see some of downtown's most recognizable structures, which are still standing, including St. Mary's School and Hall, St. Mary's Cathedral, the Granite Exchange building, and the Breen Hotel.

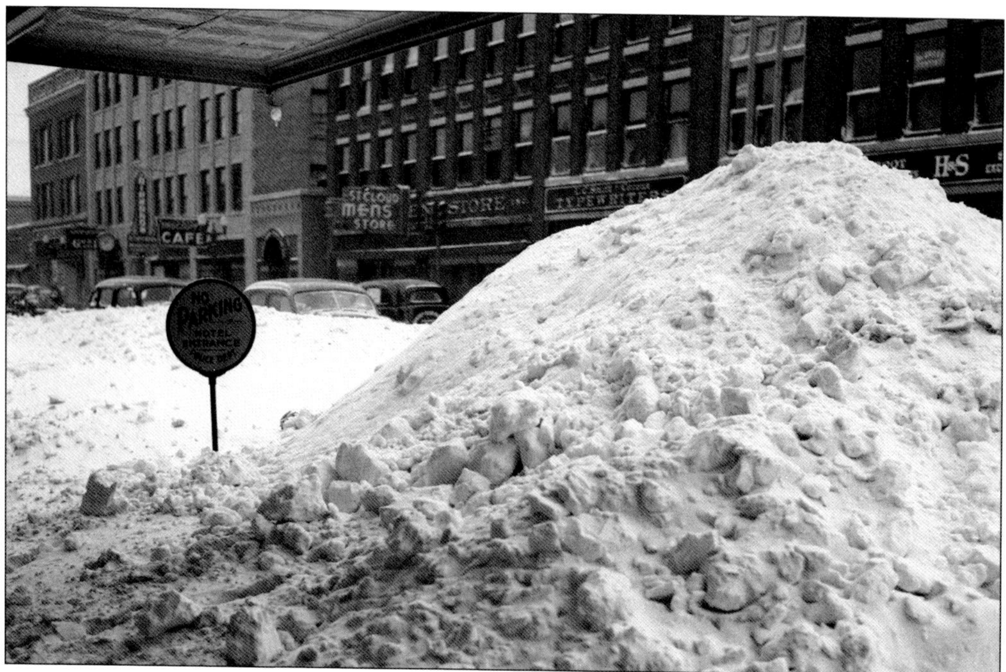

Armistice Day Blizzard, 1940. A colossal blizzard hit central Minnesota on November 11, 1940. An estimated 15.5 inches of snow fell on the region with almost 20-foot-high snowdrifts. The *St. Cloud Times* later recorded harrowing stories from that day—stories of two trains colliding head-on, students stranded inside schools, young girls losing consciousness in the outdoors as they searched for shelter, and bodies found in the thawing snow. John Fandel of St. Cloud was on his way home from St. John's University when he collided head-on with another driver, the impact throwing Fandel through the windshield. He survived but was severely injured. Another St. Cloud man, Joseph Thill, was stranded on an island in the Mississippi River near Clearwater for 25 hours when the blizzard came upon him while hunting. The blizzard killed an estimated 150 people throughout the Midwest, including 49 in Minnesota.

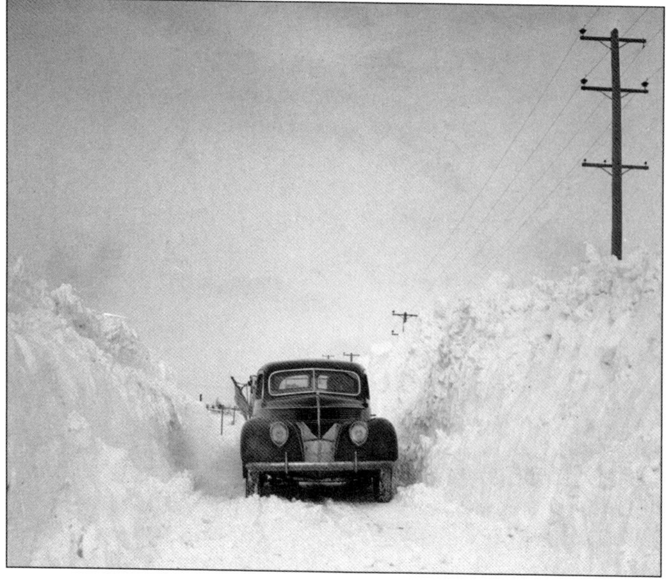

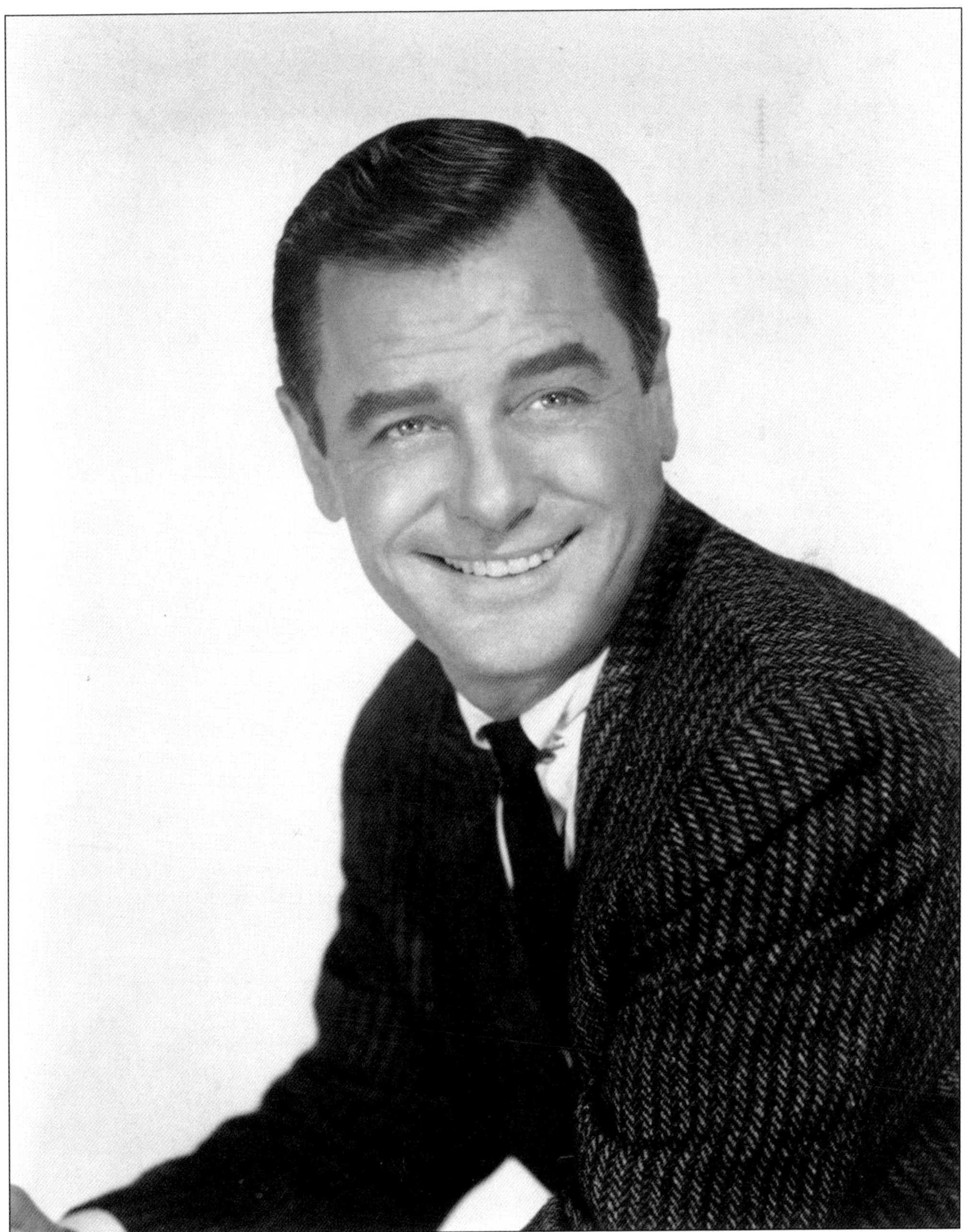

Gig Young, c. 1950. Gig Young, born Byron Barr in St. Cloud in 1913, was the son of J.E. Barr, owner of Barr Pickling Factory. He always had a desire to act but kept it a secret from the rest of his family. After they moved to Washington, DC, Young joined an acting group and received a scholarship to Pasadena Playhouse in California. In 1942, he appeared in the film *The Gay Sisters* as a character named Gig Young, his breakout role. The character name stuck to him, and it became his professional pseudonym. He was known for playing the lovable best friend of the lead and costarred with Errol Flynn, Cary Grant, and Clark Gable. Young was nominated for the Academy Award for Best Supporting Actor three times and won it for his role in *They Shoot Horses, Don't They?* (1969).

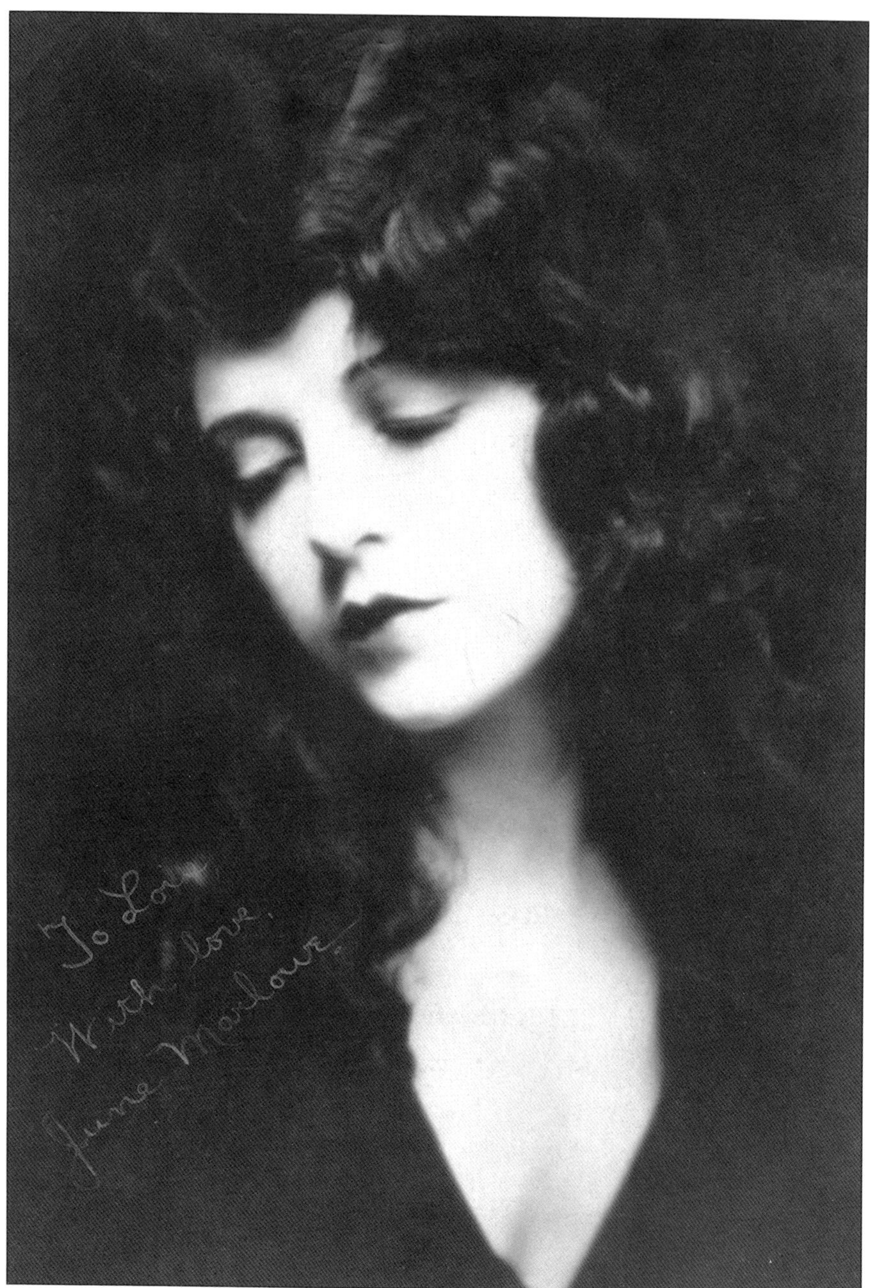

June Marlowe, c. 1926. June Marlowe was a silent film actress best known for her role as Mrs. Crabtree of the *Little Rascals* films. She was born Gisela Goetten in 1903 in St. Cloud, where her father owned the Goetten Meat Market on St. Germain Street. At the age of 16, her family moved to California, and she attended Hollywood High School, where a film producer "discovered" her during a school production of *My Ideal*. In addition to her role as Mrs. Crabtree, she appeared in multiple installments of the *Rin-Tin-Tin* film series and shared the screen with John Barrymore in *Don Juan* (1926). Marlowe appeared in a few talkies, but retired from acting after marrying Hollywood businessman Rodney Sprigg in 1933. She spent the rest of her life dedicated to philanthropy. Marlowe visited St. Cloud one last time in 1974 before her death in 1984.

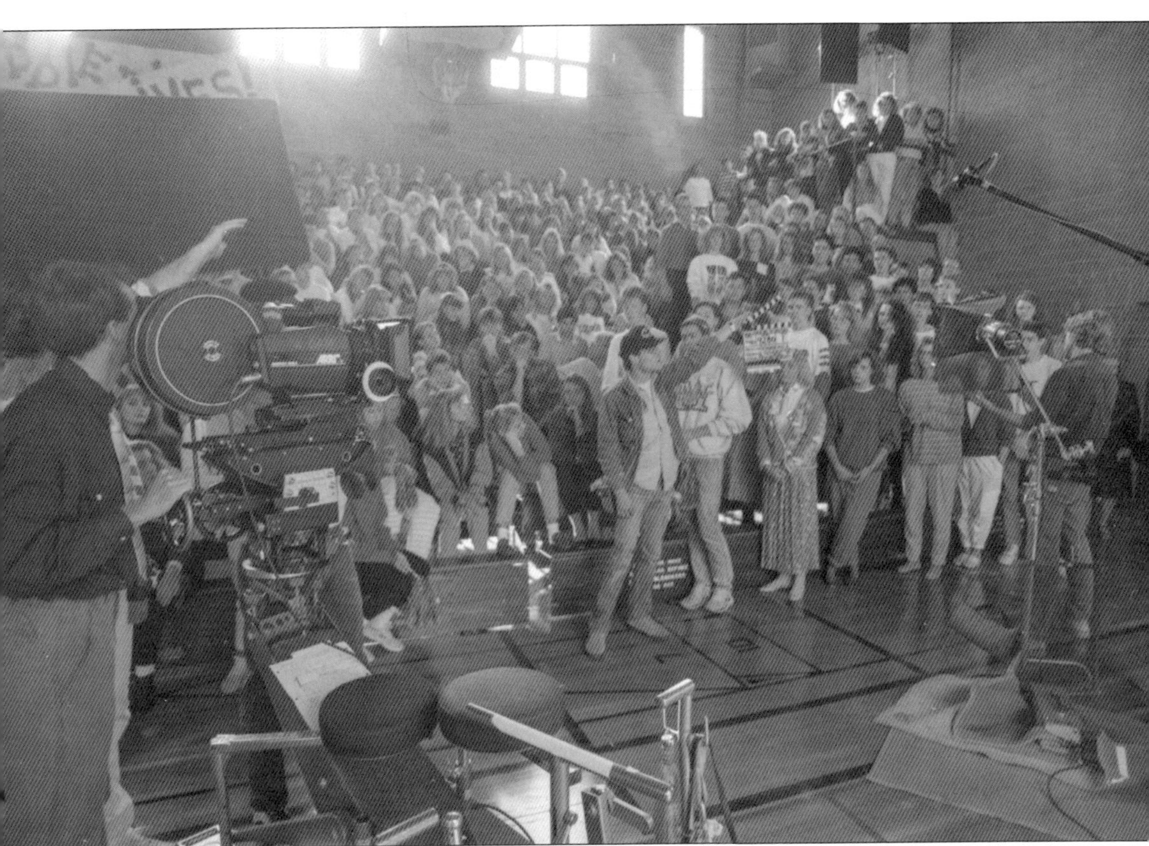

PEP RALLY SCENE, CATHEDRAL HIGH SCHOOL, 1988. St. Cloud native Stephen Sommers, director of *The Mummy* (1999), *The Mummy Returns* (2001), and *Van Helsing* (2004), directed his first feature-length film in St. Cloud in 1988. *Catch Me If You Can* (1989), not to be confused with Stephen Spielberg's 2002 film of the same name, follows the story of street racer Dylan Malone (Matt Lattanzi) and his plan to raise enough money through illegal street racing to save his local Minnesota high school from shutting down. Sommers filmed at Cathedral High School and used its students as extras for the film. (Photograph by Greg Beckel; courtesy of *St. Cloud Times*.)

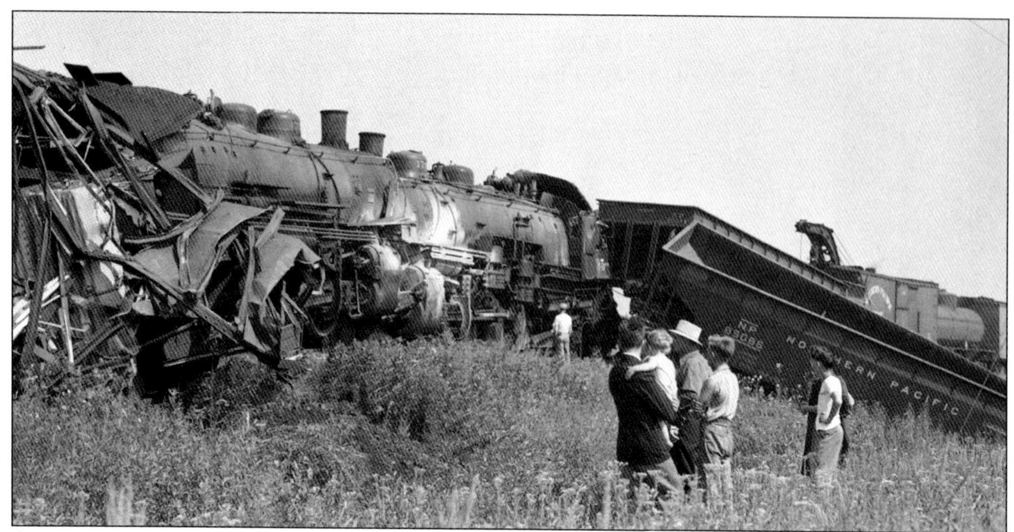

AFTERMATH OF A HEAD-ON COLLISION, 1942. Major accidents, whether vehicular or locomotive, were a common occurrence throughout the history of St. Cloud and often drew crowds to observe the scenes. In August 1942, two trains collided head-on in dense fog at a speed of 25 miles per hour. The engines telescoped into one another for several feet, and seven cars were derailed. Three trainmen were injured and taken to St. Cloud Hospital for treatment.

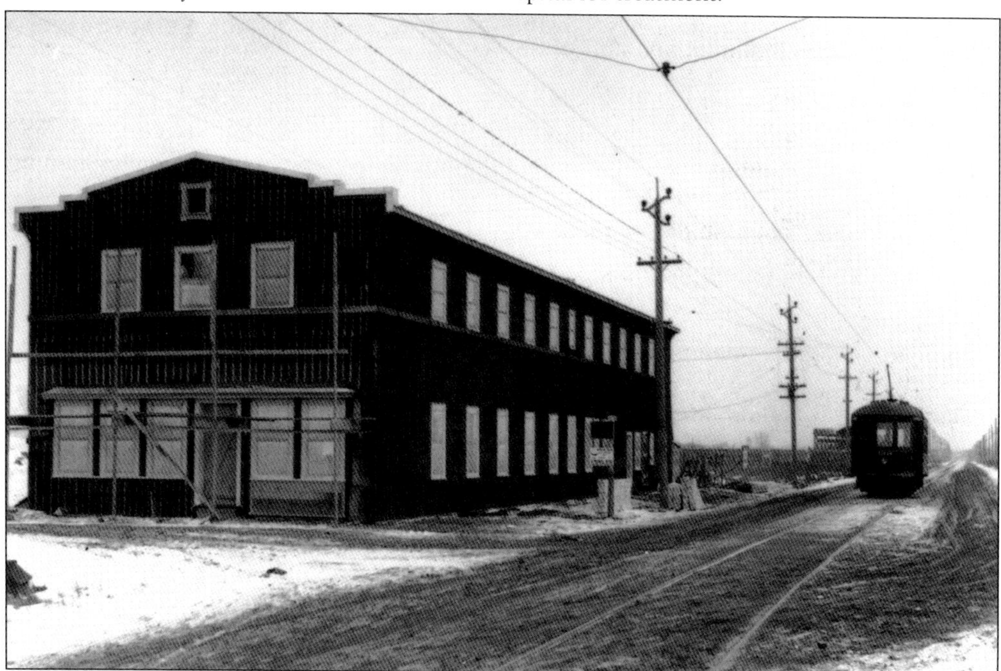

PAN MOTOR HOTEL, C. 1918. In 1933, a gangland-style shooting occurred at a St. Cloud speakeasy known as the Blue Tavern, inside what was once the Pan Motor Hotel. Fred Bukowski of Sauk Rapids got into an altercation with a patron at the tavern and left. About an hour later, two cars drove by the tavern and out of one came a volley of machine gun fire, striking an innocent bystander, Herbert Sanborn of St. Cloud. Police discovered Bukowski inside a vehicle matching the description of one of the cars involved in the incident. The car was completely armored, and in Bukowski's possession was a Thompson submachine gun, an automatic rifle, and three pistols.

Frank Capra, St. Cloud State University, 1975. Frank Capra, the Academy Award–winning director of *It's a Wonderful Life* (1946) and *Mr. Smith Goes to Washington* (1939), attended the dedication ceremony of the Kiehle Visual Arts Center at St. Cloud State University (SCSU) in September 1975. As part of the proceedings, Capra led a panel discussion on "Public Morality and Artistic Freedom." Over the years, St. Cloud State University has hosted several high-profile guests, including Don Knotts, Spike Lee, Bob Hope, and Maya Angelou.

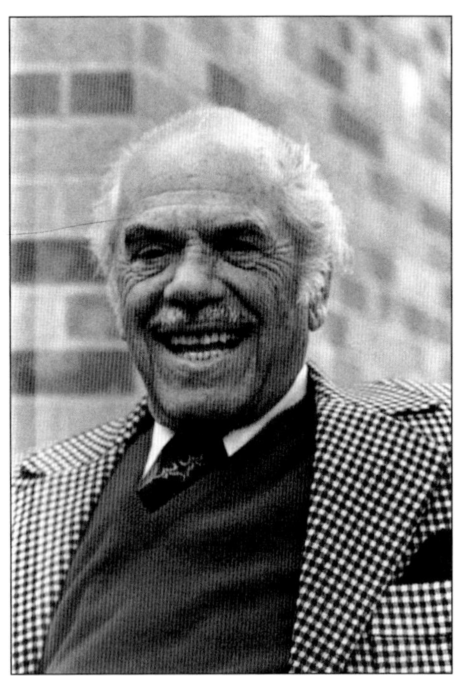

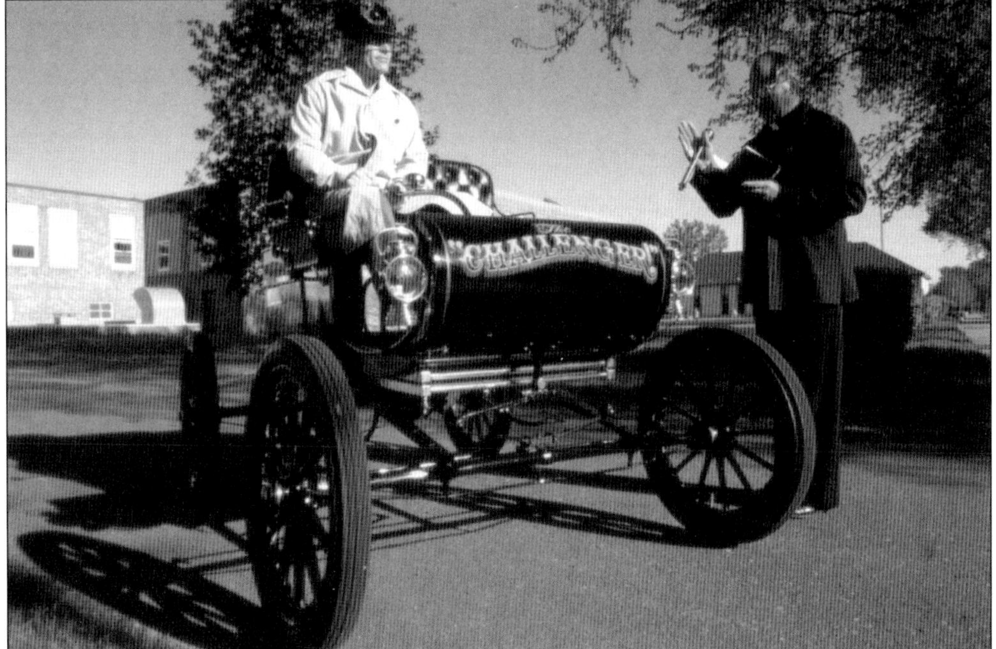

Priest Blesses Roy Bernick and His 1903 Oldsmobile, 1985. Roy Bernick, son of Francis "Snooky" Bernick and co-owner of Bernick's, was a prolific collector of antique cars. In 1985, to commemorate the 100th anniversary of the Oldsmobile company, Bernick drove from San Francisco to New York, a total of 3,800 miles, in his 1903 Oldsmobile. He purchased the car in 1940 and began restoring it in the 1970s, adding modern conveniences including an odometer and a speedometer. Bernick began the trip with two other Oldsmobile drivers on June 30, and they arrived in New York 37 days later. (Photograph by Mike Knaak; courtesy of *St. Cloud Times*.)